Further Case Studies in Psychology

This unique book offers valuable insights into the often-hidden world of forensic psychological assessment and intervention. It follows on from *Case Studies in Forensic Psychology* (2019) and presents a range of detailed clinical case studies of adults and young people across secure and community settings.

The case studies represent individuals with several different forms of offending histories, such as sexual and violent offending, and various clinical diagnoses including autism and acquired brain injury. Each chapter details the individual's personal background, offending, any relevant psychiatric or psychological diagnoses, and treatments. The chapters end with an intensive discussion on the outcomes for that case and its wider implications. This book allows the readers to understand the on-ground clinical practice and day-to-day role of a psychologist in forensic practice by demonstrating the work undertaken behind the empirical research and highlighting the complexities to which psychologists need to apply their expertise. Also, it brings together treatment models and forensic research to establish how theory translates into practice and considers whether it is effective at an individual level.

Further Case Studies in Forensic Psychology is a key reading for psychologists, clinicians, and practitioners at any stage of their career in this rapidly expanding field. It will also be useful for students of forensic psychology and those interested in the real-life work of psychologists in forensic practice.

Ruth J. Tully is a Consultant Forensic Psychologist and Clinical Lead of Tully Forensic Psychology Limited, where she and her team of psychologists work throughout the UK, in the provision of psychological assessment, treatment, consultancy, and training. She is considered a leading authority in the field of risk assessment.

Jennifer Bamford is a Forensic Psychologist who specialises in the assessment of sexual offenders. She works in private practice assessing people with forensic histories in prison, hospital, and the community for the purpose of parole, criminal court hearings, family court assessments, and mental health tribunals.

Further Case Studies in Forensic Psychology

Clinical Assessment and Treatment

Edited by Dr Ruth J. Tully and
Dr Jennifer Bamford

Routledge
Taylor & Francis Group

LONDON AND NEW YORK

Designed cover image: © Getty Images

First published 2023
by Routledge
4 Park Square, Milton Park, Abingdon, Oxon OX14 4RN

and by Routledge
605 Third Avenue, New York, NY 10158

Routledge is an imprint of the Taylor & Francis Group, an informa business

© 2023 selection and editorial matter, Dr Ruth J. Tully and Dr Jennifer Bamford; individual chapters, the contributors

British Library Cataloguing-in-Publication Data
A catalogue record for this book is available from the British Library

ISBN: 9781032081380 (hbk)
ISBN: 9781032081366 (pbk)
ISBN: 9781003213116 (ebk)

DOI: 10.4324/9781003213116

Typeset in Bembo
by Apex CoVantage, LLC

Contents

Acknowledgements

We would like to give special thanks to all contributors to this book, which includes authors, service users, and services involved. This book was written during the impact of the COVID-19 pandemic, and we would like to recognise the additional strain this put on all those involved and thank you for all your hard work and perseverance, without which this book would not be possible. If the authors and service users did not engage with the book as they did, we would not have the opportunity to share the valuable lessons the case studies can teach us all, not just about clinical practice but about being human as well. Thank you.

Contributors

Dr Lara Arsuffi
BSc (Hons), MA, MSc, ForenPsyD, AFBPsS, CPsychol

Dr Lara Arsuffi is a Chartered and Registered Forensic Psychologist in the UK. She has worked in the field of forensic mental health for 21 years. She has worked within the National Health Service (NHS) and third-sector organisations in prison, community and secure hospital settings. She is currently Principal Psychologist and Clinical Lead for the Offender Personality Disorder (OPD) and Intensive Intervention Risk Management Service (IIRMS) pathways in a service in the Midlands. She is the module leader for the undergraduate degree course in forensic psychology at Buckingham University. Dr Arsuffi has extensive experience of writing reports and giving evidence at mental health review tribunals and parole boards hearings.

Dr Sarah Ashworth
BSc (Hons), DForenPsy, CPsychol, AFBPsS

Dr Sarah Ashworth is a HCPC Registered and BPS Chartered Forensic Psychologist in the UK. She has over 13 years' experience working in adult mental health and specialises in the field of neurodiversity. She has a particular interest in increasing awareness, access to psychological interventions, and application of risk assessment for neurodiverse populations, such as individuals with learning disability, autism spectrum disorder, and neurocognitive disorders. Dr Ashworth is currently working as a principal forensic psychologist developing her clinical practice in relation to neuropsychology within locked rehabilitation neuropsychiatric services for individuals with acquired brain injuries, neurological disorders, neurodegenerative conditions, and comorbid psychiatric diagnoses.

Dr Jennifer Bamford
BSc (Hons), MSc, DForenPsy, CPsychol, AFBPsS, EuroPsy, CSci

Dr Jennifer Bamford is a Forensic Psychologist in the UK. She has worked in a variety of forensic settings for the last 13 years, including for Her

Majesty's Prison and Probation Service, the NHS, and private hospitals. Dr Bamford specialises in the assessment of sexual offenders and has published her research in multiple perpetrator sexual offending. Dr Bamford has worked in private practice for the last seven years, assessing people with forensic histories in prison, hospital, and the community for the purpose of parole, criminal court hearings, family court assessments, and mental health tribunals.

Dr Clare Holt
BSc (Hons), MSc, DClinPsy, CPsychol

Dr Clare Holt is a BPS Chartered and HCPC Registered Clinical Psychologist in the UK. Since qualifying in 2011, she has specialised in working with adolescents who are in contact with the criminal justice system. Within her varied professional roles to date, Clare has worked within the NHS, private, and third-sector organisations in both prison and community settings. Clare is passionate about adopting a whole systems approach to her day-to-day work and strives to develop responsive and accessible services that are co-produced with the individuals they are seeking to support.

Dr Faye Horsley
BSc (Hons), MSc, PhD, CPsychol

Dr Faye Horsley is a Senior Lecturer in Psychology at Northumbria University. She is a HCPC-registered practitioner psychologist and BPS-chartered psychologist in the UK with over 15 years of experience in working with men and women convicted of criminal offences in prison and hospital settings. As a practitioner, Faye specialises in firesetting, violent and sexually violent offending, along with forensic mental health. Faye's research expertise is firesetting and fire use. Faye completed her PhD in Sociology at Durham University in 2020, with a thesis titled 'Arson Reconceptualised: the Continuum of Fire Use'. She is the author of *New Perspectives on Arson and Firesetting: the Human–Fire Relationship*, published by Routledge in 2022.

Dr Gemma Luke
DClinPsych, MSc, BSc

Dr Gemma Luke is a Chartered Clinical Psychologist in the UK, registered with the HCPC and chartered with the BPS. She has worked in the field of mental health since 2001, and as a qualified clinical psychologist since 2011, developing extensive experience across community, inpatient, and forensic settings. Having worked in NHS inpatient services until 2016, Dr Luke now has a private practice where she provides psychological intervention to adolescents and adults. Alongside her clinical work, Dr Luke regularly conducts assessments for the family and criminal courts.

Dr Khyati Patel
BSc (Hons), ForenPsyD, AFBPsS, CPsychol, MBA, PGCert

Dr Khyati Patel is a BPS Chartered and HCPC Registered Forensic Psychologist in the UK. She has worked in the field of forensic mental health for over 13 years, working mainly with males. Dr Patel has worked within the NHS, private, and third-sector organisations in prison, community, and secure hospital settings. She is currently a principal psychologist working in a medium secure forensic psychiatric service and has recently been developing her clinical practice in relation to working with patients with psychosis.

Lyn Shelton
BSc (Hons), MSc, CPsychol (Foren), AFBsS

Lyn Shelton is a Consultant Forensic Psychologist (BPS Chartered and HCPC Registered Practitioner Psychologist) in the UK. She has worked in the field of forensic psychology for over 18 years and specialises in the assessment and treatment of clients with a diagnosis of learning disability and/or autism spectrum disorder. Lyn has worked in prison settings as well as medium security and low security forensic psychiatric services. She is currently a consultant psychologist working in a locked rehabilitation service.

Dr Ruth J. Tully
BSc (Hons), MSc, DForenPsy, CPsychol, EuroPsy, AFBPsS, CSci, MAE, AFEHA

Dr Ruth J. Tully is a HCPC Registered and BPS Chartered Forensic Psychologist in the UK. Dr Tully is Consultant Forensic Psychologist and Clinical Lead of Tully Forensic Psychology Ltd, where she and her team of forensic and clinical psychologists work throughout the UK, in the provision of psychological assessment, treatment/therapy, consultancy, and training. Dr Tully's wider experience includes working with adults and young people in secure forensic healthcare, social care, prison, and community settings. Dr Tully has an active research, publication, and public speaking profile. She is considered a leading authority on violence and sex offender risk assessment in relation to research, clinical work, and training professionals.

Joel Warkcup
BSc (Hons), MSc

Joel Warkcup is a Senior Assistant Psychologist currently working with adolescents in custody in the UK. He has been working with adolescents in custody for five years and benefits from experience in various roles in a custodial environment. During his professional experience to date, Joel has gained diverse experiences in various NHS community services and has been an active member of local and national groups implementing a framework for integrated care in the youth custody estate. Joel is passionate about developing accessible, collaborative, and strengths-based services for young people in custody and strives to shape trauma-informed practice at all levels of service delivery.

1   Introduction

Ruth J. Tully and Jennifer Bamford

Case studies and context

This is our second case study book. The introduction to our 2019 book *Case studies in forensic psychology: Clinical assessment and treatment* outlines various types of people who psychologists work with in forensic practice, including but not limited to people who perpetrate crime, victims, staff members, and organisations, as well as the various settings within which psychologists work.

This current book includes case studies from a range of settings; secure forensic psychiatric hospital, the community, closed prison, locked neurorehabilitation, and youth custody. This broad range of settings, and therefore broad range of client group, highlights the diverse range of people that psychologists in forensic practice work with, and this book shares with the reader the varied needs and clinical presentations of those within the justice system.

The value of forensic case studies

One of the motivators for producing a case study book was what might seem the more obvious one; to share good practice to aid practitioners and those interested in this field in their work. However, an important motivation was also that we wanted to place a spotlight on work, which as forensic work, including that with perpetrators of serious crime, is often hidden from public view. This work can often seem hidden because of the context of the assessments and interventions, with them often being delivered in secure services or linked to a court case in some way. Furthermore, forensic practitioners often struggle to find time to write up case studies for publication as they often have lots of patients to work with, within limited available time. We considered this area to be an area not only *worthy* but also to be of *critical importance* to publish in, given that forensic psychology practice can have an impact on a person's risk to themselves and other people. The case studies in this book highlight assessment and treatment approaches and how these have been adapted both to the forensic context and based on the individual person's responsivity needs/clinical presentation. We are confident that once you have read this book, if you did

DOI: 10.4324/9781003213116-1

not already agree, you too will consider this area to be of importance in relation to sharing how treatment is delivered in clinical practice in forensic settings.

A theme that comes across from the case studies presented in this book is one of responsivity; that is adapting interventions, treatment approaches, and assessments to the needs of the person accessing services. In our experience, there has in the past been a view that forensic psychology practice is all about 'standardised programmes' that leave no room to treat an individual whose presentation and history may be such that engagement in 'standardised' intervention is not successful or not possible to even attempt. In producing this book, we hope to debunk this perception by highlighting how the people detailed within the case studies have been considered as individuals. For example one chapter details the adaptation of trauma treatment protocols to account for an autism presentation, and another shows an integrated therapeutic approach to risk reduction treatment for intimate partner/intrafamilial violence.

It is essential to utilise approaches that have an empirical basis for the issue being targeted by the treatment. However, if clinicians did not carefully consider the presentation and background of the person in front of them, and instead applied a generic approach or a strictly standardised approach to treatment, it seems to us that treatment would be much less likely to be successful. This is where the skills and expertise of psychologists working in forensic practice come in. Experience working with people with various diagnoses, offending, or behavioural history and careful consideration of all of the information about the person accessing treatment, as well as consideration of the relevant literature in the area will all be brought together to devise a realistic and appropriately responsive treatment plan. The case studies presented here will serve to demonstrate this in practice. However, we also consider it essential that we do not become complacent in the manner in which treatment is adapted for a person. For instance how one person with a certain diagnosis clinically presents will differ from the presentation of another person who has exactly the same diagnosis. A person with the same criminal conviction as another person will demonstrate different attitudes and motivations for offending. Therefore, there is always a need to continue to evaluate forensic psychology practice in the real world, as well as within research, to consider what approaches and adaptations to treatment or assessment can work in general, what can work for some, what was tried but was not effective, and so on.

It is also important to consider that sometimes, and especially in forensic practice, the environment in which a client resides, or the service they are accessing, can influence treatment approaches and availability in a way that is less than ideal. This may be linked to resources, such as the person having to wait some time to access psychological intervention, which is something we have seen in practice especially during and since the COVID-19 pandemic where services are stretched, short-staffed, and under new pressures. Additionally, the service and environment may not be conducive to the most effective treatments being delivered as they are intended to be delivered. For example some therapies are designed and researched to be effective when delivered both on an individual and on a group basis to a person over a long period of time. However, the service may offer the treatment only in a group format informed by that approach, which could link to this being more cost-effective than individual therapy. Additionally, it could be the case that a service user requires a specific form or model of therapy as being best suited to meet their needs, but there might not be a psychologist in the service trained and experienced in that approach. In some cases, it may be that long-term therapy is needed for a person's risk reduction, but the service can offer only a set number of sessions as this is what is funded by the commissioning body. Added to this, for those in restricted or secure environments (e.g. prison or secure psychiatric services), the skills and development gained through therapy cannot be tested out in 'the real world' as may be possible in the community, which can be a barrier to further development and refinement of skills and learning. Sometimes, therefore, treatment involves some level of compromise and in our experience, psychologists have to work creatively with the resources they have, as well as ensuring that they are being responsive to that individual's needs as much as is possible and that they are using the time and resources available to aid that person's progress. This is not easy in forensic and secure settings, where other issues often beyond the control of the psychologist can also affect treatment such as last-minute cancellation of sessions due to operational reasons in a prison, meaning that all activity is cancelled for that day. Psychologists in forensic settings have to be able to adapt quickly to such challenges to continue to provide effective treatment and assessment within challenging systems. The chapter on youth custody in this case study book looks further at the impact of systems on psychology practice.

In working to highlight (and also to address) some of the issues described earlier, such as responsivity and adaptations being needed to support people in forensic services in accessing psychological intervention, case studies are particularly helpful. Case studies can describe approaches taken which may inspire other practitioners to consider if the same or a similar approach might be relevant in their work in terms of considering responsivity and resource needs, as well as other challenges. Moreover, we hope that if readers of this book work in the forensic field, they may be inspired to consider publishing their own work as a case study, detailing their unique and otherwise relatively hidden, but certainly valuable, work.

2   Psychological treatment relating to intimate partner violence and domestic abuse in the family court context

Gemma Luke

Role of psychologists in family courts

In England and Wales, psychologists who are registered with the Health Care Professions Council (HCPC) are often instructed as expert witnesses in family court cases. These are cases where the local authority has become involved via social care services due to concerns for child welfare. Psychologists may be instructed by the local authority during the pre-proceedings phase to assess if and how parents can be supported to meet the needs of their children without the need for the case to go to court. A psychologist may also be instructed to conduct a psychological assessment for the court proceedings and at this point would be instructed jointly by the legal representatives of all parties concerned. The overarching aim is usually to explore the presence and extent of direct and/or indirect harm caused to a child and whether the parents can make the necessary changes to support the child.

In this context, psychological assessment should be comprehensive and explore developmental, psychological, social, relational, and neuropsychological issues in complex situations (BPS, 2016). In addition to direct interviewing and observation, information is gathered from various sources to gain an in-depth understanding of the situation. This information may consist of relevant historical documentation and meetings with other professionals who are involved in the case. The psychologist should then draw on a range of psychological theories and principles to provide a theoretical framework for valid analysis and prediction through the application of psychological formulation (BPS, 2016) before making recommendations to assist, either the pre-proceedings interventions or the court, in ensuring the child's welfare remains paramount.

Following completion of court proceedings, psychological intervention may be recommended. The aim of the treatment is to support the family to stay together or come back together after court-ordered separation. During this process, the psychologist must work not only with the person referred to them but also with the local authority and potentially the wider family to ensure that the child(ren)'s needs remain paramount. This case study details the therapy process in the context of a referral relating to family court proceedings and violence risk (to partners and children) posed by the father within the family.

DOI: 10.4324/9781003213116-2

Intimate partner and family violence

Intimate partner violence (IPV) is an international public health concern. The World Health Organization defines IPV as "any behaviour within an intimate relationship that causes physical, sexual or psychological harm, including acts of physical aggression, sexual coercion, psychological abuse and controlling behaviours. This definition covers violence by both current and former spouses and partners" (WHO, 2017). In England and Wales, the law extends this definition to include abuse between relatives and where there is or has been a shared parental relationship with the same child.

Data released in 2021 indicated that over the preceding year, police in England and Wales recorded 845,734 domestic abuse-related crimes (Office for National Statistics, 2021). While this figure indicates a 6% increase from the previous year, it is likely to underrepresent the true prevalence. By comparison, the National Domestic Abuse Helpline recorded a 22% increase in access to their service, and there was a 46% increase in **multi–agency risk assessment conferences**, each over the same timeframe (Office for National Statistics, 2021). The increase in prevalence of IPV and domestic abuse has been mirrored internationally with research citing a link between this and the exacerbation of external stressors caused by the global COVID-19 pandemic (Moreira & da Costa, 2020). However, an accurate understanding of the worldwide prevalence of IPV is problematic due to the disparity in reporting, measuring, and researching.

The impact of IPV and domestic abuse is far-reaching. In addition to the risk of physical injury, partners who have been the victim of IPV are more likely to suffer from poor mental health, experience physical health complications, and increased risk of substance abuse (National Research Centre on Domestic Violence, 2021). Within the context of the family courts, the additional risks, particularly those posed to children, are paramount.

Children who live in a home where domestic abuse occurs are, by that very nature, exposed to it. The Children's Commissioner for England's (2019) Childhood Vulnerability report showed that in 2019, 831,000 children lived in homes that reported domestic abuse. The literature has identified a range of immediate and longer-term effects on children who have been exposed to domestic abuse, including emotional, behavioural, psychological, and social problems (Devaney, 2015). Bandura's (1977) learning theory has been a long-standing explanatory perspective in the literature on familial violence. It states that people can model behaviour that they have been exposed to as children and that it can continue into adulthood as a coping response to stress or as a method of conflict resolution. Therefore, in children who are subjected to living in an abusive household, externalising behaviours including aggression, temper outbursts, and oppositional behaviour can occur. Further, early traumatic experiences such as domestic abuse can alter a child's cognitive and emotional orientation to the world, impacting their capacity for healthy attachment (Bowlby, 1997) by distorting the child's sense of being able to trust in others to care for them. In addition to creating the potential for mental health problems, this may also have an important impact on a child's ability to develop healthy adult relationships. In addition, this combination of behavioural and psychological difficulties means that children from homes where domestic abuse is present often experience poorer academic outcomes (Kitzmann et al., 2003).

With regard to intervention for perpetrators of domestic violence in the UK, the Ministry of Justice and Children and Family Court Advisory and Support Service often refer perpetrators of domestic abuse to the Domestic Abuse Perpetrator Programme (DAPP), also referred to as the Domestic Violence Perpetrator Programme (DVPP). In the UK, most DAPP courses are based around the Duluth model, which originated in the USA (What Works for Children's Social Care, 2022). This model is underpinned by cognitive–behavioural approaches, which aim to change patterns of thought to change behaviour and pro-feminist approaches, which view violence as originating from patriarchal values about women's roles. These programmes usually incorporate group and one-to-one sessions. Evaluations from the USA (Gondolf, 2004) and the UK (Kelly & Westmarland, 2015) have been qualitatively positive; however, with an absence of the development of a significant evidence-base, efficacy levels cannot be ascertained and as a result, funding by stakeholders is increasingly limited (Kelly & Westmarland, 2015).

There is, however, a growing body of literature investigating the relationship between post-traumatic stress disorder (PTSD) and male-perpetrated IPV with findings suggesting a link between trauma exposure, PTSD symptomatology, and male-perpetrated IPV (Bell & Orcutt, 2009; Machisa et al., 2016; Semiatin et al., 2017). This may have important clinical implications for DVPPs, which do not address past trauma.

This case study will focus on the delivery of a one-to-one psychological intervention for risk reduction in the context of domestic abuse for a male with a history of childhood abuse who had previously completed a DAPP.

The referral

The following case study has been appropriately anonymised to maintain confidentiality. The case concerned a male who had been requested to leave the family home due to chronic concerns pertaining to violence towards partners and risk to children. Following the conclusion of court proceedings, I was instructed by the local authority to assess whether the client, who is named 'James' for the purpose of this case study, was suitable for therapy, and if so, to undertake therapy with the aim of providing James with the opportunity to reduce the risk of harm he posed to his partner and the children, such that he could co-parent.

Background information

Before meeting with James, I collated information from the case bundle to plan for the assessment of treatment suitability and aid my case formulation.

A bundle of relevant documentation was reviewed, including prior risk assessment reports, a cognitive assessment report, a probation report (as James had been supervised in the community by probation due to his criminal convictions for violence), consultation notes from professionals involved in the case, witness statements, a chronology of events, and the social worker's reports. Moreover, I had several conversations with the social worker who had been working with the family throughout the current proceedings.

Case history

James first came to the attention of social services around 20 years prior to the current referral, when his daughter, aged under one year old at the time, was assessed to have suffered non-accidental injury. James was sentenced to two-years of imprisonment for assault, which he was found to have committed against his daughter. James proceeded to have five further children with several different partners. All but one of these relationships was characterised by domestic violence and heavy alcohol use. In one of these relationships, there were also reports of James being violent towards the partner's child. Social services had been intermittently involved in each of James' relationships, with the children being subject to **child protection plans**. Further criminal court proceedings were initiated around ten years prior to the current referral, when James was convicted of assaulting his then-pregnant partner. He was sentenced to a community order for approximately two years and was required as part of this order to undertake a DAPP. In the subsequent years, there were further incidents of domestic violence, including alleged threats to kill a partner.

James' family background: James was removed from his mother's care during the first few weeks of his life due to neglect. He was subsequently cared for by his father and stepmother. Previous reports indicate that James reported "a positive relationship" with both his father and stepmother, although indicated that he had referred to himself as "a nuisance" and "did not respect anyone". James was moreover reported to describe a positive relationship with his two sisters (with whom he did not live), but he reported that there had been violence between him and his six stepsiblings.

Education: James had been disruptive at school, including engaging in acts of violence against other pupils and damaging school property. Documents indicated that James was involved with a gang which he described as a "pack of wolves" who would randomly attack others. James was temporarily suspended from school during his early teenage years. He eventually left school at the age of 16 with certificates of achievement in maths, English, and science. James was reported to experience difficulty with reading and writing and would get angry when he could not understand what was happening in class.

Employment: James joined the armed forces at the age of 16 but was discharged on medical grounds a couple of years later. James subsequently worked various manual labour jobs until his incarceration for the assault on his daughter, committed in his early twenties. Following his release from prison, James had one further position of employment before setting up his own business, which he continued to run until approximately one year prior to the assessment. Since then, James had been unemployed.

Psychiatric history: James was seen by a child psychologist while at school, but few details are known about this. His next contact with a mental health professional was following his arrest for non-accidental injury against his daughter. James was diagnosed with **Emotionally Unstable Personality Disorder (EUPD)** and was later assessed to also display 'Paranoid' personality traits. A cognitive assessment carried out indicated that James was likely to experience serious limitations in reasoning, critical thinking, planning, decision-making, and judgement. However, he was assessed to have the capacity to understand reasonably complex material, provided it is presented in a manner which is accessible to him.

Substance misuse: James had a history of heavy alcohol use. He also had a history of using amphetamines, cocaine, ecstasy, and occasionally cannabis.

Forensic history: James had prior police cautions for shoplifting and driving offences. There was documentation referring to a history of significant violence towards animals, but no charges were brought. James had prior convictions relating to possession of a knife, assaults against his daughter, assaults against a female intimate partner, and assaults against adult males.

Current concerns

Four years prior to the current referral, James commenced an intimate relationship with an adult female, who was deemed to be vulnerable due to her own history of significant domestic abuse, mental health concerns, and alcohol misuse. His partner, who will be referred to in this case study as 'Emma', had two teenage children from a previous relationship – a son and a daughter. Within months of the relationship between James and Emma commencing, concerns had been raised by Emma's children's school. These included significant alcohol use in the family home, high levels of stress and arguing between James and Emma, controlling behaviour by James towards Emma's children, and acts of aggression by James (including damaging items in the family home).

Emma's son moved out of the family home and Emma became pregnant with James' baby. Their son, who will be referred to in this case study as 'Ryan', was born approximately one year before the current referral. Following ongoing concern and an alcohol-fuelled fight involving a weapon, Emma's daughter and the baby were made the subject of an **Interim Care Order** and placed into the care of their maternal grandparents. James was required to leave the family home and permitted only supervised contact.

Assessment for suitability for therapy

The purpose of my assessment was to explore James' readiness for therapy, and his overall level of engagement with professionals, and to consider how this might impact the **therapeutic alliance**. This was done using a combination of clinical interview and psychometric assessment. Overall, James engaged well with the assessment process and was keen to demonstrate his eagerness to commence therapy. At times, this appeared somewhat overzealous and led me to consider that he was attempting to present a favourable image of himself during interview with me. In my experience, parents presenting with impression management are not uncommon within psychological assessment and treatment due to a desire to be assessed positively by professionals. Being aware of this from the outset aided my assessment of readiness for treatment and helped me to plan the therapy.

Clinical interview

Situation update

At the point of assessment, James was living with a friend. He was maintaining supervised contact sessions via video call with his baby who was still under the care of Emma's parents. James reported that he found this increasingly difficult due to feeling like he was "missing out" on witnessing his baby grow and develop. James also occasionally interacted with his stepdaughter during these contact sessions.

James reported that he and Emma continued to see each other during the supervised contact sessions and hoped to move back in together. When asked, he said they had been getting on well and not arguing, although recognised that this was because they were spending less time together. James explained that he had been asked to leave the family home because of the emotional and physical risks he posed to Emma and the children, relating this to his personality, but stating that he did not understand why he behaved in certain ways. James denied engaging in the reported controlling behaviour although went on to state that he was aware he liked to take control of some things, exampling cutting off the Wi-Fi as a way of punishing the children.

Additional family history

When discussing his reportedly close and supportive relationship with the children's maternal grandparents, James was able to link this to the lack of close relationship that he had with his own parents. I was aware that certain elements of James' self-report were not consistent with information I had previously read and so explored this further with him during the interview. James informed me that he never felt wanted by his stepmother, whom he felt treated him much less favourably than she did her biological children. James recalled few interactions with his father that did not result in him being shouted at or physically chastised. When asked whether there had been anyone in the family home whom he felt safe with, James told me that he had an older sister, whom he got along well with, adding that she died during James' childhood.

Current substance use

James informed me that on receiving the test results, which indicated that he was misusing alcohol, he had made an effort to reduce his intake. He reported that on average he would now consume approximately four cans of beer throughout a weekend, and he reported no drug use within the past 12 months. James had not undergone drug or alcohol testing recently and so his self-report could not be corroborated although I noted that he presented as sober during the assessment session.

Current employment status

James informed me at the time of assessment that he was unemployed, although he was keen to return to work on completion of therapy.

Previous therapeutic engagement

James informed me that he had completed a DAPP, which he found helpful, adding that he had learnt to use positive self-talk, to walk away from emotionally heated situations and that domestic violence also included emotional abuse and bullying. He reflected that some of his abusive behaviour had, in his mind, been an attempt to protect himself when he felt threatened or 'backed into a corner'.

Attitude towards therapy

When asked how he felt about having to attend therapy before a move back to the family home could be considered, James spoke positively about therapy. He explained that he had given this a lot of thought and that he hoped therapy would be a turning point for him. He recognised that therapy would be challenging but was able to acknowledge the need to deal with his behaviour to pose less risk of harm to those around him.

Psychometric assessment

The psychometric measures administered were selected to support the aims of the assessment; to explore James' ability to engage openly with me and his readiness for therapy. Each of the assessments described later was administered verbally to remove any pressure on James having to read as an attempt to be responsive to his difficulties with reading, as had been identified in the background documents. However, it is possible that this method of administration, which is not standard for many psychometric tests, may result in the client responding in a more socially desirable manner due to their response being more exposed to the assessor when compared to them responding with pen and paper.

Socially desirable responding

James completed the Paulhus Deception Scale (Paulhus, 1998), a self-report psychometric measure designed to assess socially desirable responding both as a response set (a temporary tendency caused by situational demands referred to as impression management) and as a response style (a trait-like tendency apparent whenever an individual gives self-reports referred to as self-deception enhancement). James scored slightly above average in relation to impression management, indicating that he may have been 'faking good' in his responses to a slight degree when compared to the normative sample of the tool. He scored above average in relation to self-deceptive enhancement, indicating an unconscious favourability bias which can be conceptualised as rigid overconfidence. Overall, individuals scoring high on both scales tend to have a trait-like style towards self-enhancement and a tendency to be influenced by situational demands to respond in a socially acceptable manner. It was my clinical opinion that while James' impression management was at play to some extent during the assessment, this was linked to his desire to be perceived as a good candidate for therapy so that it would be offered to him. Therefore, while this response style needed to be held in mind throughout therapy, I did not consider this to be a factor, which in itself, would prevent him from engaging meaningfully with therapy.

Blame attribution

To explore James' sense of responsibility in relation to previous violence, I requested that he complete the Gudjonsson Blame Attribution Inventory-Revised (1984), which is a self-report measure of an individual's blame attribution in relation to their offending behaviour. Blame attribution refers to the process of attempting to construct casual explanations for behaviours displayed by themselves and others (Gudjonsson, 1984). The inventory measures three factors: *mental element attribution* (i.e. blaming responsibility for the crime on mental illness or poor self-control); *external attribution* (i.e. blaming the crime on social circumstances, victims, or society); and *guilt attribution* (i.e. feelings of regret and remorse concerning the offence).

When completing this measure, James was asked to hold in mind the last offence of assault that he was formally charged with. James' scores on all three subscales were within the average range. This suggested that James did not attribute blame for his offending behaviour to internal factors over which he has little or no control, nor to external factors, indicating some acceptance of responsibility for his prior violent behaviour. Further, James' responses to this self-report measure indicated average feelings of regret and remorse for his offending behaviours at the time of testing. I was conscious of impression management and self-deception when considering the outcome of this measure, recognising that these scores may not be an accurate reflection of James' underlying beliefs.

Readiness for therapy

James completed two self-report measures designed to assess his readiness to engage in psychotherapy; the 31-item University of Rhode Island Change Assessment Scale, psychotherapy version (URICA; McConnaughy et al., 1989) and the 20-item Readiness for Psychotherapy Index (RPI; Ogrodniczuk et al., 2009), both of which can be used before treatment to help predict treatment outcome. James' score on the URICA measure indicated that he reported being ready to actively participate in therapy for behaviour change. James' score on the RPI indicated that he reported a willingness to work hard in therapy (perseverance), a commitment to resolving his distress, and a willingness to be open about his problems with the therapist. Again, I remained conscious of the possible impact of impression management and self-deception when considering these scores.

Case formulation

Formulation was central to the process of me being able to consider both James' motivation for therapy and to understand his risk of violence. It enabled me to identify what areas of his psychological functioning needed targeting through treatment and therefore also what model of therapy may be most suited to meeting those needs. To formulate this case, I adopted the '5 P's' model (Johnstone & Dallos, 2006). This is a structured model for formulation which encourages the clinician to consider not only the presenting difficulties but also the historical predisposing factors which increased the individual vulnerability to developing the current problem, precipitating factors known to have triggered the current problem, and perpetuating factors, which have maintained the cycle of the current problem. Importantly, this model also considers the protective factors which can include the client's resiliency, strength, and external support which can be used to increase their emotional health.

Presenting problems

James was an adult male with a chronic history of violence and aggression directed towards adults and children. At the point of assessment, he had been required to leave the family home due to concerns about the risk he posed to his partner, her children, and their baby son. James and his partner had a shared goal of coming together again as a family, but this had to be done in a manner which reduced the potential risk of harm.

Predisposing factors

James experienced a disrupted and disturbed childhood. He was separated from his birth mother due to concerns of neglect and taken into a large family in which he considered his stepsiblings were treated more favourably. James' reports of his relationship with his father and stepmother have varied; however, he has recounted numerous incidents of violence from his father, some of which carried a lasting sense of feeling frightened and powerless. These early traumatic and emotionally neglectful experiences likely resulted in an **insecure attachment style**, resulting in a long-standing deficit in the ability to develop healthy interpersonal relationships and to effectively manage his emotions within the context of others.

James' sense of not belonging appeared to be carried over to his experience in school, where the difficulties he experienced when trying to follow the lesson content created high levels of frustration. Being a perpetrator of violence created a sense of status during his time at secondary school, where James obtained a sense of belonging with a group of delinquent peers. This will have likely provided a reward for his violent behaviour, which not only predisposed the behaviour but also likely perpetuated it.

Precipitating factors

The combination of alcohol use, stress, and maladaptive coping strategies has historically been known triggers of James' violent behaviour. It seemed that at times of stress or conflict he would find himself feeling trapped or feeling a need to protect himself, which linked to his difficulties in emotional management. Additionally, it is possible that some 'in the moment justification', such as the need to 'teach the other person a lesson', also contributed to his decision to be violent.

Perpetuating factors

James had historically been considered to present with paranoid personality traits, making him more susceptible to perceived humiliation and rejection from others. Alongside this, his symptoms of EUPD appeared to make him more likely to respond in a dysregulated manner and 'lose his temper'. In addition, James' cognitive profile indicated that he was likely to experience serious limitations in reasoning, critical thinking, planning, decision-making and judgement, further affecting his capacity for clear and rational thinking in a high-arousal situation. His justification for his violence (as self-defence or acting to reduce threat) likely perpetuated the behaviour by both providing an excuse and helping him avoid recognition of the need to change his behaviour. It also seemed that punishment via the criminal justice system had not been a deterrent for James in relation to his repeated use of violence.

Protective factors

Despite the concerns highlighted by the local authority, James and Emma wanted the opportunity to try and come back together as a family. This gave James something tangible and motivational to work towards. They also had the support of Emma's parents, providing a support network. Further, although perhaps a little overzealous initially, James was demonstrating a desire to engage in therapy to better understand his actions and reactions. These factors were deemed as likely to serve as protective factors.

Treatment plan

During the assessment, it was apparent from my analysis and formulation, as well as through past assessments that had been conducted with James, that he continued to hold long-standing beliefs that he was acting in self-defence when engaging in acts of physical assault. This was therefore considered to be a key area of treatment need. Further, while James has been able to demonstrate the capacity to walk away from some heated (i.e. emotional or conflictual) situations, it was my opinion that additional intervention was required to support him to better identify and manage the early warning signs of heightened emotion and risk to deescalate a situation at an earlier stage. It was my opinion that James presented with several individual risk factors increasing the likelihood of future engagement with IPV, including low education level, unemployment, poor behaviour control, attitude justifying violence, a desire for power and control in relationships, EUPD with paranoid personality traits, historical substance misuse, and a history of an abusive childhood. These factors would need to be held in mind and addressed during the intervention.

Considering the earlier information, while holding in mind the identified EUPD and paranoid personality traits, it was my clinical opinion that an integrative therapeutic approach would be of benefit in reducing risk to others in this case. Case study evidence has supported integrated approaches as being of value in forensic cases of partner violence risk, although they also highlight that the duration of treatment offered is important in meeting the client's needs (Tully & Barrow, 2017). Based on James' identified needs and formulation of his violent and abusive behaviour, the integrated approach to therapy that I recommended was one incorporating elements of dialectical behaviour therapy (DBT) and schema therapy (described here). The local authority authorised and funded weekly intervention with James for 12 months.

Dialectical behaviour therapy

DBT was developed by Marsha Linehan in the 1980s to treat people with EUPD and since 2009, it has been the treatment recommended by the National Institute of Clinical Excellence (NICE guidelines 2009; see National Collaborating Centre for Mental Health, 2009) for this clinical presentation. DBT has also been found to be effective with other presentations, including anger management (Frazier & Vela, 2014; Ciesinski et al., 2022) and domestic abuse (Fruzzetti & Levensky, 2000).

DBT aims to help clients better manage their emotions, regulate potentially harmful behaviours, and improve their behaviours with others. A key component of DBT is skill acquisition; DBT techniques can support validation and empathy skill training through a focus on understanding the functions of emotional arousal, including aggression, identifying emotions and associated coping responses, and teaching skills in alternative ways of getting needs met (Fruzzetti & Levensky, 2000). A further component of DBT is the inclusion of mindfulness skills, which can help clients attend to their experiences in the moment and disengage from automatic negative thought patterns and impulsive behaviours, giving them space to use healthy coping strategies. Learning to foster acceptance (of the self, others, and situations) is another central element of this approach that I considered to be relevant to James' treatment needs.

Schema therapy

Developed by Jeffrey Young in 2003, schema therapy was originally developed to treat personality disorders and complex cases. With its emphasis on attachment relationships and **developmental theory**, it is considered particularly helpful for clients with chronic and enduring difficulties (Arntz & Van Genderen, 2020), experience of childhood trauma (Dadomo et al., 2016), and domestic violence (Smith, 2011). Schema therapy uses a range of strategies aimed at identifying and repairing the client's unmet childhood needs, where coping strategies which were initially developed to provide a means for survival have later developed into self-defeating patterns known as 'maladaptive schemas', which are repeated when faced with stressful triggers or events that remind them of their past.

Combining elements from these therapeutic approaches, the following key areas of focus were identified for James' treatment:

- Psychoeducation to increase James' understanding of the biological and psychological factors contributing to his presentation;
- Stabilisation and grounding intervention to equip James with coping strategies to manage his emotions and impulsive behaviours;
- Supporting James to process past trauma;
- To understand the role of adverse childhood experiences in developing James' personality structure and how this has, in turn, contributed to the violent and abusive behaviour that he has perpetrated, including his justification of his actions and the risk he poses to others; and
- To assess James' capacity for ongoing open and positive engagement with professionals.

Intervention

Psychoeducation

Early sessions aimed to provide some basic psychoeducation to increase James' understanding of the **survival response system**, including how and why stress can quickly flood both the mind and the body and the impact this can have on our capacity to think rationally. We explored the role of the autonomic nervous system and how the **sympathetic nervous system (SNS)** can be thought of in terms of being our accelerator, activating our fight/flight/freeze survival response system while our **parasympathetic nervous system (PNS)** can be thought of as our 'brake system', slowing us down and helping us return to a state of calm.

We discussed how over time, repeated activation of the SNS can result in the person not fully returning to their baseline state before subsequent activation is triggered again. In effect, the person learns to live on the edge of 'fight/flight/freeze' making them hypersensitive to the perceived threat. We discussed how at peak emotional arousal James was more likely to engage in aggressive behaviours in an attempt to achieve a sense of control in an otherwise overwhelming situation. This was discussed in relation to his experiences of feeling backed into a corner and his go-to response of fighting his way out.

Stabilisation/grounding

When a therapist adopts a stabilisation approach to therapy, focus is given to reducing shame, fear, and intrusive memories/traumas/distress by building the client's capacity to effectively recognise, reduce, and manage their symptoms/distress. Grounding techniques have become central to the early stages of trauma-sensitive approaches, such as DBT, where the client is holding onto high levels of internalised distress, which can often lead to overwhelming emotion. Grounding techniques often involve consciously engaging one or all of the senses or using a tangible object as a point of focus. The purpose is to help the client move away from overwhelming negative emotions, thoughts, or bodily sensations, bringing them into the present moment, allowing them to regain a sense of control and safety, better placing them to think clearly and make more rational decisions about their next actions.

The first technique shared with James was one known as '5,4,3,2,1', which involves consciously activating each of the five senses. James was moreover taught about diaphragmatic breathing and its capacity to provide fast and direct activation of the parasympathetic nervous system. Also, we explored the use of an 'anchor' for James, both in the form of a short phase, such as "I am in my house and I am safe" and in the form of holding a tangible object, both of which can help bring the mind away from distressing thoughts and into the present moment.

In addition to the aforementioned, we explored the importance of developing introspective awareness, gained through regular mindful attention to how James was feeling emotionally and physically, so that he was better able to notice indicators of arousal, as this is an early warning sign to potential aggression. We discussed how the regular (daily) practice of short mindfulness exercises could support this process and selected mindful practices which also served to support increased parasympathetic stimulation, including a **three-minute breathing space**, regular practice of diaphragmatic breathing, and engaging in a brief 'body scan' with progressive muscular relaxation.

Processing trauma

There is a strong focus in schema therapy for the clients to experience change, rather than just talking about it, due to an understanding that events, especially traumatic ones, can impact not only our mind but also our body, hormonal system, and nervous system. 'Imagery rescripting' is a technique used to reduce levels of distress associated with negative memories of early adverse experiences by supporting the client to rescript their autobiographical memory in line with their unmet needs (Smucker et al., 1995). Reframing James' hypersensitivity to threat and his tendency to react aggressively as a biological and learned coping mechanism, rather than as a 'personality disorder', allowed James to adopt a different stance. James had been told repeatedly that he was not a good person – by his parents, teachers, employers, and services. However, in taking this different stance, James was able to talk about the significant physical abuse he experienced as a child. One incident in particular caused him great distress. James recalled lying on his bed, at the age of eight, when his father entered his room. Shouting, his father took James by the throat and pinned him down; his father's whole weight above him. James became tearful recounting this incident, stating that at the time he thought his father was going to kill him and that he felt completely helpless to do anything about it. With this having been just one in a series of assaults, James recognised that he felt a high level of shame at not having spoken out about what was happening at home.

Over the course of six sessions, I worked with James to process the afore-mentioned memory using imagery. These sessions consisted of asking James to close his eyes and imagine himself back in that situation. James was reminded of the grounding techniques that he could engage in if he felt overwhelmed during the sessions. Then, speaking in the present tense, I supported James through the process of rescripting the situation to one whereby he was able to find the strength to push his father's hand away from his throat, move from underneath him, and tell his father that he was not going to allow him to hurt him anymore. From there, we spent time tuning into the emotions and physical sensations James' eight-year-old self was experiencing, having stood up to his father. This whole process was repeated on three further occasions until James did not experience physical arousal from the memory.

Acknowledging and understanding his risk

We discussed James' responses to situations in relation to the idea of him using an overcompensation style of coping strategy. That is he is likely to attempt to actively resist certain schemas being triggered, but when they are, he is likely to counteract vigorously, disproportionate to the situation. We discussed how in actively trying to differentiate his adult self from his child self (and the abused child schema), he adopted a rigid compensatory coping style of excessive self-assertion, status-seeking, and dominance. This was then explored in relation to James' long-standing justification of violence as self-defence and also how it is likely to have manifested in the paranoid traits, with the adoption of a 'get others before they get you' stance. Over the course of a few sessions, this discourse developed further, and James was able to recognise overt behavioural links to this theory and also more subtle ones, such as how asserting control over the children through disconnecting the Wi-Fi was an attempt to maintain this compensatory coping style.

Essential to this phase of therapy was my capacity to remain alert to James' previously highlighted tendency for impression management and self-deceptive enhancement. In my clinical opinion, the content that James was voluntarily bringing to sessions pertaining to challenges within the home appeared genuine. He spoke openly about situations he thought he could have handled differently, as well as those he thought he'd handled well. James would also frequently provide updates on situations that we had previously discussed, adding to the validity of these interactions. Reports from other professionals involved in the case also supported his positive self-development.

Developing the inner therapist

Approximately six months into therapy, conversations about our sessions ending and life post-therapy were introduced. Initially, James expressed concern about the prospect of not having a weekly meeting to discuss and explore his worries. We completed some work around what the ending would look like (i.e. that we would be taking a phased approach) and we found ways for James to develop a conviction that he was developing his own 'inner therapist' that was helping him to stop and think before reacting, using the many examples that he would often bring to the sessions, including difficulties as they arose within his relationships at home. James' ability to discuss these family disputes within sessions provided live material to explore. James took this opportunity to reflect on the nuances of what had made his responses different in recent times, which included his recollection of session content playing in his mind like a script. We discussed this internalisation of session content in the context of James developing his inner therapist.

Outcomes

Skill acquisition

As detailed earlier, over the course of therapy James was open to learning about the biological and psychological factors that had been contributing to his aggressive, controlling, and sometimes violent behaviour. He was also able to repeatedly demonstrate his capacity to employ effective coping strategies to manage emotionally arousing situations.

Processing childhood experiences

James had experienced chronic abuse as a child which had continued to manifest through high levels of anger towards his father and stepmother. Processing these experiences allowed James to move past the persistent emotional and physiological arousal he experienced in relation to this, resulting in him having more time to stop and think before reacting to stressful situations. This process also helped James to understand why certain triggers had previously pulled him into responding in a particular way.

Reducing his risk of violence and abuse

As detailed earlier, James was supported to understand his risk and importantly, his use of justification around his aggressive behaviours, using a schema therapy approach. This then formed a central component of subsequent sessions where we continued to have open discourse and explore situations which evoked a sense of James returning to the 'abused child' state. Also, we continued to develop his awareness of how this created a strong desire to protect himself via gaining control of the situation through whatever means necessary, and importantly, we continued to explore other available responses, which allowed James to relinquish control in a way that felt safe. During this stage of therapy, James began to rebuild his life in terms of finding employment, and following a risk assessment by social services, which incorporated professional meetings in which I was involved, he engaged with a phased return to the family home.

Engagement with professionals

I was still working with James at the point of it being two years since the local authority became involved with the family. We spent time reflecting on this and his approach to professional support. James was able to acknowledge that he had felt hatred and resentment towards the social worker initially and did not want to comply with her demands. However, over the course of therapy, he moved to a position of working openly with the social worker. James' capacity to reach out to professionals for support at times of need was also demonstrated towards the end of therapy when an incident occurred whereby information about his prior offending was shared publicly. James contacted me to inform me what had happened, stating that he was worried for his family's safety. I advised him to make contact with his relevant social worker to inform her, which he did. This gave me hope that James' defences had reduced enough to allow him to be willing to work with professionals in the future.

Moving back into the family home

Over the initial six months of therapy, James progressed from having supervised contact to spending increasing amounts of time in the family home with Emma and the children. This was managed through regular meetings involving the social worker, James, Emma, and me. After approximately four months, overnight stays were introduced, again closely monitored, and over the proceeding eight weeks, James progressed to moving back into the family home. Three months later it was deemed that the risk had reduced enough that social services were closing the case. I was honoured to be witness to the conversations, which included James telling the social worker how grateful he was for her input and the social worker telling James how proud she was of him.

Shortly after social services closed the case, and as planned, I reduced my input with James to fortnightly and introduced seeing James and Emma together as a couple on alternate sessions. The purpose of this was twofold; to increase the timeframe for managing without external input and to provide some ongoing monitoring of the relationship dynamics.

Discussion

This case study discussed a psychological intervention with a male presenting with chronic concerns pertaining to domestic violence, within the context of the family courts. I worked with James using a carefully integrated approach combining DBT and schema therapy over the course of 12 months. We had weekly individual sessions for approximately nine months reducing to biweekly sessions for the remaining three months, including some couple sessions. Despite having previously been resistant to making change and to authority, James engaged very well throughout the therapeutic process resulting in the family being reunited and no further allegations of aggressive, controlling, or violent behaviour being made. Social services assessed that risk had been reduced and closed the case.

IPV is a significant issue for society harming not only the immediate victim but the wider family unit (National Research Centre on Domestic Violence, 2021). This intervention helped reduce risk and reunite a family in a supported and supervised way indicating that psychological input is of value to the family court system. However, it is important to highlight that therapy is not always effective in risk reduction and not all perpetrators of family violence will be suitably assessed to reinstate child and partner contact. Therefore, suitability assessment and ongoing monitoring of effective engagement are essential, particularly given the identified challenge of impression management when working with this client group.

On reflection, it was my opinion that James' ongoing engagement with the work was aided by the nature of the protracted intervention, which aimed to facilitate his understanding of why he was driven to respond in certain ways and why he was still being pulled into certain patterns of responding, rather than adopting a 'fix the bad behaviour' approach. Research has demonstrated that having space to process underlying trauma can reduce the risk of violence (Karakurt et al., 2019). This case study has highlighted that this can indeed be the case, and it is hoped that outcomes such as this will provide further support for the need to fund and adequately resource individual psychological intervention in cases where IPV is a concern.

References

Arntz, A., & Van Genderen, H. (2020). *Schema therapy for borderline personality disorder.* John Wiley & Sons.

Bandura, A., & Walters, R. H. (1977). *Social learning theory* (Vol. 1). Prentice Hall.

Bell, K. M., & Orcutt, H. K. (2009). Posttraumatic stress disorder and male-perpetrated intimate partner violence. *Journal of the American Medical Association, 302*(5), 562–564.

Bowlby, J. (1997). *Attachment and loss. Volume 1: Attachment.* Pimlico.

British Psychological Society. (2016). *Guidance on the use of psychologists as expert witnesses in the family courts in England and Wales (standards, competencies, and expectations – Jan 2016).* www.bps.org.uk/news-and-policy/guidance-use-psychologists-expert-witnesses-family-courts-england-and-wales.

Children's Commissioner. (2019). *Childhood vulnerability in England 2019.* www.childrens-commissioner.gov.uk/report/childhood-vulnerability-in-england-2019/

Ciesinski, N. K., Sorgi-Wilson, K. M., Cheung, J. C., Chen, E. Y., & McCloskey, M. S. (2022). The effect of dialectical behavior therapy on anger and aggressive behavior: A systematic review with meta-analysis. *Behaviour Research and Therapy,* 104–122.

Dadomo, H., Grecucci, A., Giardini, I., Ugolini, E., Carmelita, A., & Panzeri, M. (2016). Schema therapy for emotional dysregulation: Theoretical implication and clinical applications. *Frontiers in Psychology, 7,* 1987.

Devaney, J. (2015). Research review: The impact of domestic violence on children. *Irish Probation Journal, 12.*

Frazier, S. N., & Vela, J. (2014). Dialectical behavior therapy for the treatment of anger and aggressive behavior: A review. *Aggression and Violent Behavior, 19*(2), 156–163.

Fruzzetti, A. E., & Levensky, E. R. (2000). Dialectical behavior therapy for domestic violence: Rationale and procedures. *Cognitive and Behavioral Practice, 7*(4), 435–447.

Gondolf, E. W. (2004). Evaluating batterer counselling programs: A difficult task showing some effects and implications. *Aggression and Violent Behavior, 9*(6), 605–631.

Gudjonsson, G. H. (1984). Attribution of blame for criminal acts and its relationship with personality. *Personality and Individual Differences, 5*(1), 53–58.

Johnstone, L., & Dallos, R. (Eds.). (2006). *Formulation in psychology and psychotherapy: Making sense of people's problems* (2nd ed.). Routledge.

Karakurt, G., Koç, E., Çetinsaya, E. E., Ayluçtarhan, Z., & Bolen, S. (2019). Meta-analysis and systematic review for the treatment of perpetrators of intimate partner violence. *Neuroscience & Biobehavioral Reviews, 105,* 220–230.

Kelly, L., & Westmarland, N. (2015). *Domestic violence perpetrator programmes: Steps towards change. Project Mirabal final report* (Project Report). London Metropolitan University and Durham University.

Kitzmann, K. M., Gaylord, N. K., Holt, A. R., & Kenny, E. D. (2003). Child witnesses to domestic violence: A meta-analytic review. *Journal of Consulting and Clinical Psychology, 71*(2), 339.

Machisa, M. T., Christofides, N., & Jewkes, R. (2016). Structural pathways between child abuse, poor mental health outcomes and male-perpetrated intimate partner violence (IPV). *PLoS One, 11*(3), e0150986.

McConnaughy, E. A., DiClemente, C. C., Prochaska, J. O., & Velicer, W. F. (1989). Stages of change in psychotherapy: A follow-up report. *Psychotherapy: Theory, Research, Practice, Training, 26*(4), 494.

Moreira, D. N., & da Costa, M. P. (2020). The impact of the Covid-19 pandemic in the precipitation of intimate partner violence. *International Journal of Law and Psychiatry, 71,* 101606.

National Collaborating Centre for Mental Health. (2009). *Borderline personality disorder: Treatment and management*. British Psychology Society.

National Research Centre on Domestic Violence. (2021). *Impact of domestic violence on health*. https://vawnet.org/sc/impact-domestic-violence-health.

Office for National Statistics Bulletin. (2021). *Domestic abuse in England and Wales overview: November 2021*. www.ons.gov.uk/peoplepopulationandcommunity/crimeandjustice/bulletins/domesticabuseinenglandandwalesoverview/november2021.

Ogrodniczuk, J. S., Joyce, A. S., & Piper, W. E. (2009). Development of the readiness for psychotherapy index. *The Journal of Nervous and Mental Disease, 197*(6), 427–433.

Paulhus, D. L. (1998). *Paulhus Deception Scales (PDS): The balanced inventory of desirable responding-7*. Multi-Health Systems Inc.

Semiatin, J. N., Torres, S., LaMotte, A. D., Portnoy, G. A., & Murphy, C. M. (2017). Trauma exposure, PTSD symptoms, and presenting clinical problems among male perpetrators of intimate partner violence. *Psychology of Violence, 7*(1), 91.

Smith, M. E. (2011). A qualitative review of perception of change for male perpetrators of domestic abuse following abuser schema therapy (AST). *Counselling and Psychotherapy Research, 11*(2), 156–164.

Smucker, M. R., Dancu, C., Foa, E. B., & Niederee, J. L. (1995). Imagery rescripting: A new treatment for survivors of childhood sexual abuse suffering from posttraumatic stress. *Journal of Cognitive Psychotherapy, 9*, 3–17.

Tully, R. J., & Barrow, A. (2017). Using an integrative, Cognitive Analytical Therapy (CAT) approach to treat intimate partner violence risk. *Journal of Aggression, Conflict and Peace Research, 9*(2), 128–140. http://doi.org/10.1108/JACPR-08–2016–0244.

What Works for Children's Social Care. (2022). *Domestic violence perpetrator programmes*. https://whatworks-csc.org.uk/evidence/evidence-store/intervention/domestic-violence-perpetrator-programmes/

World Health Organisation. (2017). *Intimate partner violence*. https://apps.who.int/violence-info/intimate-partner-violence/

3 The effectiveness of bespoke psychological intervention for an adult male convicted of internet-facilitated sex offending

Jennifer Bamford

Introduction

Prevalence of online offending

Over the last 20 years, the use of the internet has soared; between March 2000 and March 2021, there was 60.6% increase in the number of users worldwide (Miniwatts Marketing Group, 2021) and the Office for National Statistics (2018) estimates that 90% of UK adults have access to the internet. Whilst the majority of people may use the internet for legal and non-harmful reasons, the increased accessibility of online material has brought with it a rise in internet-facilitated offending behaviour (IFOB). IFOB is a term which references a very broad range of offences, from those relating to the Fraud Act (2021), the Computer Misuse Act (2011–2012), the Communications and Malicious Communications Act (2011–2012), and the Sexual Offences Act (2003). This chapter focuses on sexual offences committed via the internet, which may broadly fall into the following categories:

- The possession/making/distribution of indecent images of children or extreme pornography
- Disclosing private sexual images without consent
- Sexual communication with a child
- Causing or inciting a child to engage in sexual activity
- Arranging or facilitating commission of a child sex offence

The reported prevalence rate of online offending varies between sources, although the overall trend is, worryingly, on the increase. For example the Internet Watch Foundation (IWF) reported a 15% increase in reports of online child sexual abuse from 2019 to 2020 (IWF, 2021). The NSPCC similarly reported a 16% increase in reported online sexual offences between 2018/2019 and 2019/2020 across 44 police forces in the UK (NSPCC, 2020). Added to this increased prevalence is the IWF finding that the severity of indecent images of children (IIOC) had increased, with the prevalence of **category A**

DOI: 10.4324/9781003213116-3

images increasing from 28% to 33% in 2017. Seto (2015) and Seto and Hanson (2011) raise a pertinent issue regarding this apparent rise in internet offending; is it that internet sexual offenders represent a new type of sexual offender, or do they reflect the transformation of conventional sexual offending through new technologies? Whilst this is a complex issue to approach, recognising the evolving role of technology in the ways that people offend is another important element of considering risk and additionally, when approaching the question of preventative treatment.

Risk of contact offending in internet offenders

An ongoing focus for researchers has been about developing reliable risk assessment tools for online sexual offending, in addition to determining the ways that risk assessors might be able to predict the risk of contact offending in those who have committed internet-facilitated offences (often called 'crossover' offending). It is well established that the majority of those who have convictions for the possession of IIOC have a sexual interest in children (e.g. Seto et al., 2010) and, on this basis, it might reasonably be questioned whether that sexual interest could lead to a person with IIOC offences committing a contact sexual offence. However, studies have shown that a relatively small percentage of online offenders also have proven contact offending convictions; Seto et al. (2011) concluded that one in eight online offenders also have convictions for contact sexual offending, with this rising to four in eight when self-reported offending is considered. This of course does not account for offences for which the person is not convicted or those which the person is not willing to disclose, and the rates therefore could be higher. Indeed, the identification of 'crossover' behaviour is an issue of concern for criminal justice and social services. Exploring and formulating the function of online offending is also an important consideration within the process of psychological assessments. Briggs et al. (2011) assert there to be a clear distinction between fantasy-driven and contact-driven offenders, with the former engaging in online offending (viewing images, exchanging images etc.) that for them is gratifying in itself, with no desire to commit a contact sexual offence.

Whilst it is not possible to predict whether a person with online sexual offences will cross over to commit contact offences, research has demonstrated that crossover offenders tend to be typified by a combination of paedophilic sexual interests and general antisociality, offence-supportive attitudes, barriers to empathy, lower self-esteem, and a lack of guilt (Babchishin et al., 2015). There are also behaviours or lifestyle factors that are known to be more prevalent in those who crossover to contact offending from internet offending (Johnson, 2015; Houtepen et al., 2014; Quayle & Taylor, 2002, 2003; Long et al., 2012; Sheehan & Sullivan, 2010; Webb, 2020):

- More time spent online
- Higher number of indecent images collected

- More explicit images
- Interacting with other index image offenders
- Access to children
- Having minimal contact with others offline who do not share paedophilic interests
- Less educated
- More likely to have been abused or exposed to trauma at an early age

Importantly, there is no known threshold linking the number of factors someone may have with the likelihood of crossover offending (i.e. it is not the case that the higher number of factors present will necessarily predict crossover) and the assumption that all IIOC offenders will crossover is not empirically supported. However, risk management strategies that align with the known risks are important when working with this group of people, as is the role of psychological intervention, which forms the foundation of this chapter. The reasons an internet offender may escalate to commit a contact offence have been the source of several empirical studies. Access to a child, which may be less likely for internet-only offenders (Jung et al., 2013), is a somewhat obvious risk factor for an escalation. Smid et al. (2015) found that contact offenders were more likely to possess more deviant and a higher quantity of IIOC, which may indicate an increased likelihood of a sexual interest in children as a central motivator for those who also commit contact offences.

Risk assessment of online offenders

The majority of tools that have been tested for their ability to predict recidivism in online sexual offenders are **static/actuarial** in nature. See Tully et al. (2013) for a discussion of static and **structured professional judgement (SPJ)**-based risk tools. In 2010, Osborn et al. (2010) investigated the use of the Risk Matrix 2000 (Thornton et al., 2003; Thornton, 2007) and the Static 99 (Hanson & Thornton, 2000, 2003) with those convicted of online sexual offences. The authors concluded that both measures overestimated the risk levels in internet offenders leading to the suggestion that more bespoke measures may have greater relevance to this subgroup of sexual offenders. Seto and Eke (2015) were the first to offer such a tool in the form of the Child Pornography Offender Risk Tool (CPORT), which is also a static/actuarial risk tool. Through a five-year follow-up analysis of 266 adult male internet offenders, the authors concluded that the risk factors which increased the rate of recidivism included:

- Younger offender age
- Any prior criminal history
- Any contact sexual offending
- Any failure on conditional release

- Indication of a sexual interest in child pornography material or pubescent/ pre-pubescent children
- More boy than girl content in images
- More boy than girl content in other child depictions

Seto and Eke (2015) found a moderate predictive accuracy of the CPORT in their study. A more recent study by Savoie et al. (2021), using a population of 141 men convicted of offences relating to **child sexual exploitation material** (CSEM), concluded that the CPORT was well calibrated to predict sexual and CSEM recidivism in their overall sample of sexual offenders. It is also suggested in the literature that internet offenders reoffend less frequently than contact offenders; for example Jung et al. (2013) found that 11% of online offenders reoffended over a two-year follow-up period compared to 14% for contact offenders. Furthermore, it is suggested that the majority of reoffences by online offenders are in the form of another IIOC offence. Seto et al. (2011) found that of their sample of 1,247 internet offenders, 2% of internet offenders reoffended via a contact offence and 3.4% reoffended with another IIOC offence.

Risk assessment literature regarding internet offending is, sadly, significantly lacking when it comes to dynamic assessment, such as the use of SPJ tools. The Risk of Sexual Violence Protocol (RSVP; Hart et al., 2003) is commonly applied to those with sexual offending histories and whilst the tool is intended to include a broad range of sexual offending in its definition of 'sexual violence', including non-contact offending, it is not specifically adapted for, or designed to consider, the unique nature of internet offending. As a result, the 'Sexual Violence History' items contained within the tool, which are concerned with the nature of the offending (*physical coercion in sexual violence* and *psychological coercion in sexual violence*), could fail to capture online offending of an exclusively non-contact nature, that is possession of indecent images of children. Clinically, this leaves psychologists and risk assessors in a position where existing tools for contact sexual offenders are used with limitations with internet offenders and need to be supplemented with research-based or individual considerations in relation to this group. Further research and tool developments are required to be more responsive to this unique subset of sexual offenders.

Treatment of those with online offending histories

There has been gradual development of psychological interventions that are specific to those with internet-facilitated sexual offending. The National Probation Service in England and Wales offered a group-based programme, the **internet Sex Offender Treatment** (i-SOTP; Middleton & Hayes, 2006) until recent years, which had demonstrated moderate improvements in socio-affective functioning and a decrease in pro-offending attitudes (Middleton et al., 2009). In 2018, this was replaced by another programme named 'iHorizon', which is another group-based intervention offered by the criminal justice system for adult males with a history of internet-facilitated sexual offending.

iHorizon involves 23 sessions exploring internet use, relationship skills, the development of prosocial support, managing sexual thoughts, and developing positive self-identity. At the time of writing, there were no published studies focusing on the effectiveness of this programme.

For people with internet sexual convictions, or those who have engaged in such offending but have not been convicted (or may not have acted on this risk), who are living in the community, there is a limited range of available services in the UK outside of those provided by probation services. Those available outside of statutory services like probation often require a degree of self-funding by the person seeking treatment. For example, organisations in the UK such as The Lucy Faithful Foundation, Safer Living Foundation, and Specialist Treatment Organisation for the Prevention of Sexual Offending (StopSO) offer group and individual treatment for men with sexual convictions, those who are under investigation for sexual offences, or those who have concerns about their sexual behaviour. In 2018, Perkins et al. completed the first scoping review of interventions for online sexual offenders and identified that there was limited research into the effectiveness of interventions with internet offenders, with few providers completing systematic intervention evaluations. Perkins et al. completed interviews with staff from some of the aforementioned UK-based service providers and noted that there was positive focus placed on the targeted nature of interventions for offenders and that "clients could work with a broad range of therapists and skills, allowing for a flexible, client-centered approach" (p21).

Perkins et al. (2018) concluded that greater focus on early intervention and prevention approaches was required, including careful consideration of the language used when referencing online offending. It was noted that the term 'child pornography' which was present in some of the online literature (including this being in the title of the 'CPORT' discussed earlier in this chapter) might imply consent where there is none. Related to this issue, in 2016, Greijer and Doek (2016) from the Interagency Working Group (IWG) published the 'Terminology Guidelines for the Protection of Children from Sexual Exploitation and Sexual Abuse' and the term Indecent Images of Children (IIOC) was concluded as the most appropriate term in UK law and will be the term used throughout this chapter.

Overview

The remainder of this chapter will explore the process of assessment and treatment of an adult male, John, who had committed online sexual offending. John's details have been edited to maintain anonymity for him and any others involved in the case.

When I first met John at the point of initial assessment, he had been charged with (and was awaiting sentencing for) the possession of one indecent image of a child and for attempting to incite a child to engage in sexual activity (via online methods). He had started individual therapy with a specially trained therapist on this basis and was planning on engaging in three focused treatment sessions with another service which offer treatment and support for people at risk of sexual offending. I was asked to interview John and explore his treatment needs with a view to ensuring that his therapy had a forensic focus in terms of this being specifically targeted at reducing and managing his risk. Prior to John's sentencing date I was asked to complete an addendum report commenting on progress in therapy to that point (three months post initial assessment) and also providing my opinion on risk and whether John's risk could be managed in the community. John was further followed up for the purpose of this case study as is detailed in this chapter.

Patient history

Childhood and education

John recalled frequent relocations as a child due to his father's job. He had one younger brother. His father died when John was 28 years of age although at the time that I met John, his mother was still alive and supportive of him. John told me that his father's death was difficult for his mother to cope with, although she eventually met someone else and formed a relationship. John's mother's partner died around ten years prior to the initial assessment, and she had not had a partner since that time. John described that his mother had been emotionally and practically demanding of him over the years and that he had sometimes considered this to be excessive but could not say no to her.

When I first met John, he was residing with his mother as part of his bail conditions; he had previously been living with his wife. When asked to reflect on his childhood, John recalled a "normal and happy childhood". When this was explored, he recalled often blaming himself for his parents arguing, explaining that he would often engage in "impulsive, stupid" behaviour which would then spark an argument between his parents. John recalled an attitude whereby he liked to "test the water" and defy those who told him he could not do something. He felt that to some extent this trait was still there for him, although he was unable to offer examples of this type of behaviour after early adulthood. John reported a very good relationship with his brother whom he described as a friend to him. John showed an appreciation for the stress that his circumstances might be putting on his brother's marriage at present due to his brother spending a significant amount of time assisting John with his legal difficulties.

Employment

Due to the family frequently relocating when he was a child, John went to several schools in different parts of the country. He reported that despite these moves he was able to make friends, although he stated that he has also had a small, close group of friends rather than a wide circle of friends. John recalled some early bullying at school, and he told me that he did not report the bullying until the bully threw a brick through a window at John's home. John recalled that due to his frequent relocations, he was a year behind his peers when he went to university. After leaving university, he initially had an intention to join the armed forces but realised this was not for him and changed his career path. After leaving university, John went straight into employment working in the catering industry where he remained for several years. He described this job as very stressful, and he walked out on a couple of occasions after his working hours became excessive. His next job was in management for a different company, and he remained with this company for over 20 years. His job involved long periods of time working away from home, which he considered had increased his sense of isolation and loneliness. John explained that in the year before his offence, his travel increased and he began to find the job unmanageable, reporting that he went to his boss several times to ask for support, but it was not resolved. John reported that he found it difficult to say "no" to people at work, and the frequent international travel affected his sleeping pattern; his working pattern and stress were both considered significant in regard to his offending pathway. John was sacked from his job when he was arrested, and at the point of initial assessment, he remained unemployed.

Relationships and sexual history

John stated that he was a "late starter" and had his first relationship when he was aged 19 at university, reporting that "I was shy and lacked in confidence, and we lived in isolated villages growing up so there wasn't really the chance". John recalled that he had been in around ten relationships in his life, none of which were for longer than 1.5 years, until he married his girlfriend, when he was aged 27. His (now ex-) wife was around the same age as him, and their marriage lasted five years. John described their marriage as a mistake and said that his family had not approved of his ex-wife, recalling that even on the day of his wedding his mother had told him that it was not too late to change his mind. John stated that his ex-wife's level of interest in sex was higher than his, and that this caused some problems. She eventually had an affair and the relationship ended, with John reflecting that "I think I was glad, I wanted it to end, and I needed a reason". Two years later, John met his second wife, and they had been together for 20 years at the time of initial assessment. John does not have children although he told me that he and his wife tried for a child. He reflected that "it's something I regret; I would've enjoyed being a father". John reported that he had never been unfaithful to any of his partners until around four years before the assessment, when he began speaking online to women about sex and went on to have sex with four women he met through this method. He reported that sex with these women was not as satisfying as the fantasy and that it did not fulfil him.

John told me that he first had sex at the age of 18 and that he has had around 30 sexual partners across his life. He stated during interview that he had never engaged in bondage or violent sex and had never searched for indecent images of children, violence, or any other offence-related material online prior to his offences. He reported that he had largely not been interested in pornography and was instead aroused by the sexual conversations he would have with people online. He reported feeling as though he did not have a sexual interest in children but accepted that he was aroused by the sexualised discussions he had with children during the offending. John reported that he was not masturbating to thoughts of the victims when he was not talking to them but said that he did masturbate when talking to the victims, adding that he ejaculated during some discussions with one of the victims. John stated that at the time of the offending, he was masturbating 2–3 times a week which was significantly more than he considered 'normal' for him.

John reported that he has always had a small, close group of friends. He reported that his friends viewed him as having a glamorous job and that he did not want to tell them about his problems with work stress for this reason, wishing to maintain "bravado". He did not want them to think that he could not cope. John reported that many of his friends had maintained their support of him following his arrest, although he reported that some of his relationships had been strained, explaining for example that one of his friends works with children, which had contributed to his friend wanting some distance from him since his arrest.

Substance misuse

John said that he had never taken any type of illegal drug, and there was no evidence to the contrary. He reported that whilst he drinks alcohol, he did not drink to excess, and this had never been a problem for him.

Mental health

John had never experienced mental health problems until the time of his arrest and subsequent remand in prison. He was prescribed medication for anxiety in prison but gradually reduced the dosage of this medication over time. At the time of initial assessment, he was still taking this medication but at a low dosage. John told me that he had never attempted suicide but did have suicidal thoughts when he was apprehended for the offence and subsequently when he was released from prison on bail.

Offending history

Index offence

John pleaded guilty to internet-facilitated sex offences, including the possession of indecent images of children and attempts to incite a child to engage in sexual activity. His devices were seized and searched by the police, and he was found to have been conversing online with five individuals claiming to be female children. Three of these five individuals were decoys operated by a vigilante group, who later apprehended John after their decoy asked John to meet her.

When asked about events leading up to the offence, John reported that a year before the offence he had begun to experience erectile dysfunction during sexual activity with his wife. He reported that he felt embarrassed and after it happened more than once they stopped having sex altogether. As a result, the intimate side of their relationship began to dwindle, and they stopped being tactile with one another. John did not consult his doctor about the problem, nor did he discuss it with his friends. He said that he felt emasculated by not being able to satisfy his wife sexually and added that he pushed her away as he was worried that any physical intimacy would turn sexual, and then he would then fail to achieve an erection. John then began spending time in online chat rooms, talking about sexual content with others. He reported that he felt sexually frustrated but would not want to talking to his wife about this. The frequency of this behaviour increased until John was regularly engaging in sexualised conversations online with others, most often when he was away from home on business trips. He reported feeling aroused by the conversations he was having and the discussions of them meeting up for sex. John aligned this behaviour to an addiction, feeling as though he craved the thrill of these online discussions and the sexual gratification it afforded him. He stated that for a long time he was just having conversations as opposed to any sexual contact with those he had been communicating with online, although he eventually met up with four adult women, on separate occasions, for sex. He reported that these casual encounters did not fulfil him as much as he had expected. He said that he felt dirty and guilty afterwards, and that he eventually stopped meeting with women for sex, although acknowledged meeting socially with some women he had initially met online, without there being any sexual contact.

John began to travel more, and his online behaviour increased, coinciding with a decrease in the level of physical and verbal contact he was having with his wife. His account of how he contacted children online was that over time he came to engage more recklessly online, and through a desire to speak to "anyone" and to seek further thrills, he began speaking with female children. He reported having online sexual discussions with children and separately with adult females and that whilst he did not have a preference, he found he was aroused to both his discussions with adults and children. The transcript of his online conversations with the victims evidenced that he had engaged in grooming type behaviours with the victims, such as telling them about himself, indicating that he cared about them and their well-being, giving the victims advice, and gradually pushing boundaries in his discussions with them, including telling the victims that they could engage in whatever level of sexual contact they wanted with him.

Criminal history

John had no criminal convictions on his record prior to the index offence.

Dynamic needs assessment and progress in therapy

To formulate John's offending and to better understand his risk factors the RSVP (Hart et al., 2003) was used. This was applied initially as a guide through which to explore relevant risk factors and later to apply an overall risk rating to John's case. RSVP is a structured professional judgement sexual violence risk assessment tool designed to structure clinical judgement and to help identify relevant risk factors. The RSVP is split into five domains: sexual violence history, psychological development, mental disorder, social adjustment, and manageability. Additional risk factors relevant to the case can be added flexibly by assessors. John's offending involved using the internet to facilitate what *could have been* a contact offence. In this case, John did not commit a contact offence, but he did attend an area where he believed he was going to meet a child. In this sense, John's offending is internet-based but also has many of the hallmarks of an attempted contact offence. The RSVP was used with additional consideration of the online nature of his offending and was applied bearing in mind the limitations that this tool was not designed specifically for those convicted of internet-facilitated offending.

The RSVP, alongside clinical interview and psychometric assessment with John, helped me to formulate the following risk factors/treatment needs:

- *Cognitive distortions, which justify sexual offending*; a need to explore and challenge these in therapy;
- *Problems with insight and self-awareness*; a need to develop a greater understanding of factors contributing to offending and to develop a robust risk management plan that incorporates internal and external resources;
- *Avoidant coping and problems managing stress*; to develop a more proactive coping style, to monitor for signs of avoidance, and to develop his ability to be assertive with others regarding his needs;
- *Sexual arousal to children*; to explore his spectrum of sexual interests, specifically a sexual arousal in children, and ways of managing this sexual interest;
- *Problems with open communication with others*; to explore barriers to him showing vulnerability to others and ways of developing his social circle;
- *Difficulty achieving/maintaining emotional intimacy*; to explore his understanding of emotional intimacy, why this might have been lacking in his relationship during the offending, and how he might seek to develop intimacy in his relationship moving forward;
- *Emotional detachment from online offending*; to explore and develop his understanding of how children are victimised online, the impact of this for victims, and to develop an emotional understanding/empathy for children who are victims of abuse.

When I met John for initial assessment (time point 1), he had already completed 20 hours of individual therapy and was very motivated to continue to engage in therapy. He had developed a degree of insight into his offending, but there remained key areas where insight development was still required, and he was still trying to adjust to life after his arrest and the subsequent impact of his offending becoming known to those close to him. John was taking medication for anxiety and was recovering from a period of suicidal ideation, which had been contributed to by his apprehension by the vigilantes having been live-streamed on social media. At time point 1, I recommended that there were outstanding areas of treatment need and that he should continue to engage in a further 4–5 months of therapy. The identified needs, listed earlier, were communicated to his therapist.

By the second time we met, approximately three months later (time point 2), John had completed 20 more therapy sessions as well as six hours of intervention accessed through a different service which offers intervention and support for people with sexual convictions. He had therefore completed approximately 46 hours of therapy in total prior to his sentencing hearing. I spoke with both therapists who had worked with John to explore his level of engagement and progress in therapy, with both professionals speaking highly of his engagement and progress. I also re-interviewed John at this time point, and it was my view that he demonstrated improved insight into his risk and also improved coping ability and had evidently developed a trusting relationship with his therapist. For example, John had been able to identify the following cognitive distortions at the time of his online offending:

- *They are on an adult site, what are they here for?*
- *I'm not hurting anyone.*
- *This is a fantasy, not physical.*
- *They are here to talk about sex, or they wouldn't be here.*
- *They are here to learn; I'm helping them learn.*
- *They chose to go online for this.*
- *She was talking sexually, I don't need to push this, she's obviously grown up enough.*
- *I'm not forcing them [victims] to do anything.*

John's therapy was multi-modal, including the use of **person-centred counselling** and **transactional analysis**, as well as **CBT-based therapy**. John had also completed a relapse prevention plan informed by the **Good Lives Model** (GLM; Ward & Gannon, 2006). At this time, which was just prior to his sentencing hearing, I reviewed the RSVP and concluded that John's risk would be manageable if he remained in the community, permitting that he continued with therapy, was supervised by probation services, and engaged with the management strategies I recommended. John's case went to court and a **suspended sentence** was imposed. He was also required to be listed on the **Sex Offenders Register** for ten years and was given a five-year **Sexual Harm Prevention Order (SHPO)**. His sentence meant that he could continue engaging with therapy whilst under probation supervision and whilst adhering to the conditions of his SHPO.

Assessment of change

I completed two more follow-up meetings with John (time point 3; 15 months post initial assessment and time point 4; 21 months post initial assessment), during which I repeated various psychometric measures, described here.

As the assessment had a forensic context, a response style assessment was used to assess impression management and self-deception – the Paulhus Deception Scales (Paulhus, 1998). This did not indicate distorted responding at the time of initial assessment; however, there was a slight increase in impression management and self-deception using the PDS in the subsequent three interviews with him, which was kept in mind when interviewing him. At time point 1, the Beck Anxiety Inventory (BAI; Beck & Steer, 1990) indicated minimal symptoms of anxiety, and the Beck Depression Inventory (BDI-II; Beck et al., 1990) suggested that he was suffering from a moderate level of depressive symptoms. These measures of mental health difficulties were consistent with John's presentation and self-report, but importantly they were not of a level that appeared to impact his ability to engage with the assessment. Repeat testing found that he continued to demonstrate minimal anxiety at the subsequent three time points, and his levels of depression reduced after our first assessment to minimal. Hypersexuality was analysed through the use of the Hypersexual Behaviour Inventory-19 (HBI-19; Reid et al., 2011). John recognised that when he was offending, his behaviour had been of a hypersexual nature although at time point 1 when the HBI-19 was applied, which was six months after his arrest and after 20 therapy sessions, his level of sexual behaviour and preoccupation had reduced, and he continued to score below the clinical threshold in the following three assessment periods. At time point 1, I did not assess John's level of impulsivity although I utilised the Barratt Impulsivity Scale (BIS-11; Patton et al., 1995) at the subsequent three time points, and John scored below average on each of these occasions, indicating that impulsivity in general was not a concern.

Clinical interview

Discussion with John helped to inform my assessment of his risk and progress. By time point 4, John had found work, was having regular meetings with his probation officer, and was continuing with therapy but at a very decreased rate of once every few months as a 'check in' following core therapy being completed. He had reduced his medication and was practising **mindfulness**, which had helped him to better manage stress. Something that was important to John was his relationship with his wife and by time point 4, they appeared to be in a place of recovery and John described feeling "like we're back to where we were 10 years ago". He noted that it had taken him around a year before he could feel free to be happy again, feeling guilty for having hurt those around him. He reported that he had found pride in his therapy progress and was committed to "proving that I will never reoffend again".

John found that he developed a good relationship with his probation officer whom he felt understood him and his risk. He described feeling scared of using the internet in the first few months whilst he was under probation supervision and said that the police had checked his devices as part of unplanned visits to him, which he was happy to facilitate. John recognised that rebuilding his self-esteem had taken time and that various life events had made this more difficult, such as his neighbours frequently telling people that John was a sex offender. For John, the memories of his offending and the resulting consequences were "haunting" for him; he said that he had not detached from these memories, but rather he used them to remind himself of this difficult time, to try to keep himself focused and motivated to build a better, offence-free life.

During our last interview, John was very positive about the various forms of support and treatment he had been able to access, and it was apparent that whilst accessing therapy and making progress had potentially contributed to mitigation in relation to his sentence (i.e. may have been viewed positively by the sentencing judge), he had also found great personal benefit in understanding himself, and his offending, more than he had done before. Clinical interview, collateral information, and psychometric testing were considered against the risk framework of the RSVP. I concluded that it appeared as though the nature of the treatment provided, his progress within this, and his engagement with mandatory supervision with probation services and the police had contributed to risk reduction over time. There was no reported or convicted further offending for John during the follow-up time.

Conclusions

The case study described within this chapter has explored the process of assessing risk and treatment needs in an adult male who had used the internet to sexually offend. John had used the internet to view IIOC and had also used it to facilitate contact with someone he believed to be a child (actually a vigilante group decoy). As John had attended the scene where he believed a child was present, there was the possibility that had the child been real, he may have committed a contact sexual offence; I had considered his 'inciting' offence to be an attempted contact offence in terms of potential risk and a step towards what was described earlier in this chapter as 'crossover' offending. The RSVP, although not designed specifically for internet-facilitated offending, in my clinical view had been helpful in aiding risk formulation, which may have been contributed to by John's offending not being exclusively IIOC related. It is however clear that more research on risk tools for the assessment of people with internet-facilitated offending is needed, so that such tools can include factors specific to this group. The RSVP is however flexible in that individual risk factors or needs can be added to the list of risk factors already included in the tool, which is useful when working with people who may have broader risk factors linked to their offending profile or life history and circumstances.

If one considers John's case in the context of the research presented earlier in this chapter regarding 'crossover' offending, he does not have many of the factors associated with those who move over to contact offending. John was an educated individual, he was in his forties at the time of his offending (and therefore not 'young' as the literature defines), he had no previous convictions and no known history of antisociality, there was no evidence of sexual interest in or behaviours towards male children, he did not have a large collection of IIOC, did not have access to children in his personal life, and had not been exposed to significant early trauma. Nevertheless, John went on to arrange to meet with a child, and this highlights the importance of considering cases individually; formulating the risk factors unique to the individual being assessed and not applying risk factors as 'checklists' to determine future behaviour.

In summary, examination of treatment needs and risk indicated that John was someone with no prior offending history who, within the context of stress, hypersexuality, problems in his intimate relationship, and a capacity to be aroused to underage children, offended using the internet as a vehicle to communicate with and plan to meet someone he believed to be a child. He did not present with many of the static risk factors identified by Seto and Eke (2015) as predictors of internet reoffending, nor do we see him as someone with antisociality often seen in contact offenders. However, his offending escalated, and he attempted to meet a child. John maintained throughout the assessment and follow-up period that he would not have committed a contact sexual offence (had the victim not been a decoy), although from a risk management perspective, his attempt to meet the decoy in the 'real world' (i.e. offline) was an escalation in risk.

It is notable that John began to access treatment following apprehension; a situation that is quite common for those involved in the criminal justice system. From a cynical perspective, motivation for treatment for someone at this stage of the legal system (pre-sentence) may be influenced by an attempt to impress the sentencing judge and receive a lesser sentence than they may otherwise receive. From a positive perspective, the person may be motivated to engage in treatment due to a desire to not cause harm or reoffend in the future. Motivation could be a combination of these and other reasons, although arguably if the treatment successfully reduces risk of reoffending and the person engages in it, initial reasons for starting treatment could become less important. However, it is clear that there is a strong argument for greater resources to be aimed at preventative treatment which someone posing a risk could access before they act on offence-related thoughts or urges as well as a need for treatment being available to people after they have offended. In John's case, for example, he reported that had he been more aware of services that could have guided him away from online offending, he would have accessed these at a much earlier stage. Indeed, community-based services that work with online sexual risk have begun to advertise their services on websites hosting illicit material, which is one useful way of diverting those in the process of offending, whether it is their first time accessing such websites or whether they are a repeat offender.

John self-funded his therapy. It should therefore be noted that John was in a privileged position to be able to afford a high-quality and intensity of bespoke intervention whilst awaiting sentencing. This opportunity and his positive engagement meant that John was able to develop his insight and, in my view, reduce his risk in the 18 months between his arrest and his sentencing. He had other protective factors which likely aided him at that time, including an intimate relationship and supportive family members, the support of whom he learned to utilise more effectively as his treatment progressed. John therefore does not represent the majority of offenders who pass through the criminal justice system; in my experience, most offenders are not in a position to self-fund their legal defence or any form of therapy, and many have very little prosocial support. It is important that practitioners working in the field of internet sexual offending continue to advocate for public funding being allocated for treatment, so that there is not a class/wealth imbalance and so that treatment is accessible to those who need it, free at point of service. Public or government funding for sex offender treatment may be a controversial topic and an unpopular choice for the general public, who understandably may be keener to see public money provided to victims or other worthy causes. However, ultimately, sexual risk treatment for those who have offended (or may be at increased risk of doing so) could successfully reduce the individual's risk of sexual offending, and in turn avoid the creation of another victim. To this end, more research into the effectiveness of available treatment for internet offending risk (and sexual offending risk in general) is essential to provide an increased evidence base which practitioners can be aware of, in order to recommend certain treatments more confidently as being effective in reducing risk for those with internet offences.

References

Babchishin, K. M., Hanson, R. K., & VanZuylen, H. (2015). Online child pornography offenders are different: A meta-analysis of the characteristics of online and offline sex offenders against children. *Archives of Sexual Behavior, 44*(1), 45–66.

Beck, A. T., & Steer, R. A. (1990). *Beck anxiety inventory manual.* The Psychological Corporation.

Beck, A. T., Steer, R. A., & Brown, G. K. (1990). *Beck depression inventory-II manual.* The Psychological Corporation.

Briggs, P., Simon, W. T., & Simonsen, S. (2011). An exploratory study of internet-initiated sexual offenses and the chat room sex offender: Has the internet enabled a new typology of sex offenders? *Sexual Abuse: A Journal of Research and Treatment, 23,* 72–91.

Greijer, S., & Doek, J. (2016). *Terminology guidelines for the protection of children from sexual exploitation and sexual abuse. The interagency working group on sexual exploitation of children.* Retrieved February 2, 2022, from www.ohchr.org/Documents/Issues/Children/SR/TerminologyGuidelines_en.pdf

Hanson, R. J., & Thornton, D. (2003). *Notes on the development of a static-2002.* www.publicsafety.gc.ca/cnt/rsrcs/pblctns/nts-dvlpmnt-sttc/index-en.aspx.

Hanson, R. K., & Thornton, D. (2000). Improving risk assessment for sex offenders: A comparison of three actuarial scales. *Law and Human Behavior, 24,* 119–136.

Hart, S. D., Kropp, P. R., Laws, D. R., Klaver, J., Logan, C., & Watt, K. A. (2003). *The risk for sexual violence protocol (RSVP)*. The Mental Health, Law, and Policy Institute of Simon Fraser University.

Houtepen, J. A. B. M., Sijtsema, J. J., & Bogaerts, S. (2014). From child pornography offending to child sexual abuse: A review of child pornography offender characteristics and risks for cross-over. *Aggression and Violent Behavior, 19*, 466–473.

Internet Watch Foundation (2021, June 2). Taskforce will stop millions of the most severe child sexual abuse images and videos being shared online. *Internet Watch Foundation*. www.iwf.org.uk/news-media/news/taskforce-will-stop-millions-of-the-most-severe-child-sexual-abuse-images-and-videos-being-shared-online/

Johnson, S. A. (2015). Child pornography users & child contact offenders: Applications for law enforcement, prosecution and forensic mental health. *International Journal of Emergency Mental Health and Human Resilience, 17*(4), 666–669.

Jung, S., Ennis, L., Stein, S., Choy, A. L., & Hook, T. (2013). Child pornography possessors: Comparisons and contrasts with contact- and non-contact sex offenders. *Journal of Sexual Aggression, 19*(3), 295–310.

Long, M. L., Alison, L. A., McManus, M. A., & McCallum, C. (2012). Child pornography and likelihood of contact abuse: A comparison between child sexual offenders and noncontact offenders. *Sexual Abuse: A Journal of Research and Treatment, 25*(4), 370–395.

Middleton, D., & Hayes, E. (2006). *Internet sex offender treatment programme theory manual*. NOMS Interventions Unit, Ministry of Justice.

Middleton, D., Mandeville-Norden, R., & Hayes, E. (2009). Does treatment work with internet sex offenders? Emerging findings from the internet Sex Offender Treatment Programme (i-SOTP). *Journal of Sexual Aggression, 15*, 5–19.

Miniwatts Marketing Group. (2021, July 3). *Internet growth statistics: Today's road to e-commerce and global trade internet technology reports*. Internet Worlds Stats Usage and Population Statistics. www.internetworldstats.com/emarketing.htm.

NSPCC. (2020, September 3). Police record over 10,000 online child sex crimes in a year for the first time. *NSPCC*. www.nspcc.org.uk/about-us/news-opinion/2020/2020-09-03-cybercrimes-during-lockdown/

Office for National Statistics. (2018). *Internet users, UK: 2018*. Author.

Osborn, J., Elliot, I. A., Middleton, D., & Beech, A. R. (2010). The use of actuarial risk assessment measure with UK internet child pornography offenders. *Journal of Aggression, Conflict and Peace Research, 2*(3), 16–24.

Patton, J. H., Stanford, M. S., & Barratt, E. S. (1995). Factor structure of the Barratt impulsiveness scale. *Journal of Clinical Psychology, 6*, 768–774.

Paulhus, D. L. (1998). *Paulhus Deception Scales (PDS): The balanced inventory of desirable responding-7*. Multi-Health Systems Inc.

Perkins, D., Merdian, H., Schumacher, B., Bradshaw, H., & Stevanovic, J. (2018). Interventions for perpetrators of online child sexual exploitation: A scoping review and gap analysis. *Centre of Expertise on Child Sexual Abuse*. Retrieved February 2, 2022, from www.csacentre.org.uk/documents/online-cse-interventions/

Quayle, E., & Taylor, M. (2002). Child pornography and the Internet: Perpetuating a cycle of abuse. *Deviant Behavior, 23*(4), 331–361.

Quayle, E., & Taylor, M. (2003). Model of problematic Internet use in people with a sexual interest in children. *CyberPsychology & Behavior, 6*(1), 9–106.

Reid, R. C. Garos, S., & Carpenter, B. N. (2011). Reliability, validity and psychometric development of the hypersexual behavior inventory in an outpatient sample of men. *Sexual Addiction & Compulsivity, 18*, 30–51.

Savoie, V., Quayle, E., & O'Rourke, S. (2021). Predicting risk of reoffending in persons with child sexual exploitation material offense histories: The use of child pornography risk tool in a Scottish population. *Sexual Abuse, 34*(5), 537–567.

Seto, M. C. (2015, July). Internet-facilitated sexual offending. *SOMAPI Research Brief.* https://smart.ojp.gov/SOMAPI-brief-internet.

Seto, M. C., & Eke, A. W. (2015). Predicting recidivism among adult male child pornography offenders: Development of the Child Pornography Offender Risk Tool (CPORT). *Law and Human Behavior, 39*, 416–429. http://dx.doi.org/10.1037/lhb0000128

Seto, M. C., & Hanson, R. K. (2011). Introduction. Special issue on internet-facilitated sexual offending. *Sexual Abuse: A Journal of Research and Treatment, 23*, 3–6.

Seto, M. C., Hanson, R. K., & Babchishin, K. M. (2011). Contact sexual offending by men with online sexual offenses. *Sexual Abuse: A Journal of Research and Treatment, 23*(1), 124–145.

Seto, M. C., Reeves, L., & Jung, S. (2010). Explanations given by child pornography offenders for their crimes. *Journal of Sexual Aggression, 16*, 169–180. http://doi.org/10.1080/13552600903572396.

Sheehan, V., & Sullivan, J. (2010). A qualitative analysis of child sex offenders involved in the manufacture of indecent images of children. *Journal of Sexual Aggression, 16*(2), 143–167.

Smid, W., Schepers, K., Kamphuis, J. H., van Linden, S., & Bartling, S. (2015). Prioritizing child pornography notifications: Predicting direct victimization. *Sexual Abuse, 27*(4), 398–414.

Thornton, D. (2007). *Scoring guide for risk matrix 2000.9/SVC.* www.birmingham.ac.uk/documents/college-les/psych/rm2000scoringinstructions.pdf.

Thornton, D., Mann, R., Webster, S., Blud, L., Travers, R., Friendship, C., & Erickson, M. (2003). Distinguishing between and combining risks for sexual and violent recidivism. In R. A. Prentky, E. S. Janus, & M. C. Seto (Eds.), *Understanding and managing sexually coercive behavior. Annals of the New York Academy of Science, 989*, 223–235.

Tully, R. J., Chou, S., & Browne, K. D. (2013). A systematic review on the effectiveness of sex offender risk assessment tools in predicting sexual recidivism of adult male sex offenders. *Clinical Psychology Review, 33*, 287–316.

Ward, T., & Gannon, T. A. (2006). Rehabilitation, etiology, and self-regulation: The comprehensive good lives model of treatment for sexual offenders. *Aggression and Violent Behavior, 11*, 77–94. https://doi.org/10.1016/j.avb.2005.06.001.

Webb, R. (2020). *A review of the risk posed by internet offenders.* Retrieved February 2, 2022, from file:///Users/jenniferbamford/Downloads/RMA-AReviewoftheRiskPosedbyInternetOffenders-LiteratureReview-2018%20(1).pdf1.

4 Providing psychologically informed care in the youth custodial estate

Making 'Every Interaction Matter'

Clare Holt and Joel Warkcup

Youth custody in the UK

Whilst a detailed overview of the youth custodial estate in the UK is beyond the scope of this chapter, the information provided here is intended to provide context regarding the broader system(s) in which the case study described in this chapter took place. The authors posit that the micro and macro systems which exist within, and surround, youth custody services exert crucial influences upon the day-to-day practices in these unique settings and, most importantly, upon the children in our care. In recent years, there has been a substantial reduction in the numbers of children placed in custodial settings across the UK, with the average total population between April 2018 and March 2019 ($n = 859$) representing a 70% reduction compared to the previous ten years. The numbers fell further during the COVID-19 pandemic with the number of children in custody in the UK reported at being just 554 in June 2021 (YCS, 2021). Children detained in custody in England and Wales can be placed in one of three different placement types. Secure Children's Homes (SCHs) are the smallest facilities, each providing care for between 7 and 38 boys and girls, with the highest staff-to-child ratios. Secure Training Centre's (STCs) were built to provide care to between 60 and 80 boys and girls aged between 12 and 17, with lower staff-to-child ratios than SCHs. Young Offenders Institutions (YOIs) provide care only to boys who are aged 15–18 years old; YOIs have the lowest staff-to-child ratios and are much larger, with the largest accommodating over 300 children. The census completed by Hales et al. (2016) identified that less than 5% of children detained in youth custody in the UK were females and, reflective of broader patterns of marginalisation and exclusion, there are disproportionately more children of black and minority ethnic background in youth custody. This census identified that children are commonly placed far from home, with the furthest reported distance being in excess of 400 miles.

As the threshold for custodial placements has increased, and the population of children in these settings has reduced, there has been a simultaneous and somewhat inevitable increase in the complexity of needs presented by this cohort of children. A now well-established body of research has evidenced the impact that **Adverse Childhood Experiences (ACEs)** have upon a developing

DOI: 10.4324/9781003213116-4

child. In summary, ACEs are highly stressful events or situations that happen during childhood and/or adolescence and include single events or prolonged threats to a young person's safety, security, trust, or bodily integrity. Evidence consistently demonstrates that ACEs are associated with a wide range of health concerns (including physical and mental health) and social problems across the lifespan (British Psychological Society, 2019). Children in custody have often been exposed to neglect, maltreatment, violence, and instability in their living arrangements, often experiencing multiple placements and, therefore, fractured experiences of adult care (Chard, 2021; Hales et al., 2016). This is a group of children who have commonly experienced material deprivation, social exclusion, school exclusion, and long-standing contact with statutory services, including social care and criminal justice agencies. For example, detailed analyses of the early experiences of 80 children in contact with the criminal justice system in 2021, in the West Midlands region, identified that they experienced significantly high rates of ACEs including abuse, witnessing domestic violence, parental substance misuse, parental criminality, and parental mental health needs (Chard, 2021). Consequent to this diverse array of early experiences, children in custody demonstrate drastically increased rates of mental health and well-being needs (Leon, 2002) and a broad range of neurodevelopmental needs that are often inadequately identified and supported (Hughes & Chitsabesan, 2015). It is beyond the scope of this chapter to discuss the pathways and mechanisms through which early adversities and trauma have the wide-ranging implications they are proven to have. However, in summary, the evidence base informs us that ACEs fundamentally affect the developing brain due to maintaining a state of toxic stress in response to which the brain will employ coping mechanisms, which may be adaptive in the short term but have wide-ranging long-term implications, which can include impairment to the developing brain structures and neural pathways (Nemeroff, 2016). That is not to say that ACEs should be used as a form of checklist as to how much a child is affected by them nor do they affect people in the same way; rather, they should be considered on an individual basis.

The small cohort of children currently in custody in the UK is frequently described by terms that include 'high risk', 'high harm', and 'high vulnerability'. It is suggested that, taken alone, these labels can function to locate responsibility for the individual's needs within the child themselves; in doing so, there is an associated danger that individualised narratives and experiences are lost and that insufficient attention is paid to the systemic influences on each child's strengths and needs. There has been recognition of a need for major reform in the youth custodial estate in England, and a framework of integrated care has been implemented across the estate since 2018. The framework, titled 'SECURE STAIRS' (Taylor et al., 2018), represents a joint initiative between health and justice services and is underpinned by a number of principles that encapsulate trauma-informed and evidence-based practice. The principles describe a whole-systems approach to providing collaborative care that prioritises each child's own narrative and their relationships with key professionals. Promoting the principle that 'Every Interaction Matters', SECURE

STAIRS emphasises the pivotal importance of custodial staff being adequately trained in adolescent development and the impact of trauma and advocates for an approach to care that is underpinned by **psychological formulation**. Emphasis is turned away from specialist interventions (including psychological therapy) towards focusing efforts on ensuring that a child's day-to-day experience within the custodial setting promotes psychological and relational safety. This relies upon relationships with professionals who are able to understand and mentalise the child's position and adopt an approach to their caregiving role that emanates elements of therapeutic parenting. Integral to the framework are different forms of staff support, including group reflective practice and supervision, which are intended to ensure that self-awareness and self-care are embedded in a way that helps to ensure that staff members are best equipped to manage the inevitable emotional demands of working with children in a custodial setting. The SECURE STAIRS framework is aligned with a broader movement across health services to provide **Trauma-Informed Care (TIC)** which seeks to recognise and respond to an individual's past experiences of trauma. TIC prioritises an individual's physical, psychological, and emotional safety. Whilst different 'models' and definitions may emphasise different aspects of TIC, commonly cited themes and principles include safety; trustworthiness and transparency; peer support; collaboration and mutuality; empowerment, voice, and choice; and cultural, historical, and gender issues (Substance Abuse and Mental Health Services Administration, 2014).

Whilst the pragmatic premise of SECURE STAIRS may appear relatively simple, there are dynamics and barriers that, in practice, create somewhat inevitable complications during the implementation process. Custodial establishments typically include a number of different agencies and 'partners' that specialise in distinct areas of service provision, for example education, health, and substance use. Partner agencies are contracted to provide their service alongside the main operational provider, and it is common for each agency to hold a unique view of the 'primary task' and to be evaluated by different outcome criteria. These elements, combined with staffing and resource shortages that are commonplace within custodial settings, complicate the paradigm shift and culture change envisioned by the SECURE STAIRS framework in a multitude of ways. It is also imperative to consider the relevance of 'trauma-organised systems'; youth custody services are vulnerable to repetitive and chronic stress, and this can destabilise the cognitive and affective foundations that are necessary for groups to function in a coordinated and collaborative way (Bloom, 2010). Ultimately, SECURE STAIRS represents a re-conceptualisation of what it means to provide 'care' in the youth custodial estate, and at times, the anxiety, fear, and threat experienced by those working in these settings have culminated in defensive and rejecting responses. For example it is not uncommon for the core tasks underpinning the SECURE STAIRS framework (e.g. staff training, formulation meetings) to be cancelled at the last minute or operational staff to be prevented from attending. Additionally, staff across different professional groups have been known to be scathing of the overall aims of the framework and to be vocal about the benefits of an alternative approach, which is primarily focused on risk management and even punishment. The challenges inherent in implementing the Integrated Framework of Care are mentioned here to draw attention to the overarching context within, and dynamics amongst, the environment in which the direct and indirect clinical work of this current case study took place. As summarised by Sadie and Stokoe, "Resource shortages and the territoriality promoted by competing demands can lead to hostility between agencies that mirror the mistrust and splits between the boys" (2020, p. 23).

Meet 'Sami'

Sami was aged 15 when he was remanded to custody charged with an offence of Grievous Bodily Harm (GBH) with intent. During his period of remand, Sami was placed in an STC for three months; he was subsequently sentenced to a six-year custodial sentence and remained at the same establishment. During the offence, Sami and a group of his similarly aged peers physically assaulted the victim (a same-aged peer) with a knife; the victim sustained permanent injuries as a result of the assault. Sami reflected that the offence followed a long-standing disagreement between the victim and a close friend who was also present at the time of the offence. He described that they had unexpectedly 'bumped in to' the victim on the day of the offence and that when confrontation between his friend and the victim escalated, he felt pressured to support his friend by harming the victim.

It is noted that whilst the processes of assessment, psychological formulation, and intervention planning are separated and presented in a sequential fashion within this chapter, in practice, these processes are iterative and frequently run concurrently. As new information and 'data' is gathered (for example on the basis of clinical contact, observations, or Sami's management of and responses to particular situations), this is used to revise the working formulation and subsequently, where indicated, intervention plans.

Assessment

Sami was placed in the STC and, as is typical for all new arrivals in this setting, was offered the opportunity to engage with a range of initial admission assessments across all partner agencies within the first week of his period on remand. For Sami, whilst this assessment process began at the time of admission to custody, more specific assessments with the psychology team were conducted three months later once he had been convicted and sentenced. Amongst these initial admission assessments, Sami engaged with a process referred to as 'My Story'; a co-produced and continuously developed therapeutic assessment framework used to gather a narrative of a child's own experiences and to gain their direct input into goal setting and care planning. 'My Story' uses questions relating to significant relationships, notable previous experiences, and an individual's self-perceived strengths and difficulties to gather information relevant to a developing formulation. Completion of 'My Story' is deliberately flexible and individualised and, for example, can include the use of genograms and visual representations of thoughts or emotions to ensure that it is accessible for all young people. The hope is that such insights will allow both the child and professionals to have a contextualised and meaningful description of the child's previous and current experiences, which in turn can be used to inform intervention planning both systemically and through direct one-to-one intervention. Sami reported experiencing the process of completing 'My Story' to be therapeutic and described that it helped him to develop a narrative of some of his childhood experiences, the impact these had upon his relationships with caregivers, and the function of his offending behaviour (specific details are outlined in the 'Formulation' section of this chapter). Sami stated that he had not previously reflected on past experiences in this way and described increased self-awareness and insight because of engaging with this semi-structured assessment tool. When he was completing 'My Story', Sami recognised a particular area of current need, disclosing that he felt unsafe in the custodial environment and was fearful of moving around the custodial site. As is discussed in subsequent sections of this chapter, this lack of safety whilst in custody went on to hinder Sami's engagement in education, extracurricular activities, and ultimately his ability to engage in therapeutic intervention.

Forming another element of the admission assessment process, Sami completed the Comprehensive Health Assessment Tool (CHAT; Chitsabesan et al., 2014) with members of the healthcare team. The CHAT is a screening tool consisting of five parts that, in combination, provide an overview of an individual's physical health, mental health, neurodevelopment, and substance use. Sami's engagement with these admission assessments fluctuated, and it is understood that this was influenced by a variety of factors, including the disparity between the essence of the 'My Story' tool and more traditional forms of assessment in custody. Given that the aim of 'My Story' is to empower children in telling their own story in a way meaningful to them, Sami experienced this as therapeutic and collaborative; he was supported with the beginnings of a narrative of his past experiences and their impact. However, Sami reported experiencing other assessments as being 'done to' him, describing a lack of collaboration, a large focus on risk, and limited consideration of his childhood experiences or his many strengths. Sami conveyed an experience of these assessments as being overtly structured, prescriptive, and didactic and described that this resulted in him feeling excluded from the development of his care plan. Sami described that his experience of professional assessments was similar to his experience of community-based **Child and Adolescent Mental Health Services (CAMHS)**, explaining that he was offered several assessment-based appointments; however, due to the inflexible nature of such appointments, he felt as though he could not explore his difficulties and subsequently disengaged. In contrast to the rigidity of such assessments, Sami highlighted the need for a flexible approach, the opportunity to develop relationships, and to move through assessments or interventions at a pace with which he felt comfortable.

For example Sami had previously engaged positively with a community-based **Play Therapist**. He described that the collaborative nature of the play therapy assessment and intervention enabled him to feel sufficiently secure to explore his difficulties and to develop a meaningful relationship with a practitioner; ultimately, Sami was supported to experience safety in a therapeutic relationship.

In addition to the more structured and formalised assessments, key sources of information that helped to inform initial understandings of Sami's strengths and needs were the more informal interactions and experiences had with Sami by staff members working across all different departments and agencies. A common observation made by staff members who had interactions with Sami was his desire to provide care to those he viewed as vulnerable. A specific example of this was Sami requesting to reside in the same residential unit as another child who was struggling to adapt to the routine and structure of a custodial environment. As examples of his caring nature, Sami would provide guidance through the demonstration of how to wash clothes and cook food. Sami's ability to communicate his needs to those around him in various contexts was also highlighted as a particular skill that was evident from the early stages of his time in custody. Sami demonstrated leadership abilities by volunteering to develop the practical educational opportunities that were available in the secure environment, and in the process of planning this endeavour, he supported other children to engage in education in a positive way. A particularly notable skill Sami demonstrated through this process was his ability to communicate with others. As additional observational 'data', operational staff often offered the reflection that at times of distress, Sami could be particularly "aggressive" or "controlling". This would often be in situations in which Sami did not experience safety or did not experience staff groups to be offering him care in a way that was consistent with what he believed *should* be provided.

During the period of assessment, Sami reflected on his need for control in certain situations. Examples of this included Sami requesting to be supervised by particular members of staff and to influence decisions around potential placement moves. It was observed that within the custodial environment, these behaviours were sometimes referred to as 'needy', 'attention seeking', or 'controlling'. However, alternatively, the developing formulation drew attention to these behaviours functioning to meet Sami's hidden needs. In particular, the need for control appeared to represent attempts to try to ensure a positive outcome in otherwise threatening situations and subsequently to increase Sami's sense of safety and security. It was noted that in many cases it was Sami's experience of relational safety, and not physical safety, that was threatened. During the process of formulation (detailed further later), Sami considered how his need for control may in part be related to his experience of being placed in the care of the local authority when he was in the community and therefore becoming a **Looked After Child**, when he was aged 13. Sami described his movement through the care system as being 'done to' him and reflected that being out of control in such situations resulted in feelings of disempowerment, anxiety, and a lack of security about his care. Sami's individual experiences highlighted the importance of co-produced care planning and collaborative formulation, intended to be shared with staff to support their understanding of Sami's hidden needs and to develop a compassionate understanding of his behaviour and his needs.

On the basis of all sources of information included in the admissions process, a referral was made for additional support from the psychology team and the wider healthcare team (including physical health, mental health, and substance misuse). The request for further assessment and support referred to Sami's historical experiences of trauma, his current low mood, and self-harming behaviours which were understood to reflect his difficulties adjusting to the custodial environment.

Formulation

Psychological assessment identified that Sami had experienced a childhood characterised by neglect, emotional abuse, witnessing of domestic abuse, and parental substance abuse. Through co-production of an integrative formulation, it was possible to develop a shared understanding of Sami's strengths and needs whilst also identifying and prioritising goals and targets for intervention. Importantly, in addition to the individual meetings with Sami himself, the process of formulating also actively involved the input of operational staff and staff working with Sami who were in a range of different professional roles (for example education and chaplaincy). The rationale for working in this multi-disciplinary and multi-agency way was outlined to Sami in a transparent manner, and his agreement to the associated information-sharing protocols was a prerequisite to working in this way.

For the purpose of ease and accessibility, the '5 P's' model of formulation was used to organise and collate all sources of information. The 5 P's model provides a holistic framework that supports the systematic consideration of all factors, past and present, that may be exerting an influence on an individual's presenting needs (Weerasekera, 1996). Due to its ease of use and accessibility, this model is commonly used across diverse settings with broad-ranging professionals and service-users alike. It is important to note that the process of formulation is not intended to culminate in static statements of 'truths' or 'facts'; rather, it involves a series of informed hypotheses that can be reviewed and revised in an iterative fashion over time. Research evidence, alongside clinical experience (including in this particular case from Sami's direct feedback), identifies different benefits of collaborative formulation, which include improved working relationships and service engagement (Redhead et al., 2015; Shaw et al., 2017).

Presenting difficulties can be described as a statement relating to a child's presenting problems that may relate to emotions, thoughts, and behaviours. This initially introduces individualisation into the process of formulation and clarifies existing difficulties (Johnstone & Dallos, 2006). At the time of the initial assessment, Sami identified the following presenting difficulties from his perspective:

- Feelings of anxiety relating to a lack of experienced safety in the custodial environment
- Low self-esteem
- Low mood
- Trauma symptomatology, which included re-experiencing the offence he committed (i.e. nightmares and flashbacks), hypervigilance, and a proneness to perceiving threat from others
- Previous offending behaviour

The assessment process identified that Sami demonstrated some interpersonal difficulties when forming and maintaining relationships with others. For example he readily felt uncared for, experienced a sense of neglect by others, and he was observed to have difficulties trusting others and therefore developing meaningful relationships (with adult caregivers in particular). These interpersonal experiences were understood to be directly associated with some unwanted behaviours identified during the assessment process, for example Sami's aggression, violence, and self-harm were each understood as care-eliciting behaviours, relied upon by Sami to get his interpersonal needs met in the context of his anxiety and uncertainty within interpersonal relationships. Given the range of presenting problems, and the way they appeared to interlink, the remaining sections of the formulation attempted to make sense of these problems as a whole rather than focus on only one specific difficulty.

Predisposing factors can be summarised as the pre-existing factors which may have increased a child's vulnerability to their current problems. These may be external or internal in nature and provide a longitudinal understanding of the difficulties. Having such information in a formulation may allow for interventions to be more in depth and better able to maintain change (Johnstone & Dallos, 2006). Sami witnessed his mother being subjected to domestic abuse which was perpetrated by her partner; also, he observed parental substance use in the home from a young age. Sami was subject to emotional abuse which included an experience of being controlled by his mother and having negative comments directed towards him on a regular basis, for example "you are an evil child" and "you're not my child". Whilst in the care of his mother, Sami was subject to periods of neglect during which he would be forced to sleep outside of his family home. When Sami was aged approximately 13, his mother stated she could no longer care for him, and Sami subsequently experienced a number of different local authority care placements prior to his placement in custody. Sami described his experience of rejection by his mother (and subsequent carers) and an interpretation that he was not deserving of care. Sami said that going through multiple care placements resulted in him "losing everything", such as family, friends, and home connection; this was identified as a significant link to Sami's need for control and his strong desire to experience care as he feels it "should" be. In addition to these family based experiences, Sami described spending lots of unsupervised time with peers in the community and a pattern of antisocial behaviour developing amongst the group. Sami witnessed various assaults on friends in the community and described experiencing these as traumatic. Overall, Sami's experiences in the community appear to have exposed him to a degree of unpredictability and threat and perhaps also normalised certain types and patterns of behaviour. Sami reported frequently experiencing situations as threatening and presented a notable degree of hypervigilance. This was understood to be associated with Sami often presenting as verbally aggressive and threatening to others or in some cases, becoming physically aggressive to ensure his own safety. Sami referred to this feeling of hypervigilance as fear and anxiety and identified feeling as though he must harm another to prevent being harmed himself. Although not suggested by Sami himself, it may be hypothesised that presenting in a state of hypervigilance at least in part resulted in Sami harming the victim of the offence; Sami harmed the victim before the victim could come to harm Sami.

Precipitating factors can be described as external and internal factors that are likely to have triggered the current presenting difficulties (Johnstone & Dallos, 2006). During the assessment process, Sami identified a range of factors that had preceded the presenting difficulties outlined earlier. Of great significance for Sami was the breakdown of his relationship with his mother and his subsequent experience of multiple care placements. Prior to coming to custody, Sami had also experienced the loss of his grandfather, and this represented the loss of a supportive and protective relationship. Sami described experiencing pressure from his peers to offend, and to behave in certain ways, and he was able to reflect on the ways that his desire/need for approval and relational connection influenced his behaviour when in the company of peers. In addition to the events and experiences outlined earlier, Sami identified that his placement in custody had triggered some emotional experiences that are central to understanding some of his presenting difficulties. For example he explained that feeling anxious, hypervigilant, and perceiving potential threat from others in this novel environment were highly significant and affected his behaviour and presentation.

Perpetuating factors can be described as those that maintain the current difficulties; often referred to as a 'maintenance cycle'. Such factors may provide a focus for intervention by 'breaking' the maintenance cycle (Johnstone & Dallos, 2006). During the course of assessment, Sami identified that his experience of being placed outside of the family home, and subsequently being moved between different placements, perpetuated his perception that others did not care about him and were unable to care for him. He recognised that in response to these experiences he had made attempts to elicit care through aggression or intimidation. Subsequently, his caregivers did not respond in a way that met his needs, therefore reinforcing his perception and experience that he is undeserving of care/unable to be cared for. Sami became aware that this exacerbated his experiences of low mood and low self-esteem.

The process of assessment identified a number of core beliefs, which were understood to have been shaped by Sami's early experiences and to be perpetuating his presenting difficulties. Examples of these core beliefs included "I deserve to rot"; "others don't care about me/for me"; "I must be in control in order to be cared for"; "I must be demanding or aggressive in order to receive care". Sami reflected that as a result of his childhood experiences and subsequent belief that those in a caregiver role do not/cannot care for him, he would often seek the support of peers in the community to establish a sense of safety and to attempt to develop caring and supportive relationships. Sami moreover reflected that the peer group he sought out frequently engaged in antisocial behaviour and that, to continue to establish these relationships, he also engaged in such behaviour. Engaging in antisocial behaviour in the community often resulted in Sami being exposed to traumatic experiences, further perpetuating his belief that he is unsafe. Furthermore, Sami's willingness to engage in such behaviour to establish and maintain relationships with peers, coupled with Sami presenting in a state of hypervigilance due to his previous experience of threat and trauma, provides some insight as to how he came to harm the victim of the offence.

Protective factors include the child's resilience, support network and strengths that help to maintain emotional health. Recognition of such factors allows for interventions to build on existing resiliency, strengths, and skills. Utilising such factors provides pathways to long-term progress, including the attainment of personal goals (Johnstone & Dallos, 2006). The assessment process identified a range of strengths and positive traits demonstrated by Sami. As already outlined, he was observed to be caring towards others, particularly those who were vulnerable in some way. Despite some of the interpersonal difficulties that have been identified, Sami was open to working with professionals and at times demonstrated an ability to build meaningful and positive relationships with others. Sami was motivated to learn new skills and coping strategies, and communicate his needs more effectively. At times, he was able to communicate his needs in an appropriate and non-harmful way. Sami moreover demonstrated leadership qualities, including an ability to advocate for himself and others. Through the assessment process, Sami demonstrated insight and self-awareness and recognised his aggression to be a care-eliciting behaviour. It was theorised through the process of formulation that such behaviours were a means of eliciting care as Sami felt care *should* be provided and that any deviation from this ideology was interpreted to imply that care is not being provided at all. It was also theorised that this elicited a strong emotional response at times which contributed to aggressive behaviour, subsequently maintaining a cycle of feeling rejected.

Sami reported that the process of co-producing a formulation was therapeutic and his feedback conveyed that, in itself, this process was a meaningful intervention. He said that developing an understanding of his pertinent experiences, and their impact, helped to provide an alternative narrative to his longstanding internalisation and negative core beliefs. Furthermore, Sami reported that understanding the impact of trauma and adverse childhood experiences offered validation of his feelings and his care-eliciting behaviours. This proved to be an aspect of Sami developing his understanding of the impact of his personal experiences and developing a compassionate self-image. Due to Sami's positive engagement in the process of co-producing a psychological formulation, this was reviewed and further developed as subsequent interventions were evaluated and further assessments took place, as is generally considered to be best practice (Johnstone & Dallos, 2006).

Intervention planning

Principles

Before outlining some of the specific facets of the intervention plan for Sami, it is pertinent to highlight some of the broader fundamental principles that underpin the provision of psychological care in an STC, as shaped by the SECURE STAIRS framework:

- *Every interaction matters.* As already outlined, the SECURE STAIRS model emphasises the pivotal importance of operational staff and strives to ensure that a child's moment-to-moment and day-to-day experience of care is emotionally containing, trauma-informed, and underpinned by a sensitive understanding of their individual strengths and needs. This fundamental principle dictates that a primary task running alongside any individual psychological intervention is staff training and support; details regarding the relevance of this to Sami's care are provided later.
- *Collaboration and centrality of the child's voice.* It is recognised that as a result of various societal, cultural, and political influences, children in secure care have frequently experienced marginalisation and disempowerment. The custodial system itself can perpetuate and exaggerate these patterns with children placed in custody being exposed to inherent power imbalances and frequently experiencing a lack of autonomy and personal agency. It is proposed that, in this context, it is imperative that all efforts are made to ensure the child's voice is central at all stages of assessment, formulation, and intervention.
- *Sequencing support.* As emphasised by the trauma recovery model (TRM; Skuse, 2015), it is deemed necessary to sequence both direct and indirect interventions with all children in secure care. The TRM highlights the necessary layers of support that act as prerequisites to more formal forms of support. For example daily structure and routine typically contribute to a readiness to form relationships with adults, who are then able to begin to provide an experience of safety and stability which, in turn, will contribute to trust and containment. These experiences of relational safety and security assist a young person who has experienced past trauma to access direct interventions and, where relevant, learn strategies

to regulate their own emotional experiences. An individual's working formulation can be used to guide which forms of intervention are indicated at any one time and to ensure that prerequisite layers of support and containment are in place prior to more formal forms of support being offered/attempted.

- *Evidence-based and individually responsive care.* As already outlined, the children placed in custody have frequently experienced a complex array of adverse experiences and commonly present with a range of social, emotional, and behavioural needs. In the context of their early experiences of adversity (often including abusive and/or neglectful adult care), the children engaging with services in the secure environment may experience great difficulty trusting adult caregivers, in addition to reluctance and/or ambivalence about engaging with professional support. There is also a reality that the challenging process of adjusting to and managing life in custody can often detract focus from other areas of need and distress that may have been identified. For these reasons, it is necessary for clinical assessment and intervention to adopt a highly flexible approach that prioritises the development of trust and collaboration, whilst simultaneously utilising evidence-based best-practice guidelines (e.g. *National Institute for Health and Care Excellence [NICE] Guidelines*) most relevant to each young person's presenting needs.
- *Developmentally informed care.* This chapter is focused on children and adolescents, and it is imperative that an individual's current stage of development is continuously considered during all stages of assessment, formulation, and intervention. It is commonplace for children and adolescents who have experienced an array of adverse and complex childhood experiences (such as those common amongst those in the youth custodial estate) to present with an uneven developmental profile across domains of social, emotional, and behavioural development. Furthermore, the experience of detention in custody has been demonstrated to affect adolescent development in various ways (Dmitrieva et al., 2012; The Howard League, 2015). International literature has drawn attention to 'adultification bias', where adults or professionals assume a healthy development and overestimate levels of maturity in children. This can affect children in contact with the criminal justice system in a variety of ways (Antolak-Saper, 2020). The current developmental stage and profile of the children placed in secure services must continually be held in mind to ensure responsive and appropriately tailored care.

Indirect and whole systems interventions

In line with the principles of SECURE STAIRS, the indirect interventions delivered across the system of care to best meet Sami's needs will be outlined prior to details of the more individualised and direct forms of psychological intervention that were indicated by his working formulation.

The inclusion of operational and multidisciplinary staff in the formulation process was an integral element of ensuring that a shared understanding of Sami's strengths and needs underpinned all aspects of his care. It was invaluable to combine a range of perspectives and experiences within the formulation itself. Additionally, this process offered opportunities to impart information and understanding regarding attachment, trauma, and adolescent development. Members of the mental health and psychology teams had a very deliberate and regular presence on Sami's residential unit. This aspect of care is delivered to all young people in the environment and helps to create opportunities for informal and ad hoc consultation and guidance with operational staff. This is intended to assist a psychological understanding of each child's strengths and needs which, in turn, can inform staff members' approach to care.

The custodial environment is rife with stresses and challenges. Additionally, Sami presented with some specific care-eliciting behaviours with the potential to create barriers to consistent, thoughtful, and containing adult care. In other words, there was a risk that staff could find Sami's behaviours (e.g. those posing a risk to himself or others) difficult and stressful to work with, further risking that they may respond from a non-compassionate or punitive position. Given the potential impact of this on Sami's progress, for instance this reinforcing his belief that adults do not care and that he is unsafe, there was a strong recognition of the need for all staff to be working with Sami from an emotionally regulated position. This was also important in ensuring that Sami did not maintain a sense that his needs are not understood, acknowledged, or met. This further emphasises the need for operational staff to work from an emotionally regulated position and also highlighted a need to work from a place of compassion, often derived from an understanding of need through a psychological formulation. To support the achievement of this, operational staff were provided the opportunity to engage with regular clinical supervision and reflective practice. The focus of such interventions was to:

1   Develop a safe and containing space where staff are able to express and reflect upon their experiences of working with Sami, and how this relates to the working formulation of his strengths and needs;
2   Explore any particular challenges or successes;
3   Ensure an outlet for their own emotional experiences to avoid these same emotional experiences impeding their provision of care to Sami in any way.

These forums for supervision and reflective practice provided an opportunity to review the shared understanding of Sami's needs, formulate care-eliciting behaviour, and support staff in the regulation of their own emotions when working with a traumatised population. Within the framework of the TRM, these elements of indirect intervention are pivotal in supporting the staff to deliver the moment-to-moment and day-to-day care that creates a sense of safety and containment, without which more specific and direct interventions will not have optimal impact. A particular theme raised throughout supervision and reflective practice was the challenging nature and understanding of Sami's care-eliciting behaviours. Staff groups often interpreted these behaviours as 'needy' or 'attention seeking' and struggled to conceptualise the function of such behaviours. Staff members often reflected that clinical supervision with an emphasis on gaining an understanding of the function of Sami's behaviours, as well as an understanding of the impact of past experiences, allowed space to foster a sense of empathy and compassion opposed to labelling such behaviours. During the reflective spaces, staff members frequently shared a common experience that the wider system failed to recognise how challenging it was to support Sami and his needs on a day-to-day basis. They made reference to a lack of consistent physical support when working with Sami, a difficulty exacerbated by staff sickness and turnover. Staff members described feeling isolated and alone when providing care to Sami, and whilst the reflective and supervisory spaces made available to staff provided opportunities for these feelings and experiences to be expressed, they did not (and could not) provide practical solutions or support in isolation.

Direct interventions

In addition to the more formal psychological therapy that was completed with Sami, a pivotal aspect of the direct intervention offered to him was the frequent, informal contact which was mainly facilitated on his residential unit. Sami had direct contact with multidisciplinary staff members from across the mental and physical healthcare team; this informal contact was vital in gaining a dynamic sense of Sami's current physical, emotional, and mental well-being. Also, it provided him with an increased sense of collaboration and co-production regarding care plans and appointment scheduling. The formulation of Sami's presenting needs highlighted his experiences and expectations of professionals in caregiving roles as a significant and perpetuating factor. Therefore, it was deemed important that the support offered to Sami by the team was facilitated very flexibly; in practice, this was often provided upon Sami's request, particularly in the earlier stages of relationship building. It is important to note that consistent consideration of professional boundaries was required by the whole team, often within reflective and formulation-driven conversations with one another. Whilst such considerations are always a vital aspect of providing appropriate care, they were particularly pertinent given the intensive and flexible way the team was required to work with Sami to gain his engagement. It was recognised that professional boundaries could easily become blurred, and therefore Sami's experience of the relationships being forged could be confused or unhelpful. For example given Sami's model of relationships, it was important to avoid a situation whereby the team reinforced his expectations about how care 'should' be provided, and consistent reflection was deemed important to avoid Sami developing unrealistic expectations about how professional care *can* be delivered. In our professional experience, the broader systems of care (both in the adult custodial estate and community) are often restricted to more rigid and inflexible ways of working. There was an awareness amongst the multidisciplinary team that the high levels of flexibility and responsivity experienced by Sami would likely not be replicated by future services/professionals, and there was a risk that Sami could experience this as rejecting.

The likes of '**active monitoring**' are detailed as effective interventions by best practice guidelines (e.g. NICE, 2018), and the positive impact of such interventions for Sami was apparent. However, the benefits of such interventions are thought to be dependent on robust professional boundaries and the recognition that interventions that are frequent and informal place emotional and practical demands on the professionals involved. Sami's feedback demonstrated the true significance of these informal elements of 'intervention', and he described experiencing these as regular demonstrations of care which, as previously discussed in the formulation section of the chapter, was of great significance to him. Available information indicated that this experience of being cared for and held in mind helped to challenge Sami's beliefs that he must be aggressive to elicit care and, overall, he reported experiencing many professionals as caring and responsive to his needs.

Shaped by the outcome of the psychological assessment and subsequent formulation, the interventions provided to Sami included direct therapeutic work drawing on principles and skills from **cognitive behavioural therapy (CBT)** and **dialectical behavioural therapy (DBT)**. Such interventions included the delivery of psychoeducation, mindfulness, emotion regulation skills, and an assessment of suitability for **eye movement desensitisation and reprocessing (EMDR)** therapy. The modality of therapy offered to Sami was influenced by the presenting difficulties identified during assessment in combination with NICE guidelines (2018), which state that in the treatment of trauma-related symptomology, both EMDR and CBT including psychoeducation are most appropriate. Furthermore, the NICE guidelines (2011) state that DBT skills are also effective in managing the distressing feelings and acts of self-harm of those who have experienced trauma.

Initially, Sami was offered work around **stabilisation** and **scaffolding**. This work included a focus on mindfulness skills to allow Sami to anchor his attention on a specific task or mindful experience and ultimately work from a regulated position. Coupled with these skills, Sami engaged in a psychoeducational intervention intended to provide insight into the symptomology and impact of trauma. Sami reported finding both of these interventions incredibly useful and often cited analogies used in trauma psychoeducation to make sense of his day-to-day experiences. Also, Sami was offered DBT skills-based intervention around emotion regulation in both a group setting and on an individual basis. Sami found it challenging to engage in this aspect of the intervention for several reasons. DBT skills-based interventions are primarily offered in a group setting; however, Sami reflected that without a pre-existing relationship with a professional and the group members, he felt unable to engage in such interventions. Subsequently, DBT skills for emotion regulation were offered on a one-to-one basis with a familiar and trusted professional. Sami later reflected that this flexible and integrated approach to working with, and listening to, his concerns about working in a group-based setting was fundamental in fostering a trusting therapeutic relationship and was central to him feeling empowered and experiencing a sense of agency.

Moreover, Sami was offered EMDR therapy to begin the processing phase of trauma treatment. Initially, this began with an assessment of suitability and the beginnings of resource installation. Resource installation in EMDR therapy is intended to support in the development of internal resources and increased affect tolerance in clients; essentially ensuring that Sami had all the necessary skills to successfully engage in the processing aspect of trauma therapy. Sami engaged well in the initial assessment of suitability and initial stages of resource installation work. However, after he had completed this work and at a time he was deemed ready to process the trauma, Sami transitioned to the adult custodial estate, meaning the processing aspect of therapy could not be completed. This highlights the problematic impact that the unpredictability and uncertainty inherent to the custodial system can have upon the delivery of psychological therapy; external factors and considerations frequently take priority over individual psychological needs. Examples of such factors include the risks of harm to self and others that an individual may demonstrate at any one time, the age of an adolescent, as well as the expected sentence length.

Therapy in any environment requires careful consideration of the time available to account for psychological safety being achieved and the therapeutic ending of relationships. The safe and well-constructed ending of therapy allows a young person to review progress in relation to therapeutic goals and to work through any challenging feelings which may be experienced due to the therapeutic relationship ending (Vasquez et al., 2008). However, in an environment and system where considerations of risk and operational demands are often prioritised over and above the therapeutic benefits of psychological therapy, transitions to other establishments can often interrupt psychological practice in an unavoidable way. Sometimes, this is necessary such as to avoid harm; however, where it is not, this represents a lack of understanding from the wider system, with its competing priorities and aims, as to the necessity of sequencing interventions and ensuring sufficient time is allowed for endings.

Outcomes and reflections

Sami's care

Sami fed back his views about some of the main features of the care offered to him whilst in custody that he felt were supportive and therefore effective. A particular reflection from Sami was the significance of working flexibly and often informally outside of scheduled therapeutic appointments. Sami reflected that being able to speak with a mental health professional outside of such appointments not only offered him continued emotional support but also demonstrated being "held in mind" and genuine care and compassion. Sami suggested that working in such a manner was one of the primary factors that supported the development of a therapeutic relationship and his subsequent engagement in more formal and structured therapeutic support. Sami moreover highlighted the significant therapeutic impact of the co-production of care plans. He reflected that initially not being involved in the development of his care plans resulted in an experience of these plans being "done to" him and resulted in a feeling of being out of control with regard to his care. This mirrored his childhood experiences of being in local authority care and his life feeling (and being) out of his control. Also, Sami reflected that being involved in the initial creation of his care plans whilst also having a voice in how these plans developed provided him with a sense of ownership and empowerment over his care.

Sami reported finding certain aspects of direct intervention very useful and reflected that he had previously struggled to engage in therapeutic intervention due to experiencing the environment as unsafe or chaotic. He recognised that exercises such as mindfulness allowed him to anchor himself in the present moment and subsequently find therapeutic intervention(s) more accessible. Sami stated that previously he felt overwhelmed by his thoughts and feelings relating to past experiences and struggled to make sense of these experiences and the impact they may have had. Sami experienced the psychoeducation intervention as containing and said that it provided an understanding of his experiences and the impact they had on him, both physically and psychologically. Finally, Sami reflected on the value of the initial EMDR resource installation intervention offered. Sami stated that learning skills to feel safe when he experienced thoughts of traumatic experiences was particularly useful; however, the most significant aspect of this intervention was what it demonstrated to Sami. He had requested trauma therapy as a means of processing his traumatic experiences for some time; however, given the importance of sequencing interventions, this was not offered immediately. When Sami was offered the initial EMDR resource installation, this not only represented achieving progress in his care plan, but it also enabled him to experience that his views and requests for such therapy had been listened to. Sami reflected that having his requests responded to, and being offered therapy, resulted in him feeling as though he was in control of his care, and an increased confidence that professionals aimed to support him and cared about the support and intervention being offered.

Sami moreover provided reflections on the challenges to integrated and collaborative care. As previously mentioned, by their very nature, secure environments are commonly trauma-organised and staff groups frequently become 'burned out' due to the emotionally demanding nature of caring for traumatised children. Burnout of operational staff members who are tasked with caring for children with a multitude of different needs on a daily basis often results in high staff turnover. Sami reflected that the turnover of staff members hindered his development of safe and secure relationships with operational staff.

Children who have perpetually experienced a lack of relational security and traumatic circumstances have often not experienced the co-regulation of their emotions with a caregiver at times of distress. In turn, this results in children receiving inadequate support to develop their own capacity to regulate their emotions. Sami reflected that at times of distress and challenge, he required the support of adults in a caregiving role to regulate his emotional and behavioural responses. However, Sami elaborated that he did not feel able to turn to staff members in times of need if an established relationship did not exist, for example due to the infancy of the relationship.

There is recognition that outcome measures in forensic settings are often quantitative in nature; however, in this case outcomes are qualitative and based around Sami's reflections of the care offered. Formal psychometric test measures were attempted to be completed with Sami on different occasions, but he was reluctant to engage, and this was understood in the context of his past experience of care and interventions as being "done to" him. Therefore, as a responsive measure to ensure that Sami felt his choices were being respected, these measures were not persisted with.

The Short-Term Assessment of Risk and Treatability (START:AV; Webster et al., 2009) was completed as a means of measuring strength and vulnerability factors throughout Sami's time in custody. This measure was completed as a multidisciplinary team comprising psychology, health, resettlement, education, and operational staff. Quantitative and qualitative information relating to the positive changes in Sami's self-harm behaviour, aggressive behaviour, relationships with professionals, and engagement in education and extracurricular activities informed the assessment. During the regular reviews of the START:AV, professionals working with Sami identified an increased degree of regulated behaviour; specifically Sami demonstrated less self-harming behaviours and aggression towards others. The team also discussed a shared experience of increased trust and engagement from, and with, Sami. For example Sami would talk more openly about his day-to-day emotional experiences and was described as encouraging other young people to seek support from the professionals working within the centre. At times of particular challenge, Sami would proactively seek out the support of professionals from across different disciplines; behaviour that was not apparent during earlier stages of his time in custody. Furthermore, professionals within the team would provide reflections about Sami's engagement with psychology specifically, stating that Sami demonstrated a strong desire and motivation to engage with psychology and found value in the therapeutic work completed. Custodial team members and community professionals provided some reflections as to some of the skills Sami demonstrated, such as reflecting on behaviours, communicating his needs in an appropriate manner with the support of a professional, more positive interactions with other young people, and decreased levels of anxiety in situations that Sami would have previously experienced as threatening and debilitating.

The wider system

It has been well documented that the criminal justice system in the UK is facing a broad range of challenges that include high staff turnover, insufficient resource, and increased rates of violence and instability (Shilson-Thomas, 2020); many of these challenges afflict the youth system in the same way they afflict the adult system. For example whilst Sami's experience of fear and threat in the custodial setting is partly understood in the context of his personal history, it is also viewed as a typical and understandable emotional response to an environment which is permeated by different forms of violence and aggression. A child being placed within an environment that is experienced as frightening and threatening will prevent the attainment of true safety and security; conditions which we would posit are crucial foundations for achieving optimal therapeutic benefits and change. It is acknowledged that, despite the many forms of intervention and support outlined, Sami continued to experience the custodial environment as unsafe, and this appeared to have a fundamental impact on the outcomes that were achieved.

Whilst it was possible to implement various indirect forms of support and intervention as part of Sami's care plan (for example staff supervision and consultation), it is important not to overlook the ongoing challenges with accessing operational and multidisciplinary support to deliver these vital aspects of children's care. It was not uncommon for planned meetings to be cancelled due to operational staff shortages and for pivotal meetings (e.g. care plan reviews, formulation reviews) to be held without the presence of operational staff. This can contribute to disparities across staff members' understanding of the child's presentation and also risks insufficient support being provided for staff members' emotional needs. Without these indirect aspects of care being provided in a consistent and predictable manner, children will not receive optimal care and containment. Unfortunately, in a secure environment where all stakeholders face the challenges and demands outlined in this chapter, not all barriers to optimal care can be overcome.

In line with best practice guidance, there are efforts to try to ensure that every child's resettlement planning is considered from the very beginning of their time in custody, includes true engagement and collaboration with the child themselves, and involves the coordination and collaboration of partner agencies (e.g. Goodfellow et al., 2015). This is vital to ensuring a child is being sufficiently supported to consider, form, and work towards a prosocial identity and goals for their future (Hazel, 2017), in addition to maximising the likelihood of sufficient continuity of care and their individualised needs being met in the community. In practice, this is hard to achieve; in relation to Sami, it was our clinical experience that his immediate, day-to-day needs frequently became the sole focus of intervention planning and delivery and that broader resettlement goals easily got neglected. Upon reflection, this pattern appears to mirror the reactive nature of the custodial system in which we are providing care; a system that is perpetually and, at many times, necessarily responding to and managing unpredictable events and incidents. It is not uncommon for the custodial environment to be chaotic and volatile, and this appears to perpetuate a focus on immediate risk management and containment at the cost of more holistic and future-based planning. It is recognised that recent reforms in youth custody have created scope and opportunity to provide a high level of support and intervention whilst children are in custody. However, unfortunately, community-based resources are often not equitable, and it is not uncommon for the high level of support within custody to end at the point of transition to the community, despite frequently made attempts to establish ongoing support. This is an aspect of care that requires constant consideration and reflection throughout a child's time in custody to avoid potential unintended consequences of any support provided (e.g. dependence or over-reliance) and also to plan for the potential impact of the often suddenly reduced levels of support and care upon release from custody.

Final reflection

A historical perspective on the custodial system as a whole reveals some highly relevant debates and perspectives regarding the central purpose of incarceration and whether it should be, for example punishment, public protection, and/or reform and rehabilitation (Coyle et al., 2016). Whilst beyond the scope of this chapter to explore these differing perspectives in detail, there can be ongoing tensions and conflicts within and between different agencies and individuals within the youth justice system, despite well-meaning intentions, and it is important to consider the practical implications of such. Overall, there can remain a lack of shared vision, purpose, and aims, and this is perhaps somewhat inevitable in a system that comprises multiple agencies, each with its own contractual requirements and objectives. It is important to recognise that the SECURE STAIRS framework, and the approach to providing care that is outlined within this chapter, represents a fundamental shift of the model of service delivery in the youth custodial estate. The modes of assessment and intervention that are outlined within this chapter were all undertaken within the broader aim of cultural and organisational change to enable a truly therapeutic environment. As summarised by Sadie and Stokoe (2020), 'having used locks, bars and gates to contain the emotions of frightened and aggressive boys [children] for so long, the idea of using words and relationships alongside them can feel dangerous and threatening' (p. 23).

References

Antolak-Saper, N. (2020). The adultification of the youth justice system: The Victorian experience. *Law in Context a Socio-Legal Journal*, *37*(1), 99–113.

Bloom, S. (2010). Trauma organised systems and parallel process. In N. Tehrani (Ed.), *Managing trauma in the workplace: Supporting workers and organisations* (pp. 139–153). Routledge.

British Psychological Society. (2019). *Evidence briefing: Adverse childhood experiences*. www.bps.org.uk/news-and-policy/adverse-childhood-experiences-aces.

Chard, A. (2021). *Punishing abuse: Children in the west Midlands criminal justice system*. West Midlands Combined Authority.

Chitsabesan, P., Lennox, C., Theodosiou, L., Law, H., Bailey, S., & Shaw, J. (2014). The development of the comprehensive health assessment tool for young offenders within the secure estate. *Journal of Forensic Psychiatry and Psychology, 25*(1), 1–25.

Coyle, A., Fair, H., Jacobson, J., & Walmsley, R. (2016). *Imprisonment worldwide: The current situation and an alternative future*. Policy Press Shorts Insights.

Dmitrieva, J., Monahan, K. C., Cauffman, E., & Steinberg, L. (2012). Arrested development: The effects of incarceration on the development of maturity. *Development and Psychopathology, 24*(3).

Goodfellow, P., Wilkinson, S., Hazel, N., Bateman, T., Liddle, M., Wright, S., & Factor, F. (2015). *Effective resettlement of young people: Lessons from beyond youth custody*. Beyond Youth Custody.

Hales, H., Warner, L., Smith, J., & Bartlett, A. (2016). *Census of young people in secure settings on 14 September 2016: Characteristics, needs and pathways of care*. NHS. www.england.nhs.uk/publication/secure-settings-for-young-people-a-national-scoping-exercise/

Hazel, N. (2017). *Now, all I care about is my future: Supporting the shift*. Nacro/Beyond Youth Custody.

Hughes, N., & Chitsabesan, P. (2015). *Supporting young people with neurodevelopmental impairment*. Centre for Crime and Justice Studies.

Johnstone, L., & Dallos, R. (Eds.). (2006). *Formulation in psychology and psychotherapy: Making sense of people's problems*. Routledge.

Leon, L. (2002). The mental health needs of young offenders. *Mental Health Foundation Briefing, 3*(18).

National Institute for Health and Care Excellence. (2011). *Self-harm in over 8s: Long-term management*. nice.org.uk/guidance/CG133.

National Institute for Health and Care Excellence. (2018). *Post-traumatic stress disorder*. nice.org.uk/guidance/NG116.

Nemeroff, C. B. (2016). Paradise lost: The neurobiological and clinical consequences of child abuse and neglect. *Neuron, 89*(5), 892–909.

Redhead, S., Johnstone, L., & Nightingale, J. (2015). Clients' experiences of formulation in cognitive behaviour therapy. *Psychology and Psychotherapy: Theory, Research and Practice*, 1–15.

Sadie, C., & Stokoe, P. (2020). Creating therapeutic environments in youth custody: The SECURE STAIRS programme. *Monitor*, 20–23.

Shaw, J., Higgins, C., & Quartey, C. (2017). The impact of collaborative formulation with high risk offenders with personality disorder. *The Journal of Forensic Psychiatry and Psychology, 28*(6), 777–789.

Shilson-Thomas, A. (2020). *The prison system: Priorities for spending*. Reform Public.

Skuse, T. (2015). The Trauma Recovery Model: Sequencing youth justice interventions for young people with complex needs'. *Prison Service Journal, 220*, 16–24.

Substance Abuse and Mental Health Services Administration. (2014). *Concept of trauma and guidance for a trauma-informed approach*. https://store.samhsa.gov/sites/default/files/d7/priv/sma14-4884.pdf.

Taylor, J., Shostak, L., Rogers, A., & Mitchell, P. (2018). Rethinking mental health provision in the secure estate for children and young people: A framework for integrated care (SECURE STAIRS). *Safer Communities, 17*(4), 193–201.

The Howard League. (2015). *Healthy sexual development of children in prison*. https://howardleague.org/publications/healthy-sexual-development-of-children-in-prison/

Vasquez, M., Bingham, R., & Barnett, J. (2008). Psychotherapy termination: Clinical and ethical responsibilities. *Journal of Clinical Psychology, 64*(5), 653–665.

Webster, C. D., Martin, M.-L., Brink, J., Nicholls, T. L., & Desmarais, S. L. (2009). *Manual for the short-term assessment of risk and treatability (START) (Version 1.1)*. British Columbia Mental Health and Addiction Services.

Weerasekera, P. (1996). *Multiperspective case formulation: A step towards treatment integration.* Krieger.

Youth Custody Service. (2021, August). *Youth custody report.* www.gov.uk/government/statistics/youth-custody-data.

5 Treatment of delusions of exceptionality in an adult male with sexual offences against children in a secure psychiatric setting

Khyati Patel

Overview

This case study chapter will describe the assessment, formulation, and treatment of a patient who has sexually offended against children and who has been diagnosed with paranoid schizophrenia within a medium secure hospital setting from a cognitive behavioural therapy (CBT) perspective. The literature on CBT will be presented, along with a specific focus on the Garety et al. (2001) model and the more recently published work on grandiose delusions by Isham et al. (2019). A brief case history will be presented followed by relevant formulations that guided subsequent intervention completed with him. A description of the session content will be presented, and the chapter will end with a reflective analysis and conclusion.

Introduction

Cognitive behavioural therapy was pioneered in the 1960s by Dr Aaron T. Beck and has been used to treat many forms of mental health difficulties. Early forms of CBT incorporated a stronger behavioural emphasis, which focused on aspects such as coping strategies, graded activity for negative symptoms, and building social and independent living skills, with a clear secondary focus on relevant cognitive factors (Tai & Turkington, 2009). Further, as the widely held belief at the time was that positive symptoms remained outside the realms of normal functioning, the focus on cognition and incorporation of cognitive techniques were not yet established (Tai & Turkington, 2009). This perspective altered after the introduction of seminal cognitive models incorporating the development and maintenance of psychosis including: Garety et al.'s (2001) 'Cognitive Model of Positive Symptoms of Psychosis', Morrison's (2001) 'Cognitive Model of Psychosis', and Freeman et al.'s (2002) 'Cognitive Model of Persecutory Delusions'. Although these models differ visually, the most significant common link between them was that the *appraisal* formed at the time constitutes the experience as being psychotic rather than the anomalous experience itself.

DOI: 10.4324/9781003213116-5

Cognitive models of psychosis

In Garety et al.'s (2001) model, they proposed that there were two routes to the development of positive symptoms within the context of psychosis; in both pathways, they postulate a role for biopsychosocial vulnerability and triggering factors, but in one route, this is via affect alone whilst the other is through anomalous experiences and affective changes (Garety & Hemsley, 1994). They presented a clear association between emotional changes and the anomalous experience which trigger the individual to seek an explanation of its cause. It is here where thinking errors or cognitive biases are significant, and which are worsened by negative emotional states. A further important concept encompassed in this model is the role of schemas and core beliefs. Schemas can be described as a set of cognitive frameworks that allow us to make sense of the world around us. It is widely researched and accepted that those who experience psychosis are more likely to have negatively held schemas about themselves and often accept their subordinate position within society, resulting in low levels of self-esteem and confidence (Fowler et al., 1998). Finally, appropriate emphasis on maintenance factors and their link to positive symptoms is clearly distinguished within the model. When initially published, this first-generation CBT model of positive symptoms was welcomed and provided a comprehensive underpinning from previously conducted research and literature.

Morrison's model, which was published in the same year, stated that information was inaccurately misinterpreted by the patient due to the faulty self and social knowledge rather than faulty perceptions (Phiri et al., 2017). Both models were exceptionally important at the time they were published as they emphasised the central role of cognition in the maintenance of positive symptoms, stipulating that it was the appraisal of the experience which was key rather than the experience itself. Prior to this, there were some concerns that talking about psychotic experiences could be harmful to the patient. These early cognitive models and subsequent efficacy trials found the opposite to be true; they were not harmful to patients and even had a small, positive effect on improving positive symptoms (van der Gaag et al., 2014).

Within the last ten years, there has been a paradigm shift from treating psychosis from a general CBT perspective to the development of specific models that are associated with a defined set of symptoms. This has been welcomed, as results from first-generation CBT for psychosis were not significant enough, and although there was a small positive benefit from treatment as usual, advances made in other areas of cognitive treatment, for example in depression and anxiety, demonstrated that further improvements in this area were key to developing truly effective interventions for psychosis. Factor analysis, conducted by Ronald et al. (2014), demonstrated that specific psychotic symptoms are independent of one another, meaning that psychotic experiences are distinct and do not necessarily occur together. Further, twin studies also suggested different heritability estimates for varying experiences (Zavos et al., 2014). This precipitated a move away from diagnostic approaches and facilitated the development of experience-specific models. Currently, there is good quality evidence for translational treatments for persecutory delusions and command hallucinations, and results from interventions in these areas are far greater than the first-generation CBT for psychosis approaches (Freeman, 2016; Freeman et al., 2021; Birchwood et al., 2018). Other symptom-specific models are still being developed, including one on grandiose delusions, which is of particular relevance to this case study chapter.

Grandiose delusions

Grandiose delusions have been described as, "unfounded beliefs that one has special powers, wealth, mission, or identity" (Isham et al., 2019, p. 120). Although it has been suggested that this psychotic experience affects about half of patients diagnosed with schizophrenia (Knowles et al., 2011), there has been limited research and literature focus on the maintenance and treatment for this type of delusion. There may be several reasons for this, including the inaccurate perception that this type of delusion is not harmful or distressing to the patient and therefore the focus of research should lie elsewhere (Isham et al., 2019). To address this shortcoming, Isham et al. (2019) conducted a qualitative study which aimed to explore whether grandiose delusions have harmful consequences to patients and what patients want from clinical services. Also, the published work sought to identify relevant maintenance factors associated with grandiose delusions that may be amenable to psychological intervention. These maintenance factors have been presented in Figure 5.1.

Isham and colleagues have proposed that not all maintenance factors need to be present, and it is likely that a combination of these factors may be relevant

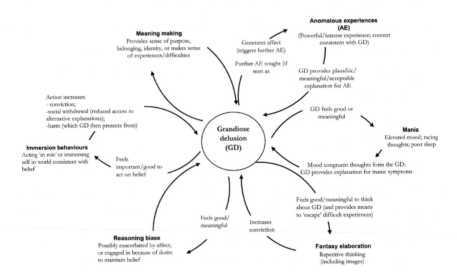

Figure 5.1 Hypothesised maintenance factors of grandiose delusions (Isham et al., 2019)

to different patients. They also proposed that the term, "grandiose delusions" should be replaced with "delusions of exceptionality", suggesting that "grandiose" has become a derogatory term and one that is often considered synonymous with arrogance, superiority, and entitlement which did not accurately describe the participants within their study. Therefore, the term 'grandiose delusions' will be replaced with the term 'delusions of exceptionality' for the remainder of this chapter. Their work found that experiences related to delusions of exceptionality can be harmful in a number of ways and that the belief itself was highly meaningful and important as it provided a sense of identity and purpose. This is a hypothesised model based on a qualitative interview of 15 patients and will necessitate development and refinement as further research and testing in larger-scale clinical samples is conducted. That said, it is the most up-to-date contribution to the literature in this area and appears highly relevant in relation to Theo's experiences.

Case presentation

Introduction to Theo

Theo is a 35-year-old male currently residing on a medium secure forensic ward with an established diagnosis of paranoid schizophrenia. Theo has a history of drug and alcohol misuse, and a forensic history of sexual offending against children. In 2015, Theo was remanded in custody after a conviction for a sexual offence. Whilst in prison, Theo became non-compliant with his prescribed antipsychotic medication and his mental state deteriorated significantly. Due to his presentation in custody, Theo was assessed and admitted to hospital under Section 47/49 of the Mental Health Act.

Presenting problems

On admission to hospital, Theo presented as hypervigilant, had thoughts to harm others, reported thought insertion and thought withdrawal, as well as auditory, visual, and tactile hallucinations. Theo continued to have these experiences during the initial weeks of his admission to hospital with symptoms relating to hypervigilance, harming others, and tactile hallucinations, which subsided subsequent to compliance with the anti-psychotic medication he was prescribed. It was reported by nursing staff that he had been heard making loud noises, particularly at night, responding to unseen and unheard stimuli. Theo stated that he was having problems sleeping due to his experiences. Theo did not display any concerning behaviours on the ward although he did report hearing a voice of a "bad God" that fantasises about hurting women and children. Theo reported a varied number of symptoms that he was experiencing. These included beliefs that he was in communication with 'bad Gods' who had previously been able to control him, had access to his thoughts, and would send him intrusive thoughts. Theo described constantly hearing a large number of voices of those whom he believed were these Gods. He also reported occasionally being able to see things that he believed were visions from the Gods or the workings and mechanisms of the universe. Theo understood these experiences as him being in the process of completing a transformation into a God. He believed he was required to have these experiences as part of the transformation process and because he was responsible for saving humanity from 'bad Gods'.

Theo had displayed little insight into his difficulties, although he reported hospital was the most appropriate place for him. He stated this was because his index offence had upset his family and reported that his mother was, "stressed by [me] speaking to myself and banging around". Theo did not believe that his experiences could be attributed to psychosis and reported, "It is completely impossible to be Schizophrenic". He stated that his difficulties were caused by God rather than having a medical or psychological causation.

History of problem development

Theo did not have a religious upbringing and did not affiliate himself with any religion. He reported his first auditory hallucination occurred in 2013. His first recorded contact with psychiatric services was in 2014, after being admitted to hospital under Section 2 of the Mental Health Act following concerns from a family member. It was reported that he was using a large quantity of drugs and consuming increasing amounts of alcohol; Theo stated that this heightened use of substances was precipitated by a breakdown in his intimate relationship and losing his job. At this time, he also believed he was 'Jesus' and was observed responding to unseen stimuli. It was during this admission that Theo was diagnosed with schizophrenia. A short time after he was discharged from hospital, he committed the index offence and was incarcerated. It appears that Theo initially attempted to cope with symptoms by using substances in the community and whilst an inpatient, he had been isolating himself in his bedroom. More recently, he had begun to meditate to relieve distress caused by his experiences but initially could only do this for ten minutes, twice per day. His participation in activities on the ward had also increased.

Previous interventions

Theo had never participated in psychological intervention before; he had previously only been treated from a medical model perspective.

Risk assessment

Due to Theo's previous forensic history, a Historical Clinical Risk-20 version 3 (HCR-20v3; Webster et al., 2013) assessment was conducted upon admission. This assessment comprises 20 items that are relevant to ascertain risk of future violence. Theo was unable to collaborate with the assessment due to his level of preoccupation and distress at the time. A further assessment of Risk of

Sexual Violence Protocol (RSVP; Hart et al., 2003) was also completed to aid understanding and formulation around his sexual offending. Outstanding risk factors that were identified included extreme minimisation or denial of sexual violence, problems with self-awareness, sexual deviance, major mental illness, and problems with intimate relationships. Due to Theo's level of preoccupation and severity of mental health symptoms, he was not able to complete focused work around this sexual violence risk factors. Instead, initial work with Theo was centred on improving his level of distress so that he could be in a better position to engage in focused interventions around reducing his future risk to children. When Theo was admitted to hospital, his risk of harm to others was also comprehensively assessed and a **Positive Behavioural Support (PBS)** plan was co-produced with Theo to help staff to manage his behaviour and risks on the ward.

Suitability for CBT

After the PBS plan was completed with Theo, the possibility of participating in CBT sessions was discussed. As the ward psychologist, I was tasked with this intervention. Initially, Theo declined psychology sessions but after we built a rapport, he agreed to meet with me regularly. We spent time discussing our mutual expectations from participating in sessions. Theo reported a high level of distress from his experiences and stated, "it's taking over everything". He stated that he would like to work on this during sessions. Initially, his goal was to increase his ability to distract himself from some of his experiences. However, as time progressed the goals for therapy evolved; this will be described in further detail later in this chapter. After trust was built, through motivational interviewing techniques, Theo was keen to take part in an assessment that involved obtaining a history of his life experiences as well as the development of his presenting problems and completing relevant psychometrics.

The National Instituted of Clinical Excellence (NICE) recommends that patients presenting with psychosis should be offered CBT (NICE, 2014) and, in the case of Theo, his self-reported high level of distress and level of motivation made CBT a suitable intervention for him.

Outcome measures

Table 5.1 denotes the psychometric results from questionnaires that were completed.

Formulation

When Theo was admitted to the service, the HCR–20v3 risk assessment was completed, and a formulation was produced based on historical information. After preliminary assessment, I then moved on to introducing him to the basic principles of CBT. From the Isham et al. (2019) work on delusions of exceptionality, it was recommended that therapists spend extra time discussing

Table 5.1 Theo's pre-treatment psychometric test results

Test name	Test description	Test results
The Schedule for Assessment of Insight – Extended Version (SAI-E); Kemp and David, (1997)	The SAI-E is a 12-item semi-structured interview, exploring the respondent's clinical insight, including their compliance with treatment.	Theo's score on the SAI-E suggests a low level of insight into his personal symptoms.
The Voice Power Differential Scale (VPDS; Birchwood et al., 2000)	The VPD is a self-report scale that provides a measure of the respondent's perception of the disparity of power between themselves and their voice.	Theo's scores on this indicated that between Theo and his most prominent voice at the time, he felt there was a greater power differential in favour of the voice.
The Brief Core Schema Scale (BCSS; Fowler et al., 1998)	The BCSS is a 24-item questionnaire assessing both negative and positive schemas about self (e.g. "I am vulnerable", "I am successful") and others (e.g. "Other people are devious", "Other people are supportive").	Theo's scores on the BCSS indicated that he had a positive view of himself but did hold the negative self-belief that he is vulnerable. Theo's beliefs about others do not appear skewed to be either positive or negative.
The Psychotic Symptom Rating Scale (PSYRATS; Haddock et al., 1999)	The PSYRATS is an interview-based set of clinician-rating scales which provides a more detailed examination of the respondent's voices and delusions.	The PSYRATS auditory hallucinations subscale revealed that Theo reported continuously hearing a large number of voices that he identified as Gods. The PSYRATS delusions subscales revealed that Theo believed he was experiencing a transformation into a God for the purpose of saving humanity from 'bad Gods'. His overall score was 25.
Belief About Voices Questionnaire–Revised (BAVQ–R; Chadwick et al., 2000)	The Beliefs About Voices Questionnaire–Revised (BAVQ–R) is a self-report measure of the respondent's beliefs, emotions, and behaviour about auditory hallucinations.	Theo's scores indicated that he found his most dominant voice to be malevolent and with some omnipotence. Theo reported that he engaged in some resistance to the voice but that he was engaged with the voice just by being born.

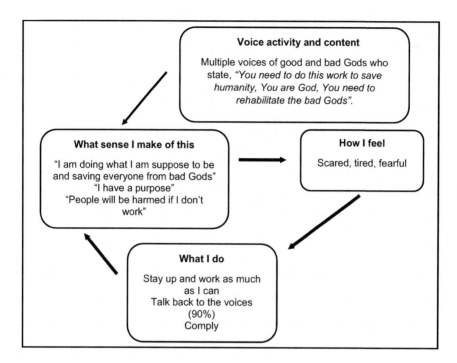

Figure 5.2 Theo-shared ABC formulation

patients' experience as it facilitates trust within the therapeutic relationship. Therefore, Theo and I spent a period of time speaking about his experiences in detail and we co-produced a simple ABC formulation together (Figure 5.2). ABC is an acronym for Antecedents, Behaviour and Consequences and is used to assist with the formulation of a specific behaviour. This helps to make sense of the experience for the patient. It was helpful to ascertain a scale (0%–100%) of how frequently he heard the voices and how much he responded to the voices so that this could be measured throughout intervention sessions. This simpler formulation allowed Theo to be involved with completing a shared understanding of his experiences during a time of increased instability.

As our sessions progressed, I was able to gain further information that aided a more detailed formulation based on Garety et al.'s (2001) cognitive model of positive symptoms of psychosis. This model was used because it clearly outlines key causal and maintenance mechanisms for positive symptoms for psychosis which were highly relevant for Theo (e.g. role of anomalous experiences and reasoning biases). Further, although still a hypothetical model, the specific model for delusions of exceptionality developed by Isham et al. (2019) was also used to guide assessment, and again, it became evident that many of the maintenance factors presented in this model were relevant for Theo.

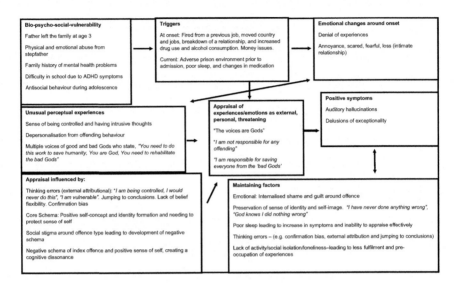

Figure 5.3 Theo's Garety et al. (2001) informed formulation

The onset of Theo's experiences was precipitated by specific events, such as a relationship breakdown, loss of employment, increased substance misuse, and financial problems. These factors, coupled with his biopsychosocial vulnerabilities including significant trauma and a family history of mental illness, have a likely role in the development of psychosis; both by biological inheritance and by experiences of trauma and family experiences which affected his core beliefs and the way in which he interpreted the world. The hypothesised link between Theo's experiences and his offending behaviour are a significant factor to consider in his formulation. Following his sexual offending and subsequent detention in custody, he is likely to have experienced high levels of shame and guilt, although this was hypothesised. It was reported that an unusual perceptual experience of depersonalisation from the sexual offence followed, and this led to Theo stating that he was not responsible for the sexual offending he committed, and he stated that his body was being controlled by a "bad God". It is hypothesised that when Theo began to consider this possibility of being controlled, it provided an acceptable alternative explanation for his actions. This enabled Theo to resolve his cognitive dissonance of doing actions that went against his positive sense of self and allowed him to retain a sense of purpose and meaning. It is likely that his current experiences provide a protection from the reality that he is a man who has committed a sexual offence. The cognitive biases and maintenance factors were discussed with Theo in detail. This formulation, depicted in Figure 5.3, was also presented to the clinical team to assist their understanding of Theo's experiences and the development of his difficulties over time.

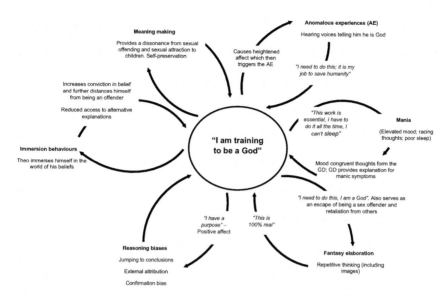

Figure 5.4 Theo's delusions of exceptionality maintenance cycle

Source: Based on Isham et al.'s (2019) work

After spending time speaking with Theo about his unusual experiences, it became clear that delusions of exceptionality were an important part of his presentation. Theo believed that he was making a transformation into God and after this was complete, that his job would be to save humanity and get rid of all the 'bad Gods'. As he stated, "the Gods are 100% powerful", which was a belief he held with a high level of conviction; it seemed appropriate to consider his case from a delusions of exceptionality perspective. Although there is little research conducted in this area, Isham et al. (2019) have developed a hypothesised model for delusions of exceptionality, identifying six key potential maintenance mechanisms. Although they stated that no patient had to encompass all six maintenance factors, it appeared as though all of these were relevant in the case of Theo (see Figure 5.4). A clear strength of Isham et al.'s (2019) work was that the maintenance factors were easy to explain and use collaboratively with Theo. Theo was involved in ascertaining some of these maintenance factors (anomalous experiences, mania, reasoning biases, fantasy elaboration and immersion behaviours) but one that included a link to his offending (meaning making) required a more sensitive approach and was not shared with him at the time. Because of Theo's likeness for the model and his ability to formulate his maintenance factors, he was keen to explore these further in treatment; therefore, we decided collaboratively to base our interventions around the delusions of exceptionality framework and more specifically Isham et al.'s (2019) work.

Meaning making

This factor is related to the experiences of delusions of exceptionality having a significant meaning for patients. It is proposed that the experience provides a sense of identity, purpose, and belonging. It was also stated that these delusions may have occurred at a time of increased stress and negative circumstances, providing a protective function for the patient. In the case of Theo, he had recently committed further offences of sexual violence against children, and it was highly likely that his delusions protected him from feelings of shame, guilt, and negativity from society and the community he lived within. Of note was that his experiences centred around saving humanity and getting rid of 'bad Gods', whom he has stated had fantasies around raping women and children. It is likely that his delusions were a way to absolve himself from past offending.

Anomalous experiences

Theo's experiences included hearing voices coupled with a felt **sense of salience**. Theo described these experiences as intense and powerful, occurring all day, every day. This is likely to have made the experiences more likely to be appraised as significant. In the case of Theo, when he had these experiences, it reinforced the message that he has important work to do, and because he engaged in this as much as he could, he lacked access to evidence to the contrary.

Mania

Theo had exhibited mania on many occasions and nursing staff had described his mood as highly elevated. Theo had self-reported racing thoughts, an inability to sleep, and increased levels of energy. Also, he spent a lot of time in his room writing his life story, which he stated he had to do as part of his work as a God. This was an intense time for Theo, and he produced hundreds of pages of material during a three-month period. He described wanting some time to himself and wanted to achieve some 'peacefulness' in his life. This was an indication of how all-consuming his delusions were. As Theo believed that these negative outcomes were a necessary consequence of the important work he was doing, he was initially reluctant to work on this area in therapy.

Fantasy elaboration

Theo stated that his work on saving humanity was extremely important and therefore took up all of his time, leaving him unable to take part in any meaningful activity. He spoke a lot about banishing "bad Gods" into space through visual imagery and making, what sounded like, swooshing noises. He stated that this part of his role was significant and took a lot of concentration. It is likely that this was a method of avoiding the consequences of his sexual offending and his sexual attraction to children, and gave him a sense of responsibility and purpose.

Reasoning biases

Theo's self-report highlights a number of reasoning biases, such as confirmation bias, jumping to conclusions, and external attribution that act to maintain his beliefs and which are further reinforced by positive affect. Theo would sometimes state that he had not slept well and attributed this to not working hard enough to banish bad Gods during the day rather than considering a likely alternative explanation which was that he drank a large amount of caffeine just before attempting to go to sleep.

Immersion behaviours

Theo had fully immersed himself in his delusion resulting in social withdrawal and isolation. Theo spent most of his time in his room unless he was eating in the dining room or going to get his medication. His activity level on the ward was extremely low which served to further increase his conviction in his beliefs and preoccupation, which in turn reduced his ability to consider alternative explanations.

Treatment plan and intervention

Aims and goals of therapy

Theo was extremely affected by his experiences, which he described as "all consuming". Although he stated he was pleased to have been selected to do the work of God, with the aim of saving humanity, he admitted that he would have liked more respite and for his life not to have been completely taken over by this mission. His overarching goal was to feel less pressure from his mission to save humanity and when we discussed this in more detail, Theo expressed that he would like to learn how to distract from his experiences and be able to concentrate on other things. As such, Figure 5.5 illustrates the first goal for therapy using SMART (Specific, Measurable, Achievable, Realistic and Timely) as a template.

Goal 1 – Increase ability to distract from experiences

S: Try different strategies to distract from voices

M: Diaries and feedback on tasks

A: Highly motivated

R: One psychology session per week and weekly focus on progress

T: In one month

Figure 5.5 Distraction goal

Goal 2 – Increase meditation time

S: Increase meditation time from 10 min x2 to 10 min x3 a day

M: Feedback sheets and monitoring

A: Highly motivated

R: One psychology session per week and weekly focus on progress

T: In one month

Figure 5.6 Meditation goal

Goal 3 – feel more like myself and more peaceful

S: Complete activities (swimming, cooking, mindfulness group, cleaning job, ground leave) once per week. Continue to meditate 10 min x4 per day. Increase social interaction

M: Social interaction diary, feedback sheet in relation to activities and linked with goal. Meditation diary

A: Highly motivated and accessible resources

R: One psychology session per week and weekly focus on progress

T: In three months in time for CPA meeting

Figure 5.7 Identity goal

After achieving this goal, and through further discussion in sessions, Theo decided that he would like to focus on increasing the duration for which he was able to meditate throughout the day. Initially, he was able to complete this task for ten minutes twice a day. Figure 5.6 presents this goal during therapy.

After we were able to increase the time, Theo was able to meditate to a period that he was content with, he reflected that his experiences had made him feel like his thoughts were racing and his mood was elevated and he stated that he would like to feel, "more like myself and more peaceful". We spent some time gaining a shared understanding of what these concepts meant to Theo, and, after this time, were able to develop a goal which is presented in Figure 5.7.

This then paved the way for work to centre around his reasoning biases with the aim of giving him access to alternative explanations for some of his experiences. Luckily, through our work we were able to target his anomalous experiences, some aspects of mania, fantasy elaboration, immersive behaviours, and reasoning biases maintenance cycles from Isham et al.'s (2021) work, which also cover many of the maintenance factors presented in Garety et al.'s (2001) formulation.

Engagement and trust (sessions 1–3)

Theo had not seen a psychologist in the past and initially declined to see me. Due to his suspicion around my motives, I attempted to develop an informal therapeutic relationship with Theo which involved more ad hoc informal open interactions instead of sessions in a confidential space. It took five weeks before Theo agreed to meet with me for a more formal session and we spent time talking about my role and goal setting. As evidenced by Evans-Jones et al. (2009), therapists are able to establish a good therapeutic relationship with patients with psychosis, irrespective of the severity of symptoms. They moreover found that concepts such as empathy and collaborative goals were important factors when developing a therapeutic relationship within this context. Further, providing a clear explanation that I was not aiming to invalidate his experiences or try to make his voices go away but was just there to guide him through a process of achieving a more balanced life, where both doing his work as God and achieving his own goals were possible, helped his engagement. Theo stated during our first session that he did not trust me, and it took several sessions for Theo to agree to speak to me about his experiences. Because of this, very early on, we developed a Trust scale through which we came to a shared understanding of trust within this context and measured it at the end of every session. Also, we developed the use of a symbolic pause button (safe word) that gave Theo control over the discussions of his experiences. He was able to use this word if he felt any negative sensations or experiences during our discussion. This allowed me to know when Theo was distressed and to pause the conversation and redirect if necessary.

Assessment and formulation sessions (sessions: 4–6)

After a period of engagement and therapeutic rapport building, Theo completed several psychometric tests identified as relevant for his case. We then spent time developing a collaborative formulation, which was presented earlier in Figure 5.2.

Coping with voices (sessions: 7–10)

As Theo's first goal was focused around enhancing his ability to distract himself from the content of his delusions, we spent three sessions on coping strategies.

When I explained the different strategies that we could start with, Theo stated that we would like to try the 'earplug technique' first. Initially, I bought ten different pairs of earplugs for Theo to try, and we conducted a behavioural experiment within the session to ascertain if the strategy was at all effective. He then spent the week trying it on his own but stated in the following session that it did not work as it blocked out all the external sounds in his environment, making the voices more prominent. It was helpful to go through this process together as it taught us that there was no negative outcome from the strategy not working and that we had learnt something from completing the experiments. I believe that it also helped Theo's confidence to disclose when something I had suggested was not effective; I was conscious that in secure services, a power imbalance exists between patients and professionals, and that autonomy within treatment was considered hugely important. The next strategy that we focused on was setting boundaries and allocating a certain amount of time to the voices. However, due to increased social isolation and lack of meaningful activity at the time, this strategy was also not effective for Theo. I wondered if this was more likely to be successful if Theo was not in his room all day and had some structure to his life. I returned to this strategy later in therapy. Theo informed me that he enjoyed listening to music and felt he could focus on the sound as a distraction technique. As a result, we worked to increase his use of music and I bought him some guided imagery CDs, which was the strategy that was the most used and most effective for Theo during therapy. We also spent time developing our own imagery CDs based on Theo's favourite places and experiences.

Mindfulness for psychosis (sessions: 11–16)

As Theo's next goal was focused around increasing the amount of time he could meditate for and to clear his mind, the next few sessions were centred around **mindfulness**. Initially, Theo could meditate for ten minutes twice a day and through teaching the principles of mindfulness from Morris et al.'s (2013) **Acceptance and Commitment Therapy (ACT)** from a psychosis perspective, he was able to increase this to ten minutes four times a day. This work started by completing mindfulness activities together during the session and then Theo practising the skills outside of sessions. After he was familiar with this, we worked on noticing exercises focusing away from the voice and towards the voice without resistance or response. He was able to apply these skills well and reported that he found this work very valuable.

Increasing activity (sessions: 17–22)

During the mindfulness sessions, however, it became apparent that although Theo wanted to increase his meditation time, he also wanted to feel more like himself by completing activities he enjoyed and to feel more peaceful. We spent some time creating a shared meaning of these concepts, which involved participating in activities on the ward and increasing his social interaction with others. Theo moreover agreed to do a cleaning job on the ward on a daily basis, which assisted in structuring his day and gave him more of a purpose and identity on the ward. During this time, it was deemed that his current engagement was at a good-enough level to allow Theo escorted ground leave which appeared to significantly improve his well-being and his ability to cope with his experiences. It was during these sessions, that I reintroduced setting boundaries and a period of time to listen to the voices. This appeared to help with Theo's anxiety about missing important information from the voices about his work. It also proved an important strategy from a therapeutic perspective, as Theo's initial beliefs were that I was going to try to stop him from doing his work. Theo found the sessions helpful and was pleased to be living a more fulfilled existence on top of the work he believed he was doing as God. The increase in his social interactions and activities was giving him more of a purpose and identity; this was imperative, as if his beliefs around being God were to alter, he was considered more likely to fall into a state of low mood and depression. These new aspects of his life will, in my view, act as protective factors if he does come to learn that he is not God and also in relation to coming to terms with the sexual offences he has committed. It is imperative, in any CBT work, that relapse prevention and blueprinting are ongoing skills developed throughout the course of therapy and not just at the end of psychological treatment. Blueprinting is a CBT tool that helps to summarise the work the patient and therapist have completed together. Figure 5.8. illustrates an example of Theo's blueprinting at this point in treatment.

Blueprint

What have I learnt so far?

There can be a balance between meeting my goals and doing my work. This is not a bad thing, it makes me feel better when I can do activities and go on ground leave. I don't have to be stuck in my room all day, this isn't good for me. I don't have to work all the time, and I feel better when I am engaging with other people.

Top three strategies for feeling more like yourself
1. Keep a schedule of daily activities and complete them
2. Keep practising mindfulness and flexible thinking
3. Stick to boundaries of listening to the voices and working

Support from others

I can talk to the nursing team or psychologist

Figure 5.8 Theo's blueprint

Reasoning biases (sessions: 23–30)

Throughout intervention sessions, Theo demonstrated an ability to be flexible with his thinking and he agreed to complete some work on reasoning biases. He was keen to complete this intervention and admitted that he had lost some of his previous ability to think flexibly. We spent eight sessions completing metacognitive work, which is work on knowledge and regulation of one's cognitive processes, and Theo showed a capability to think about his experiences more critically. He was able to build his ability to ascertain 'evidence for' and 'evidence against' concepts. As a result, he presented as being able to think with greater flexibility around his experiences and admit that his assumptions were not always right. Theo was able to consider alternative explanations regarding situations within the ward environment. This intervention was based on Moritz et al.'s (2012) work on individualised metacognitive therapy for psychosis.

Ending and outcomes (sessions: 31–32)

After completing work on reasoning biases, the staff team was informed that Theo would be imminently transferred to another setting. So, for our final sessions we discussed our work together and Theo stated that his belief in the content of the voices had decreased from 100% to 90%, which although was not our target for intervention was interesting to discuss with Theo. Also, we spent a session completing post treatment psychometric tests (discussed later).

Intervention considerations

It is important to remain aware that if Theo's appraisal of his experiences changes, then there is a high likelihood of him becoming very low in mood. Therefore, it was noted as important to incorporate a self-compassionate perspective in any future work. Finally, Theo did describe sleeping problems during our formulation sessions; however, his sleep significantly improved after an increase in activity and social interaction.

Outcomes

The outcomes for intervention with Theo were assessed from four different perspectives described as follows:

1   The first from his beliefs associated with his experiences from the joint formulation (Figure 5.2);
2   From the Trust scale we developed initially and recorded throughout therapy on a weekly basis;
3   From the three goals that Theo wanted to achieve through therapy which set the focus for our sessions; and
4   From psychometric tests completed with Theo during the assessment stage and again after session 31.

Table 5.2 Belief ratings

Formulation stage results	After session 32 results
The voices are 100% powerful. I believe this 100%. I talk back to the voices 90% of the time. I hear voices 100% of the time.	The voices are 100% powerful. I believe this 90%. I talk back to the voices 60% of the time. I hear voices 80% of the time.

Information and data will be presented from these four perspectives in turn in relation to his beliefs associated with his experiences and are presented in Table 5.2.

These results indicated that although there was no change in the power, Theo did hear and respond to voices less than at the start of therapy and his conviction in the belief reduced. Although these were not aspects directly targeted in treatment, it is clear that an increase of social interaction and activity and work around mindfulness and reasoning biases had a positive impact on Theo's well-being.

Due to Theo's suspicions around my intentions and a lack of trust, we developed a Trust scale at the start of therapy. We initially spent some time thinking about the concept of trust in this therapeutic relationship which involved the following aspects:

1   You want the best for me.
2   I believe you are not trying to take my role as God away and tell me I am mentally unwell.
3   You will be honest if I ask you something.
4   You will be accountable and see me when we have agreed.
5   You will tell me what information you will pass onto the team.
6   You will not be judgemental.

We looked at these factors and every week Theo rated how much he trusted me on a scale from 1–10. The results are displayed in Figure 5.9.

It was positive to see a steady increase in trust within the therapeutic relationship. Theo had not worked with a psychologist in the past and had declined to see me on a number of occasions so a significant aspect of or work together was the achievement of him gaining trust within the therapeutic relationship. His perspective on psychology had completely altered and his positive experience of therapy will hopefully allow him to engage in meaningful work more readily in the future.

In relation to his own goals and the main focus of therapy, Theo was able to distract himself from the voices and concentrate on other things more as he used the guided imagery CDs I supplied and those that we created. I believe that his ability to engage in more social interactions, his use of mindfulness, an increase in his level of activity, and his awareness of his reasoning biases had a

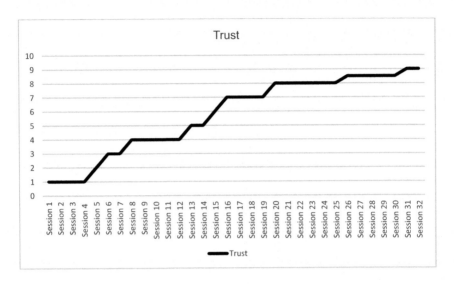

Figure 5.9 Trust scale outcomes

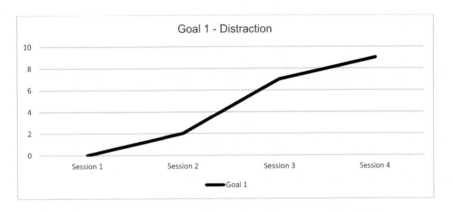

Figure 5.10 Goal 1 scale outcomes

direct impact on the results presented in Table 5.1, as well as meeting his third goal of feeling more like himself and feeling more peaceful. The progress of his goals is illustrated in Figure 5.10, Table 5.3, and Figure 5.11.

Finally, a re-administration of all the psychometric tests conducted during the assessment stage was completed, with the tests used detailed in Table 5.1. All scores remained unchanged except Theo's PSYRATS score was reduced from 25 to 20 when reassessed, and his level of insight improved on the SAI-E. These results indicated that he was less preoccupied with his experiences, that it caused less disruption to his life, and that he was not hearing them as often.

Table 5.3 Goal 2 outcomes

Session	Meditation time achieved
5	10 min x2 daily
6	10 min x2 daily
7	10 min x2 + 5 min x1 daily
8	10 min x2 + 10 min x1 daily
9	10 min x2 + 10 min x1 daily
10	10 min x2 + 10 min x2 daily

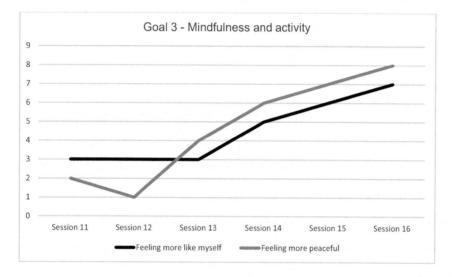

Figure 5.11 Goal 3 scaled outcomes

This outcome was positive as it suggested that his well-being was increased as a result of the interventions he had completed.

Reflective analysis

Challenges

The reflective analysis has been extremely pertinent in this case; particularly considering the systemic environment Theo was treated within. As Theo resided in a secure forensic service, there were a number of professionals involved in his care and treatment. One of the most difficult factors involved in this work with Theo was an issue that several members of his clinical team held an ongoing and unwavering view that he was feigning his symptoms to remain in hospital and as a way of dissolving responsibility for his sexual offending. The reflection I had about this, and experiences I have had previously, made me realise that when a patient is reporting multiple psychotic experiences which medication is not treating, when the patient has committed a serious offence, and the patient has a high level of intelligence, the clinical team might sometimes falsely believe that the patient is either exaggerating, or, in this case, feigning symptoms. To address these views, I ran a number of reflective practice and formulation sessions for staff. Further, Theo gave consent for staff to listen to our recorded therapy sessions, and this assisted in understanding his experiences and strengthened the view that Theo was extremely unwell and highly distressed. Also, I spent a lot of time explaining to staff his working formulation and how his symptoms were linked to his offending. This work continued for several months and after this time, most staff had the consistent perspective that Theo was not being deceptive. Most notably, I observed an increased level of compassion and empathy, which in turn had a positive impact on the relationship and interactions between Theo and nursing staff.

Conclusion

This case study has presented the assessment, formulation, and treatment overview for an adult male with a diagnosis of paranoid schizophrenia. Intervention was informed by using two specific formulation models relevant for this case. Of note, Isham et al.'s (2019) work is applicable within a forensic population and the model is highly relevant and accessible to patients; this case study demonstrated the application of the model in clinical practice. Psychometric test data and self-report indicated that Theo's level of conviction in his unusual belief reduced, with less occasions of hearing voices and responding. Additionally, he demonstrated increased insight with an overall improvement to his quality of life and well-being. This work is imperative to better equip Theo to engage with work around developing insight and completing treatment in relation to his future risk to children. Finally, some important reflections were presented which highlight the challenges of multidisciplinary team working and the importance of truly patient-focused psychological treatment.

References

Birchwood, M., Mohan, L., Meaden, A., Tarrier, N., Lewis, S., Wykes, T., Davies, L. M., Dunn, G., Peters, E., & Michail, M. (2018). The COMMAND trial of cognitive therapy for harmful compliance with command hallucinations (CTCH): A qualitative study of acceptability and tolerability in the UK. *British Medical Journal Open, 8*(6).

Birchwood, M., Spencer, E., & McGovern, D. (2000). Schizophrenia: Early warning signs. *Advances in Psychiatric Treatment, 6*, 93–101.

Chadwick, P., Lees, S., & Birchwood, M. (2000). The revised beliefs about voices questionnaire (BAVQ-R). *British Journal of Psychiatry, 177*, 229–232.

Evans-Jones, C., Peters, E., & Barker, C. (2009). The therapeutic relationship in CBT for psychosis: Client, therapist and therapy factors. *Journal of Behavioural Cognitive Psychotherapy, 37*(5), 527–540.

Fowler, D., Garety, P. A., & Kuipers, E. (1998). Understanding the inexplicable: An individually formulated cognitive approach to delusional beliefs. In C. Perris & P. D. McGorry (Eds.), *Cognitive psychotherapy of psychotic and personality disorders* (pp. 129–146). Wiley.

Freeman, D. (2016). Persecutory delusions: A cognitive perspective on understanding and treatment. *Lancet Psychiatry, 3*(7), 685–692.

Freeman, D., Emsley, R., Duamond, R., Collett, N., Bold, E., Chadwick, E., Isham, L., Bird, J. C., Edwards, K., Kingdon, D., Fitzpatrick, R., Kabir, T., & Waite, F. (2021). Oxford cognitive approaches to psychosis trial study group. Comparison of a theoretically driven cognitive therapy (the Feeling Safe Programme) with befriending for the treatment of persistent persecutory delusions: A parallel, single-blind, randomised controlled trial. *Lancet Psychiatry, 8*(8), 696–707.

Freeman, D., Garety, P. A., Kuipers, E., Fowler, D., & Bebbington, P. E. (2002). A cognitive model of persecutory delusions. *British Journal of Clinical Psychology, 41*, 331–347.

Garety, P. A., & Hemsley, D. R. (1994). *Delusions: Investigations into the psychology of delusional reasoning.* Oxford University Press.

Garety, P. A., Kuipers, E., Fowler, D., Freeman, D., & Bebbington, P. A. (2001). Cognitive model of the positive symptoms of psychosis. *Psychological Medicine, 31*, 189–195.

Haddock, G., McCarron, J., Tarrier, N., & Faragher, E. B. (1999). Scales to measure dimensions of hallucinations and delusions: The psychotic symptom rating scales (PSYRATS). *Psychological Medicine, 29*, 879–889.

Hart, S. D., Kropp, P. R., Laws, D. R., Klaver, J., Logan, C., & Watt, K. A. (2003). *The risk for sexual violence protocol (RSVP).* The Mental Health, Law, and Policy Institute of Simon Fraser University.

Isham, L., Griffith, L., Boylan, A. M., Hicks, A., Wilson, N., Byrne, R., Sheaves, B., Bentall, R. P., & Freeman, D. (2019). Understanding, treating, and renaming grandiose delusions: A qualitative study. *Psychological Psychotherapy, 94*(1), 119–140.

Kemp, R., & David, A. (1997). Insight and compliance. In B. Blackwell (Ed.), *Treatment compliance and the therapeutic alliance in serious mental illness* (pp. 61–84). Harwood Academic Publishers.

Knowles, R., McCarthy-Jones, S., & Rowse, G. (2011). Grandiose delusions: A review and theoretical integration of cognitive and affective perspectives. *Clinical Psychology Review, 31*, 684–696.

Moritz, S., Bohn Vitzthum, F., Veckenstedt, R., Leighton, L., Woodward, T. S., & Hauschildt, M. (2012). *Individualized metacognitive therapy program for psychosis (MCT+).* Van-Ham Campus Press.

Morris, E. M., Johns, L. C., & Oliver, J. E. (Eds.). (2013). *Acceptance and commitment therapy and mindfulness for psychosis.* John Wiley.

Morrison, A. P. (2001). The interpretation of intrusions in psychosis: An integrative cognitive approach to hallucinations and delusions. *Behavioural Cognitive Psychotherapy, 29*, 257–276.

National Institute of Clinical Excellence. (2014). *Psychosis and schizophrenia in adults: Prevention and management* [CG178]. www.nice.org.uk/guidance/cg178.

Phiri, P., Rathod, S., Carr, H., & Kingdon, D. (2017). A brief review of key models in cognitive behaviour therapy for psychosis. *Acta Psychopathologica, 3*, 84.

Ronald, A., Sieradzka, D., Cardno, A. G., Haworth, C. M., McGuire, P., & Freeman, D. (2014). Characterization of psychotic experiences in adolescence using the Specific Psychotic Experiences Questionnaire: Findings from a study of 5000 16-year-olds. *Schizophrenia Bulletin, 40*, 868–877.

Tai, S., & Turkington, D. (2009). The evolution of cognitive behavior therapy for schizophrenia: Current practice and recent developments. *Schizophrenia Bulletin, 35*(5), 865–873.

van der Gaag, M., Valmaggia, L. R., & Smit, F. (2014). The effects of individually tailored formulation-based cognitive behavioural therapy in auditory hallucinations and delusions: A meta-analysis. *Schizophrenia Research, 156*(1), 30–37.

Webster, C. D., Douglas, K. S., Eaves, D., & Hart, S. D. (2013). *HCR-20: Assessing risk for violence version 3*. Mental Health, Law and Policy Institute, Simon Fraser University.

Zavos, H. M., Freeman, D., Haworth, C. M., McGuire, P., Plomin, R., Cardno, A. G., & Ronald, A. (2014). Consistent etiology of severe, frequent psychotic experiences and milder, less severe manifestations: A twin study of specific psychotic experiences in adolescence. *JAMA Psychiatry, 81,* 1049–1057.

6 The psychological recovery journey of a patient detained in low secure forensic mental health service

Lara Arsuffi

Introduction

In its broadest term, the recovery paradigm is founded on principles of hope, empowerment, healing, and connection (Jacobson & Greenley, 2001). It promotes patient choice, responsibility, and self-determination, opposing coercive forms of treatment (Pouncey & Lukens, 2010). The term 'forensic population' is often used to refer to people who have been charged with a crime and are detained either in prison or a secure mental health hospital or those who are managed by probation or by a forensic mental health team in the community. Service users in forensics settings, in general, present with a range of complex difficulties, including a history of aggression and/or other antisocial behaviour, limited educational and employment achievements, substance abuse issues, a complex trauma history, problems with impulse control (i.e. high impulsivity levels), difficulties in developing trusting, healthy relationships in general, and difficulties with people in a position of providing care or authority.

Recovery when experiencing these difficulties can be complex. This can involve all of the usual elements of recovery, including reduction in acute symptoms, finding medication that is effective, and gaining insight into their illness, personality, and the need for treatment. However, forensic clients must also define a 'life worth living' for themselves, overcome problems with functional impairment, find vocational support, and foster healthy relationships with family and friends (Simpson & Penney, 2011). They may have to engage in additional tasks, including understanding the origins and effects of their offending and the legal oversights imposed upon them (Simpson & Penney, 2011).

Forensic 'mental health psychiatric patients' are generally detained in secure hospitals and can experience lengthy periods of inpatient care. This chapter presents part of Mr Jones' recovery journey during his stay in an NHS low secure mental health ward and subsequently in an open rehabilitation setting over a period of three years and the psychological interventions he accessed before his discharge into 24-hour supported housing in the community, under the care of the local forensic mental health team. 'Mr Jones' is a pseudonym to protect his identity; identifiable information has been edited.

DOI: 10.4324/9781003213116-6

Patient history

Childhood

Mr Jones is a Caucasian 50-year-old man. He was raised by his single mother and has never met his father. Mr Jones reported that his mother physically and emotionally abused him during his childhood, which included burning him with cigarettes, locking him in cupboards, not feeding him (this resulted in him eating his own faeces), and beating him with household items. Furthermore, he has reported that his mother sexually abused him from the age of nine years. Mr Jones' only positive memories about his childhood relate to when he was spending time with his grandmother, whom he used to visit on an occasional basis.

Education and employment

Mr Jones attended school until the age of 12 years old. He then left school to go to work. He worked in a shop for three years and subsequently worked in a factory for a year but left because he thought "the machines were talking to" him. He has not held other periods of employment.

Substance misuse

Mr Jones reported that he started snorting heroin when he was 11 years old, progressing onto injecting it, until his early forties. Mr Jones was also a regular user of crack cocaine and cannabis. He has used LSD and ecstasy occasionally and has a history of abusing prescribed medications. Mr Jones stated that he used to be addicted to alcohol, drinking at some points up to six litres of cider per day.

Relationship history

Mr Jones' first consensual sexual relationship was when he was 17 years old. Overall, he reported having had three serious relationships in his life. When he was in his early twenties, he met Daisy. They lived together for about three or four years and had two children together. Daisy wanted to get married and arranged for a ceremony without letting him know. When he discovered this, he walked out and ended the relationship. He then met Anna. They developed a relationship, lived together for about four years, and had two children together. Mr Jones reported that they both drank alcohol to excess. When the relationship with Anna ended, Mr Jones entered a relationship with another woman, Carla, whom he married. They were together for approximately five years, and they were both heroin users. This was a volatile relationship and Mr Jones admitted hitting Carla on occasion. The relationship ended when he was remanded in prison for the index offence (described later). Carla died of a drug overdose whilst Mr Jones was in prison. He was unable to attend her funeral and reported for several years feeling guilty about her death (as he had introduced her to heroin) and that he reported that he had not grieved about losing Carla.

Mental health

Mr Jones has had several short psychiatric hospital admissions due to his poor mental health, experiencing symptoms such as hearing voices, low mood, and paranoia. At times, there have been concerns regarding him expressing intent to harm and/or kill others, as well as concerns regarding self-harm and suicide (overdosing and cutting himself). During his hospital admissions, Mr Jones received several diagnoses including **borderline personality disorder**, **depression**, **paranoid schizophrenia**, **post-traumatic stress disorder (PTSD)**, and opiate and alcohol dependence.

Mr Jones reported that he had suffered a few head injuries throughout his life. When he was 16 years old, he fell and lost consciousness for five to ten minutes. He was taken to hospital and was diagnosed with a concussion. He remembers having a swelling on his head for some time after this incident. Subsequently, as an adult, he was involved in a few fights and lost consciousness for five minutes on at least three occasions. During one of these fights, an assailant punched him in the head and jumped on his head.

Offending history

An 'index' offence refers to the offence for which the person is detained or which caused them to come to the attention of services; therefore, it is the most recent offence. Mr Jones' index offence is attempted robbery. Mr Jones entered a shop and ordered the cashier to open the till. The cashier refused, at which point Mr Jones pulled a knife out of his pocket and threatened the cashier with it. The cashier became frightened for his life and ran out of the store. Images of the event were recorded on CCTV and the police later arrested Mr Jones who was initially remanded in prison but was subsequently transferred to an NHS medium security hospital to access treatment due to poor mental health. Mr Jones was disposed via a hospital order for the index offence under Section 37/41 of the **Mental Health Act 2007**; therefore, instead of being sentenced to prison, he was detained in hospital for treatment.

Mr Jones has a long history of violence. He has stated that when he was a teenager, he stabbed a man in the stomach. No further information is available about this incident apart from Mr Jones' self-report. Police records detail the following convictions relating to violence: assault with intent to rob; several offences of possession of an offensive weapon in a public place; and several offences of assault on police. Mr Jones has also threatened to be violent to staff and patients in hospital and prison.

Assessment

Upon transfer to the low secure ward from a medium secure setting, Mr Jones was assessed for a period of three months by his multidisciplinary team, composed of nursing, occupational therapy, medical, and psychology staff. The HCR-20 version 3 (Douglas et al., 2013) was used to establish risk and treatment targets. The HCR-20 is a systematic guide for assessing risk for violence. It contains 20 risk items organised around three scales – historical (ten items), clinical (five items), and risk (five items). The ten historical items (H) are mainly static in nature and are therefore unlikely to fluctuate over time. The five clinical items (C) refer to current (within the past 6–12 months) mental, emotional, and psychiatric status and include risk markers that are dynamic and are, therefore, likely to be amenable to intervention and change over time. The five risk items (R) are concerned with the future (usually within the next 6–12 months) social, living, and treatment circumstances as well as anticipating the person's reaction to those conditions. The R items are scored based on the context the person is going to live in moving forward, for example IN (if they remain in a secure setting) or OUT (if they are released in the community). As the H scores on the HCR-20 tend to remain relatively static, the main focus when it comes to planning interventions for risk minimisation and evaluating treatment tends to be on the more changeable C and R factors (Muller-Isberner et al., 2007). The 20 items on the HCR-20 are scored as follows:

N =   No evidence of this risk item.
P =   The item possibly is present or is present only to a limited extent.
Y =   Yes, definitely present.
Omit =   Item is not scored due to insufficient valid information.

During his stay on the low secure and open rehabilitation ward, Mr Jones was assessed with the HCR-20v3 approximately every 6–9 months, for a total of five times, to evaluate how he was responding to various medical and psychological treatment interventions and as a means of planning his future pathway. Table 6.1 presents Mr Jones' dynamic (C and R) HCR-20 scores at assessment (three months post admission), mid-treatment (18 months after admission), and pre-discharge into the community (three years after admission). A score of 'Y' (meaning yes, present) or 'P' (possible/partially present) indicates a treatment target.

Based on the initial HCR-20 assessment, the following treatment targets were identified:

1   Developing greater insight into mental health and how to remain mentally stable when released in the community
2   Stabilising mental health by reducing active symptoms of mental disorder in the here and now, including symptoms of depression, paranoia, and PTSD

3   Reducing cognitive instability, for example jumping to negative conclusions, not thinking of consequences, feeling hopeless
4   Improving social and professional support
5   Developing stronger stress management skills

These treatment targets were met through provision of various individual and group psychological interventions delivered by a team of assistant psychologists, trainee forensic psychologists, and a principal forensic psychologist, in addition to input from other multidisciplinary team colleagues, that is nursing staff, responsible clinician/consultant forensic psychiatrist, and occupational therapists. The psychological interventions accessed by Mr Jones will be described in the next section of this chapter.

Because of his trauma history, poor academic achievement, early onset and long-term substance abuse, and history of head (and therefore possible brain) injuries during the assessment period, Mr Jones engaged in a cognitive assessment to assess whether or not adjustments needed to be made to how interventions would be delivered and to maximise responsivity and treatment benefit. Mr Jones' overall intellectual functioning was assessed using the Wechsler Adult Intelligence Scale–4th Edition (WAIS–IV UK; Wechsler, 2008). The WAIS-IV provides a global measure of intellectual function in addition to several index scores, which examine more specific cognitive skills including verbal comprehension, perceptual reasoning, working memory, and processing speed. Mr Jones obtained a Full-Scale Intelligent Quotient (FSIQ) score within the *low average* range. A closer look at his scores on the different indexes revealed weaknesses with **processing speed**.

Table 6.1 Mr Jones' dynamic C and R scores at assessment, mid-treatment, and pre-discharge

HCR-20 dynamic risk items	Assessment	Mid-treatment	Pre-discharge
C1 Recent problems with insight	Y	P	N
C2 Recent problems with violent ideation	N	N	N
C3 Recent problems with symptoms of major mental disorder	Y	P	P
C4 Recent problems with instability	P	P	N
C5 Recent problems with treatment response	N	N	N
R1 Future problems with professional services	N (in)	N (in)	P (out)
R2 Future problems with living situation	N (in)	N (in)	N (out)
R3 Future problems with personal support	Y (in)	Y (in)	Y (out)
R4 Future problems with treatment response	P (in)	N (in)	P (out)
R5 Future problems with stress and coping	P (in)	P (in)	P (out)

Mr Jones' memory was assessed using the Wechsler Memory Scale–4th Edition (WMS-IV UK; Wechsler, 2010). The WMS-IV provides several sub-scales of memory functioning including auditory memory, visual memory, visual working memory, immediate memory, and delayed memory. Mr Jones' profile on the WMS-IV was not a balanced one. His scores revealed that Mr Jones was much better at remembering things that were presented to him in a visual format rather than in a verbal format. The assessment also revealed problems retrieving information from memory, especially after a delay. Weaknesses in processing speed, as revealed by the WAIS-IV, suggested that Mr Jones was likely to be overwhelmed by too much verbal information. Therefore, when communicating with him, staff were advised to use short sentences, regular pauses, to ask him to repeat back what he understood, allow him to ask questions, and use visual aids to communicate the main points of a conversation.

Psychological treatments

Bereavement counselling

After the assessment period, Mr Jones was presented with his treatment plan and to promote autonomy was asked if he wanted to engage in treatment, and if so, to choose what psychological treatment he wanted to access first. He requested bereavement counselling to help him process the passing of his ex-partner Carla. This intervention took place over the course of ten sessions of 45 minutes duration. Sessions were scheduled at the same time/day every week, where possible, to be responsive to his cognitive needs. At the beginning of the intervention, to assess his level of symptoms of depression/low mood, Mr Jones was asked to complete the Beck Depression Inventory-II (BDI-II) (Beck et al., 1996) psychometric test. His score fell in the *severe* range for depression. He was offered pharmacological support to alleviate his depression, but he declined.

During bereavement work, Mr Jones was provided with psychoeducation about the five stages of the grief model (Kubler-Ross, 1969). He was sup-ported to develop a new sense of identity without Carla; this was aided by his recent re-establishment of contact with one of his daughters and by him making positive future plans to contact his now-adult children. Mr Jones was unable to connect with the emotional aspects of processing the bereavement due to his childhood trauma experiences. He was offered **EMDR therapy** to help him to reprocess painful memories. However, he declined, preferring to "keep the past in the past". However, Mr Jones was able to accept Carla's death, at least cognitively, if not emotionally. A celebration of her life was planned, and Mr Jones chose to say goodbye to Carla by praying with the pastor and by releasing a balloon with a personal message attached to it. Mr Jones again com-pleted the BDI-II at the end of this intervention. It was noted that his score on the BDI-II had lowered, now falling in the *moderate* range for depression, indicating some symptom reduction over the course of the intervention.

'I Can Feel Good' group

The I Can Feel Good group (Ashworth et al., 2018) is a **Dialectical Behavioural Therapy (DBT)-**informed skill training programme for people with intellectual disabilities and problems managing their emotions. The programme draws in part on the structure and themes of the Skills Training Manual for Treating Borderline Personality Disorder developed by Marsha Linehan (1993); however, the concepts and exercises have been adapted for the needs of people with impairments in their cognitive functioning. The programme is composed of four modules: (1) mindfulness skills, (2) managing feelings, (3) coping in crisis, and (4) people skills. Mr Jones attended the first module of this programme.

The aims of the mindfulness skills module are to (1) teach group participants mindfulness skills, (2) increase awareness of internal states and external events, which may impact our thoughts and behaviour, and (3) increase emotion awareness and expressive vocabulary. The module moreover provides the opportunity to practise social skills with other group members. It comprises 12 individual one-hour sessions. The group is interactive and uses lots of visual prompts/cues throughout. To maximise learning, the group repeats mindfulness practices in each session and encourages group members to try each skill learned during their independent time.

Mr Jones attended every session on time and abided by the group rules throughout. He found it difficult to complete homework tasks independently because of his literacy and memory difficulties, and despite support being offered in between group sessions, he declined these. Mr Jones was initially a quiet observer within the group; however, he quickly became more confident sharing his views and opinions spontaneously, and he was supportive of others. Mr Jones engaged in all tasks set, including discussions, mindfulness exercises, and written tasks. For the written tasks, he was provided with extra staff support.

Mr Jones engaged well in visualisation tasks, stating that he enjoyed these (e.g. listening to calming music and visualising a halo slowly moving down his body). Mr Jones was able to show good understanding of the 'hot mind' (led by emotions) and used specific examples from his own experiences to share with the group when he had been in a 'hot mind' state in the past. Likewise, he was able to think of alternative solutions, showing problem-solving abilities. Furthermore, Mr Jones was able to successfully use the 'emotion wheel' to identify how he was feeling, the thoughts that were occurring whilst experiencing the emotion, and how this affected his behaviour. He gave the following example, "feeling low in mood – thinking 'keeping to myself is best' – not using leave/self-isolating". Following the intervention, the nursing team observed that Mr Jones was putting mindfulness strategies into practice in his everyday life, for example by practising mindful walking, visualising, and deep breathing.

Understanding Mental Health Group

The Understanding Mental Health Group is a psychoeducational intervention aimed at increasing participants' insight into emotional well-being, developing coping strategies, and enhancing recovery of clients with Axis I diagnoses (DSM-IV; APA, 1994). The group covers various topics including the stress-vulnerability model, sleep, anxiety, depression, various psychotic illnesses, medication, relapse prevention, and recovery, over 20 one-hour sessions. Each participant completes the group with an individualised relapse prevention plan.

Bauml et al. (2006) describe the concept of psychoeducation as a "therapeutic programme with a focus on the didactic and skilful communication of relevant information". Psychoeducation is considered a paradigm shift from traditional forms of therapy to a more "holistic approach which stresses health, collaboration and empowerment" (Dixon, 1999). The primary guiding principle of psychoeducation is that everyone has the right to receive information about their difficulties and evidence-based treatment options so that they may be able to take a more active and informed role in their recovery (Aho-Mustonen et al., 2008). It is also thought to be among the most effective evidence-based practices that have recently emerged in both inpatient and community settings (Luken & McFarlane, 2004).

A further consideration of psychoeducation is that group dynamics can be helpful to facilitate opportunities for within-group dialogue, social learning, and the potential for positive group reinforcement and peer support (Luken & McFarlane, 2004). By doing so, it is suggested that such groups could serve to reduce social isolation and provide a forum for recognising, understanding, and normalising mental health experiences. The concept of psychoeducation is supported by **NICE** guidance, for example NICE guideline CG138 (2012) and CG178 (2014), which recommends the inclusion of information on psychosis, effective use of medication, identifying and managing symptoms, coping with stress, individualised recovery goals, relapse prevention, and building social support networks. Mr Jones was invited to attend the Understanding Mental Health Group because during the assessment phase on the low secure ward, it was noted that developing insight into his mental health needs was a treatment target, as measured by the initial HCR-20v3 assessment.

Mr Jones attended the group spontaneously, with little encouragement; he was on time for the sessions and followed the group rules throughout. Mr Jones presented as quiet during the group, but as sessions went on, he grew in confidence, sharing his views. Mr Jones was able to identify his early warning signs and high-risk situations for mental health deterioration, demonstrating insight that it is important to recognise warning signs so as to be able to implement coping strategies at the earliest opportunity, to help avoid a relapse. He was also able to recognise that people become unwell quickly if they don't know their 'relapse signatures'. Mr Jones emphasised the importance of asking for help, relating this back to his own experience of returning to hospital on several occasions historically because he did not ask for help when needed. He was able to identify personal coping strategies that he could use when distressed. The treatment team considered that he had made good progress through this intervention.

Behavioural Treatment for Substance Abuse

The Behavioural Treatment for Substance Abuse (BTSA) (Bellack et al., 2006) is an evidence-based treatment programme addressing substance misuse for people with psychosis. BTSA is based on harm reduction principles rather than abstinence and is highly repetitive to account for the cognitive deficits often associated with individuals with a psychotic disorder, particularly schizophrenia (Bellack et al., 2006). Research highlights that treatment programmes for people with a history of offending should include motivational interviewing and a contingency management component (Bahr et al., 2012). Two core components of BTSA are motivational interviewing and contingency management.

Research also highlights that treatment programmes should include different interventions targeting multiple needs, provide intensive treatment, and include an aftercare component (Bahr et al., 2012). BTSA runs for 35 sessions, twice weekly across five to six months and covers various topics aimed at improving goal setting skills, emotional management, and drug refusal/social skills in programme participants. Engagement in social activities not associated with substance use, and the development of a social network of non-substance using individuals, is encouraged. BTSA also incorporates a psychoeducation component about the effects of substance misuse on physical and mental health and behaviour for the self and others. The last module of BTSA is relapse prevention training, during which participants are supported to develop detailed, individualised relapse prevention plans to minimise the likelihood of relapse. The BTSA group was delivered in the community from the premises of a charity supporting people with substance abuse problems. In addition, the programme was delivered by NHS staff alongside Recovery Champions (i.e. former substance abusers who are now recovered) employed by this charity. For a detailed description of the BTSA programme attended by Mr Jones, please see Arsuffi & Scarborough (in press).

Mr Jones was encouraged to attend the BTSA group because substance abuse had been identified as a treatment target, the reduction of which was considered likely to minimise mental health decompensation and reduce risk of future aggressive behaviour. Mr Jones was referred to this intervention only when he had official permission to leave the hospital grounds and travel into the local community to attend it. Mr Jones attended the BTSA group 'on leave' from the hospital, initially with the support of an escort but over time more independently. He complied well with all group rules. Mr Jones did not generally complete written exercises in between sessions, despite help being offered. He paid attention throughout the programme, being particularly interested in the Recovery Champions' disclosures about how they managed to overcome their addictions and turn their life around. Mr Jones openly shared his personal experiences with heroin and crack cocaine, including having delusions, seeing things that were not there, and engaging in offending behaviour. Mr Jones generated short-term goals during the BTSA programme and managed to achieve a few, including taking his medications regularly, saving money, avoiding alcohol and drugs, getting a passport, and engaging in various occupational therapy activities and nursing sessions as agreed with his treating team. However, it was noted that Mr Jones was resistant to working towards more medium–term goals such as developing a constructive routine in the community. During the programme, he identified several reasons/motivators/strategies for abstaining from drugs and alcohol, demonstrating consistent commitment to abstaining, for example,

> I want to improve my relationship with my family. I've had enough of using drugs and alcohol. I have been involved in criminal behaviour and I don't want that anymore. I lost touch with my family and I lost my self-respect (due to substance abuse). I want to stay out of hospital. Staying drug free will help me to save money and see my children [...]

Reasoning and Rehabilitation 2 Mental Health Program (R&R2MHP)

The Reasoning and Rehabilitation Mental Health Program (R&R2MHP; Young & Ross, 2007) is a structured, manualised cognitive behavioural therapy (CBT) programme, which aims to reduce antisocial attitudes and behaviours, as well as improving cognitive and problem-solving skills in antisocial people with mental health problems. The programme includes a module on neuro-cognitive skills, focusing on improving cognitive deficits and executive dysfunction common within psychiatric forensic patients (e.g. attention, memory, and planning). The programme moreover aims to teach participants to detect their 'thinking errors' and to gain skills in critical reasoning, social perspective-taking, and alternative and consequential thinking. A number of studies have shown promising evidence about R&R2, including self-reported improvements on measures capturing violent attitudes, anger cognitions, rational problem-solving and locus of control, and decrease in nursing-reported disruptive behaviour for forensic patients (Young et al., 2010; Rees-Jones et al., 2012; Yip et al., 2013) in medium and low security hospitals.

R&R2 MHP is composed of 16 sessions of 90 minutes duration. It consists of individual and group treatment, whereby each participant is met in between sessions by an assistant psychologist or trainee psychologist to transfer the skills learned during the group into their daily lives practice. Mr Jones was invited to attend this intervention to improve his thinking skills and decrease cognitive instability. During the R&R2 group, Mr Jones appeared to understand problem-solving skills and provided several examples of how to implement these to both hypothetical and real-life situations. He recognised one of his thinking errors as 'jumping to conclusions' and found the skill 'stop and think of the consequences for you and others' particularly useful. During the programme, Mr Jones was observed as able to consider different perspectives about an issue and capable of empathic understanding.

Eye Movement Desensitisation and Reprocessing (EMDR)

Throughout his stay on the low secure and open rehabilitation wards, Mr Jones was encouraged to engage in EMDR therapy (which is recommended by the NICE guidelines; Nice Guidelines NG116, 2018) on several occasions to reprocess his childhood trauma and improve his mental health. Mr Jones took up this offer when he was on the rehabilitation ward, after having worked with the lead psychologist during various group interventions for a couple of years. It is proposed that by this time he had developed a working alliance with his psychologists, which was helpful in increasing his motivation and readiness to engage in trauma therapy. This hypothesis is supported by literature. For example, rapport between client and therapist has been found to be related to greater engagement and higher motivation and readiness to participate in treatment (Simpson et al., 2009). The working alliance has also been linked to retention in treatment programmes and more positive treatment outcomes (Joe et al., 2001).

Mr Jones attended 14 EMDR sessions. To help him with remembering to attend these meetings, they occurred at the same time/day of the week. Mr Jones was always ready for these sessions. His response to EMDR was evaluated with the IES-R (Weiss & Marmar, 1997), a psychometric trauma scale, which was administered on three occasions during treatment; at baseline, mid-treatment, and end of treatment (see Table 6.2). The first three appointments were used to plan for EMDR, that is what it was and how it worked, the seating arrangements, the bilateral stimulation, and the stop signal. Mr Jones reported that he was not keen on eye movements or tapping but agreed to use earphones with sounds for bilateral stimulation. A 'calm/safe place' was developed and enhanced. Mr Jones was shown various grounding techniques, that is the light stream, which worked for him; the spiral technique, which did not work; and deep breathing, which Mr Jones found helpful. In subsequent sessions, Mr Jones identified the complaint he wanted to work on, namely the sexual abuse perpetrated by his mother. He explained that his mother used to beat him if he did not do what she asked. His mother told him that he would lose his grandmother if he said anything about the abuse. Therefore, he was scared to speak to anyone. He reported feeling "violated, ashamed, dirty, cheated, resentful, sad, and horrible". Mr Jones reported that he tried to put the memories of the abuse "on the back of my mind but every day the memories come back". He still dreamt about the abuse and had

Table 6.2 Mr Jones' scores on IES-R during EMDR treatment

Psychometric	Baseline	Mid-treatment	End of treatment
Impact of events scale–revised	Avoidance–2.75	Avoidance –2	Avoidance –1.63
	Intrusion–2.625	Intrusion–2.25	Intrusion–1.75
	Hyperarousal–2.66	Hyperarousal–1.67	Hyperarousal–0.83
	Total mean–8.035	Total Mean–5.92	Total Mean–4.21
	Total IES-R–59	Total IES-R–44	Total IES-R–32

memories of it when he was in bed in the evening. This was a particularly emotional session for Mr Jones as he reported that he had never spoken to anybody about the abuse in such detail. At the end of the session, to alleviate distress, he was supported to put himself into his 'calm place', which was enhanced with bilateral stimulation. A 'body scan' revealed no outstanding distressing feelings. Mr Jones reported that he felt as if a weight has been lifted from his shoulders and expressed insight that he needed to do trauma work to become emotionally well.

Mr Jones reported that current triggers for memories of the abuse included seeing sexual content on TV, smelling the perfume that his mother used to wear, and he gave other examples in session. The negative cognitions he tried to reprocess during EMDR therapy included: "I am permanently damaged", "it's my fault, I must have done something wrong to deserve the abuse". These were replaced with the positive cognition: "it's not my fault, there was nothing wrong with me, it's something to do with her, e.g., she suffered from depression, was an alcoholic, had a high sex drive".

Mr Jones' recovery journey during bilateral stimulation was emotionally painful for him. He experienced feelings of anger and hate, memories of abuse he had forgotten, and thoughts such as "she was a bitch", "I am glad she is dead", "there is hope". Distancing techniques were used to alleviate distress, for example thinking of the abuse in black and white and thinking of it as if it was on TV, with Mr Jones moving his chair backward, progressively more away from the TV. Mr Jones was encouraged to say (to his mother) things that had been left unsaid. He quietly cried, subsequently reporting that he had never been able to cry in his life because his mother used to hit him more if he did cry.

This course of EMDR therapy was concluded with the installation of positive resources that could help him move forward in his recovery journey. Despite Mr Jones liking the Superman character, when he was a child, he was not able to use Superman as a resource because Mr Jones "didn't trust Superman as he did not save me from the abuse". Instead, Mr Jones found thinking about his first dog as a useful resource because "my dog kept me out of the house, away from the abuse, for hours". This resource was enhanced with bilateral stimulation. Mr Jones reported feeling at peace at the end of this session. During bilateral stimulation, he was observed twice saying "it's not my fault, she was the problem" when referring to the abuse, suggesting that the positive cognition he tried to install during EMDR may have started to take effect.

At the end of this course of EMDR, Mr Jones was offered additional EMDR sessions to reprocess other traumatic events he experienced. Mr Jones reported that he did not want to access additional EMDR sessions because he had noted improvements in his symptoms including:

> [S]ome days the memories go away quickly rather than lingering. I don't dream as much about the abuse; before it used to pop in my mind 6 days a week, just before going to sleep and in the middle of the night at around 3/4 am, now this happens only 2 days a week.

Mr Jones also reported feeling "more patient, not getting as fed up, and better able to concentrate". To assess the impact of EMDR, Mr Jones was administered the IES-R on three occasions, at baseline, mid-treatment, and at the end of the intervention. His scores can be found in Table 6.2. As can be seen, there was a decrease in all scores from baseline to end of treatment, with the total score on the IES-R at the end of treatment being one point below the cut-off suggestive of PTSD symptoms.

Outcome of the case

After three years as an inpatient on the low secure and open rehabilitation wards, Mr Jones was discharged into 24-hour supported accommodation under the care of the local Community Forensic Team (CFT). Because of his trust difficulties, several attempts were made to handover his case to the CFT psychologist before discharge, so that the two could develop a working alliance. However, this was not possible. Unfortunately, once in the community, Mr Jones did not engage with the psychologist attached to the CFT.

In the community, Mr Jones received some bad news about the welfare of one of his daughters, with whom he had resumed contact whilst on the low secure ward. She stopped contacting him, and he was unable to speak to her. Mr Jones felt powerless and guilty at not being able to help her. During this time, a local drug dealer had also started putting pressure on Mr Jones to buy drugs from him, managing on a couple of occasions to get into the building where Mr Jones was residing, despite this being 24-hour (staff) supported accommodation. Additionally, no cover was put in place when Mr Jones' community psychiatric nurse was off work. Overwhelmed by his feelings and thinking that he did not have anyone to talk to, Mr Jones absented himself from his residence for three days during which time he binged on crack cocaine. Upon returning to his accommodation, he was returned to the same low secure ward.

Mr Jones was reassessed with the HCR-20v3 and began working again with his treating team. His mental health was found to be stable and risk unchanged. Mr Jones worked with a psychologist on formulating his recall to hospital, with the aim of identifying what needed to be in place before being discharged again. A new community psychiatric nurse was identified and the two began working together before discharge. Mr Jones was referred to the **Assertive Outreach Team (AOT)** and was supported to develop a working relationship with their psychologist. After nine months on the low secure ward, Mr Jones was discharged to a different 24-hour supported accommodation, under the care of the CFT, with the additional support of the AOT.

Discussion

This chapter has outlined the psychological assessments and treatments accessed by a forensic mental health patient during his three-year stay on an NHS-run low secure and open rehabilitation ward before his discharge in the community. It highlights that recovery for this population is multifaceted and it involves clinical recovery (i.e. recovery from mental health issues and physical health problems), functional recovery (i.e. being able to manage life tasks such as planning/organising one's time, shopping, cooking, paying bills, etc. in the community), social recovery (i.e. developing and maintaining a non-professional, prosocial support network, comprising family, friends, colleagues etc.), and personal recovery (i.e. developing meaning and purpose in life, beyond illness and offending behaviour), alongside coming to terms with one's risky behaviours and their impact on other people (Drennan & Alred, 2012). This case study has also highlighted that progress is not linear for many patients. Lapses can occur as mental and emotional stability are not static variables and can change depending on life stressors, coping strategies, and support available. However, **lapses** do not need to mean 'failures' as they are different from full-blown **relapses.** Lapses can be used as learning opportunities to reflect, as was the case for Mr Jones, on how to further augment recovery so that the likelihood of future lapses is minimised.

It is noted that Mr Jones was discharged with a limited social support system (apart from professional relationships). Despite attempts to support him in engaging in prosocial, structured activities in the community, which may have led to the development of new supportive friendships, Mr Jones was resistant to engage in community-based activities. After many months of encouragement, when he finally agreed to explore the possibility to volunteer to walk dogs for people, because of his offending history, he was not able to pursue this interest. The only available voluntary role involved looking after rescued dogs, but Mr Jones found this job emotionally difficult, as seeing dogs held in cages reminded him of when his mother used to lock him in cupboards. Mr Jones' case demonstrates the need to increase occupational opportunities for people with offending histories to help them develop a purposeful sense of self and connectedness through greater access to meaningful vocational activities, as this is likely to help improve their social and personal recovery (Clarke et al., 2016).

In addition, based on the literature highlighting the importance of the therapeutic alliance for better treatment outcomes (e.g. Arsuffi, 2016; Baldwin et al., 2007; Castonguay et al., 1996), an argument can be made for shifting the focus of forensic services from the biomedical, risk-reduction model, where people are assumed to be afflicted by a range of specific disorders (e.g. mental health issues, personality disorders) that require evidence-based treatment in specific doses to a model where, alongside treatment provision, there is a greater focus on investing in the development and maintenance of compassionate, trusting, consistent working relationships between staff and service users. This task is not an easy one in the current climate, specifically relating to the COVID-19 pandemic, with long waiting lists and high staff vacancies in the NHS and National Probation Service, where staff are holding high caseloads and therefore may not have the time to get to know their clients and invest in building robust working relationships with them, before they are released back into the community.

Finally, there is an argument for improving how recovery is evaluated within forensic populations. The HCR-20v3 is a useful tool to assess risk, formulate risk management plans, evaluate the impact of treatment on risk over time, and inform decision-making as to whether someone is ready to be discharged. However, other measures may be more meaningfully related to the concept of recovery. Quality of life indicators, for example, could also be used as outcome measures. In this respect, Bouman et al. (2009) demonstrated that subjective well-being indicators (specifically satisfaction with health and life fulfilment) predicted decreased self-reported violent and general recidivism in forensic psychiatric outpatients. It appears that a range of measures can be useful in considering risk and recovery for forensic mental health patients.

Conclusion

This case has highlighted that recovery for forensic mental health patients is a lengthy process which requires the input of a full multidisciplinary team, including access to several psychological interventions, aiming to help the patient address treatment needs, for example through developing insight, decreasing impulsivity, strengthening emotional resilience, increasing motivation to abstain from substance misuse, overcoming trauma symptoms, to mention a few. This case study also highlights the importance of giving patients the time and opportunity to develop working relationships with staff involved in their care, as these relationships may increase their motivation to engage in treatment they have avoided for years, alongside reducing the likelihood they engage in future risky behaviours (Arsuffi, 2016). This seems especially important in cases where, as is sadly often the case, the person has very limited personal support; professional relationships may become even more important for patients in this position, as appeared to be the case for Mr Jones.

References

Aho-Mustonen, K., Miettinen, R., Koivisto, H., Timonen, T., & Raty, H. (2008). Group psychoeducation for forensic and dangerous non-forensic long term patients with schizophrenia: A pilot study. *European Journal of Psychiatry*, 22, 84–92. https://doi.org/10.4321/s0213-61632008000200004.

American Psychiatric Association. (1994). *DSM-IV: Diagnostic and statistical manual of mental disorders* (4th ed.). Author.

Arsuffi, L. (2016). *What is the relationship between relational security, attachment, ward incidents and treatment outcomes on forensic psychiatric wards?* University of Birmingham. https://etheses.bham.ac.uk/id/eprint/7129/1/Arsuffi17ForenPsyD_Redacted.pdf.

Arsuffi, L., & Scarborough, N. (in press). A service evaluation of the Behavioural Treatment for Substance Abuse (BTSA) programme for forensic dual diagnosis populations. *Journal of Forensic Psychology Research and Practice*. Published online. DOI: 10.1080/24732850.2021.2017551.

Ashworth, S., Brotherton, N., Ingamells, B., & Morrissey, C. (2018). *I can feel good* (2nd ed.). Pavilion Publishing and Media Ltd.

Bahr, S. J., Masters, A. L., & Taylor, B. M. (2012). What works in substance abuse treatment programs for offenders? *The Prison Journal*, 92(2), 155–174. https://doi.org/10.1177/0032885512438836.

Baldwin, S. A., Wampold, B. E., & Imed, Z. E. (2007). Untangling the alliance-outcome correlation: Importance of therapist and patient variability in the alliance. *Journal of Consulting and Clinical Psychology, 75*, 842–852. https://doi.org/10.1037/0022-006x.75.6.842.

Bauml, J., Frobose, T., Kraemer, S., Rentrop, M., & Pitschel-Walz, G. (2006). Psychoeducation: A basic therapeutic intervention for patients with schizophrenia and their families. *Schizophrenia Bulletin, 32*, 1–9. https://doi.org/10.1093/schbul/sbl017.

Beck, A. T., Steer, R. A., & Brown, G. K. (1996). *Manual for the Beck Depression Inventory-II.* Psychological Corporation.

Bellack, A. S., Bennett, M. E., Gearon, J. S., Brown, C. H., & Yang, Y. (2006). A randomized clinical trial of a new behavioral treatment for drug abuse in people with severe and persistent mental illness. *Archives of General Psychiatry, 63*(4), 426–432. https://doi.org/10.1001/archpsyc.63.4.426.

Bouman, Y. H. A., Schene, A. H., & de Ruiter, C. (2009). Subjective well-being and recidivism in forensic psychiatric outpatients. *International Journal of Forensic Mental Health, 8*(4), 225–234. https://doi.org/10.1080/14999011003635647.

Castonguay, L. G., Goldfried, M. R., Wiser, S. L., Raue, P. J., & Hayes, A. M. (1996). Predicting the effect of cognitive therapy for depression: A study of unique and common factors. *Journal of Consulting and Clinical Psychology, 64*, 497–504. https://doi.org/10.1037/0022-006x.64.3.497.

Clarke, C., Lumbard, D., Sambrook, S., & Kerr, K. (2016). What does recovery mean to a forensic mental health patient? A systematic review and narrative synthesis of the qualitative literature. *The Journal of Forensic Psychiatry and Psychology, 27*, 38–54. http://dx.doi.org/10.1080/14789949.2015.1102311.

Dixon, L. (1999). Providing services to families of persons with schizophrenia: Present and future. *Journal of Mental Health, 2*, 3–8. https://doi.org/10.1002/(SICI)1099-176X(199903)2:1<3::AID-MHP31>3.0.CO;2-0.

Douglas, K. S., Hart, S. D., Webster, C. D., & Belfrage, H. (2013). *HCR-20v3: Assessing risk for violence.* Mental Health, Law, and Policy Institute, Simon Fraser University.

Drennan, G., & Alred, D. (2012). *Secure recovery: Approaches to recovery in forensic mental health settings.* Routledge.

Jacobson, N., & Greenley, D. (2001). What is recovery? A conceptual model and explication. *Psychiatric Services, 52*, 482–485. https://doi.org/10.1176/appi.ps.52.4.482.

Joe, G. W., Simpson, D. D., Dansereau, D. F., & Rowan-Szal, G. A. (2001). Relationships between counselling rapport and drug abuse treatment outcomes. *Psychiatric Services, 52*(9), 1223–1229. https://doi.org/10.1176/appi.ps.52.9.1223.

Kubler-Ross, E. (1969). *On death and dying.* Scribner.

Linehan, M. M. (1993). *Skills training manual for treating borderline personality disorder.* Guilford Press.

Luken, E. P., & McFarlane, W. R. (2004). Psychoeducation as evidence-based practice: Considerations for practice, research, and policy. *Brief Treatment and Crisis Intervention, 4*, 3. https://doi.org/10.1093/brief-treatment/mhh019.

Muller-Isberner, R., Webster, C. D., & Gretenkord, L. (2007). Measuring progress in hospital treatment: Relationship between levels of security and C and R scores of the HCR-20. *International Journal of Forensic Mental Health, 6*, 113–121. https://doi.org/10.1080/14999013.2007.10471256.

NICE Guidelines CG138. (2012). *Patient experience in adult NHS services: Improving the experience of care for people using NHS services.* www.nice.org.uk/guidance/cg138/resources/patient-experience-in-adult-nhs-services-improving-the-experience-of-care-for-people-using-adult-nhs-services-pdf-35109517087429.

NICE Guidelines CG178. (2014). *Psychosis and schizophrenia in adults: Prevention and management.* www.nice.org.uk/Guidance/CG178.

NICE Guidelines NG116. (2018). *Post traumatic stress disorder.* www.nice.org.uk/guidance/ng116/chapter/Recommendations#management-of-ptsd-in-children-young-people-and-adults.

Pouncey, C. L., & Lukens, J. M. (2010). Madness versus badness; The ethical tension between the recovery movement and forensic psychiatry. *Theoretical Medicine and Bioethics, 31,* 93–105. https://doi.org/10.1007/s11017-010-9138-9.

Rees-Jones, A., Gudjonsson, G., & Young, S. (2012). A multi-site controlled trial of a cognitive skills program for mentally disordered offenders. *BMC Psychiatry, 12*(1), 44. https://doi.org/10.1186/1471-244X-12-44.

Simpson, A. I. F., & Penney, S. R. (2011). Editorial; The recovery paradigm in forensic mental health services. *Criminal Behaviour and Mental Health, 21,* 299–306. https://doi.org/10.1002/cbm.823.

Simpson, D., Rowan-Szal, G. A., Joe, G. W., Best, D., Day, E., & Campbell, A. (2009). Relating counsellor attributes to client engagement in England. *Journal of Substance Abuse Treatment, 36*(3), 313–320. https://doi.org/10.1016/j.jsat.2008.07.003.

Wechsler, D. (2008). *Wechsler adult intelligence scale* (4th ed.). Pearson Clinical.

Wechsler, D. (2010). *Wechsler memory scale* (4th ed.). Pearson Clinical.

Weiss, D. S., & Marmar, C. R. (1997). *Impact of event scale-revised.* APA, PsycTests. https://doi.org/10.1037/t12199-000.

Yip, V. C., Gudjonsson, G. H., Perkins, D., Doidge, A., Hopkin, G., & Young, S. (2013). A non-randomised controlled trial of the R&R2 MHP cognitive skills program in high risk male offenders with severe mental illness. *BMC Psychiatry, 13*(1), 267. https://doi.org/10.1186/1471-244x-13-267.

Young, S., Chick, K., & Gudjonsson, G. (2010). A preliminary evaluation of reasoning and rehabilitation 2 in mentally disordered offenders (R&R2M) across two secure forensic settings in the United Kingdom. *The Journal of Forensic Psychiatry & Psychology, 21*(3), 336–349. https://doi.org/10.1080/14789940903513203.

Young, S. J., & Ross, R. R. (2007). *R&R2 for youths and adults with mental health problems: A prosocial competence training program.* Cognitive Centre of Canada.

7 Utilising EMDR to address trauma with an autistic person with a history of sexual offending

Lyn Shelton

Introduction

Autism spectrum disorder

In the UK, the Mental Health Act (MHA, 1983, as amended 2007) allows someone with a mental health condition to be admitted, detained, and treated in hospital even where this may be against their wishes. In such cases, suitable professionals need to have deemed this to be necessary to protect them or the public, and this is a decision made after a comprehensive mental health assessment. This process is similar in many countries, and the law allows this type of detention where an individual is deemed to be suffering from what is often termed a 'mental disorder', which warrants their detention in a hospital for assessment or treatment. In relation to people who have committed a crime, the process of mandatory detention under the MHA can occur at various points in the criminal justice system in the UK, such as whilst they are waiting for trial, post-trial when awaiting sentence, or during a prison sentence (i.e. post-sentence). A judge can also sentence a person to indefinite treatment in hospital, instead of a prison sentence, when recommended by healthcare professionals. Table 7.1 outlines the sections of the MHA that are used within forensic mental health settings. When a person is transferred from prison to secure psychiatric services, this is with the aim of ensuring that the person who has a severe mental health problem can have access to the right treatment and care whilst they and the public are protected from harm.

Mental health and neurodevelopmental conditions that patients may be diagnosed with within secure psychiatric settings are summarised in Shelton (2019), but in essence, a range of mental health diagnoses are present including autism spectrum disorder (ASD). Although other terms are often used in the literature, for instance autism spectrum condition (ASC), the term ASD will be used within this chapter. Patients with ASD often have a comorbid presentation, meaning that they have additional mental health difficulties/diagnoses (Glaser & Florio, 2004) as well as ASD.

ASD is a neurological and developmental disorder that affects social interaction, communication, how an individual learns, and their behavioural

DOI: 10.4324/9781003213116-7

Table 7.1 Sections of the Mental Health Act utilised within forensic mental health settings in the UK

MHA Section	Definition	Length of detention
37	The client can be sent to hospital for treatment; this could be before or after they have been convicted (Crown Court) or after conviction (Magistrate's Court). Two doctors need to provide evidence to the court that the client has a mental disorder of a nature or degree that makes detention for medical treatment appropriate and that appropriate medical treatment is available for them.	Up to six months, can be renewed for a further six months, and then for one year at a time
38	The Crown Court can remand an individual following conviction for offences leading to imprisonment (except for murder) under Section 38. This means that the client will be transferred to hospital for assessment and treatment. The client will then return to the Court for them to determine whether to sentence them to prison or under a hospital order.	Renewable to a maximum period of one year
41	If the Crown Court has made a hospital order under Section 37, it can also impose a 'restriction order'. This means that the client can only be discharged, transferred, or given Section 17 leave with permission from the Ministry of Justice (MoJ). This is usually imposed to protect the public.	No fixed time limit
47	The MoJ can order the individual to be transferred from prison to hospital for treatment of their mental health problems.	Up to six months, renewable for a second six months, and then one year at a time
48	If a prisoner is on remand, two registered medical practitioners need to agree that the client is suffering from a mental health problem of a nature or degree which makes it appropriate for them to be urgently admitted to hospital for medical treatment.	N/A
49	If the MoJ has ordered an individual to be transferred from prison to hospital under Section 47, at the same time it can also impose a 'restriction direction' on them under Section 49. This means that they can only be discharged, transferred, and given leave from hospital with permission from the Secretary of State for Justice.	Until the end of the Section 47 or the date when they should be released from prison

presentation. Autism can be diagnosed at any age; however, it is described as a developmental disorder because symptoms are usually prevalent during the early stages of childhood (National Institute of Mental Health; NIMH, 2018).

According to the *Diagnostic and Statistical Manual of Mental Disorders* (DSM-5; APA, 2013), people with ASD tend to experience the following symptoms:

- Persistent deficits in social communication and social interaction across multiple contexts;
- Restricted, repetitive patterns of behaviour, interests or activities, currently or by history;
- Symptoms must be present in early developmental period;
- Symptoms cause clinically significant impairment in social, occupational, or other areas of functioning.

ASD is known as a 'spectrum' disorder due to the variation in the type and severity of symptoms people experience. Additionally, these disturbances are not better explained by intellectual disability or global developmental delay. Males continue to be diagnosed more frequently than females, with three males for every one female receiving the diagnosis (Loomes et al., 2017).

Forensic inpatients with ASD appear to be over-represented in mental health facilities (Dein & Woodbury-Smith, 2010). Dein and Woodbury-Smith (2010) found that 30% of their sample of detained patients had ASD; Over 40% of these individuals had a history of abuse. Additionally, over 40% had a history of sexual violence, compared with 26% of those who did not have a diagnosis of ASD. Also, they noted that there was a lower prevalence of ASD inpatients being subject to criminal sections or restriction orders compared to inpatients without ASD inpatients, suggesting that the Criminal Justice System treated those with ASD less harshly.

Historically, Asperger's syndrome was a separate diagnosis under the umbrella of ASD. The main diagnostic criteria of Asperger's syndrome included a "qualitative impairment in social interaction and restricted, repetitive and stereotyped patterns of behaviour, interests, and activities". These deficiencies and patterns caused "clinically significant impairment in social, occupational or other important areas of functioning" (DSM IV; APA, 2000). However, with the introduction of DSM-5 (APA, 2013), Asperger's syndrome was removed as a separate diagnosis; it has been absorbed into the diagnosis of ASD. Research has identified that whilst people with ASD do commit sexual offences (Hare, 1999; Murphy, 2007), the rates of sexual offending in general (Hare, 1999), and specifically of sex offences against children (Elvish, 2007), are lower among offenders diagnosed with ASD. Whilst being diagnosed with ASD does not increase the risk of sexual offending behaviour, there is a recognised link between ASD and sexual offending behaviours (Higgs & Carter, 2015). It has been identified that individuals with an ASD diagnosis can often have a desire for sexually intimate relationships but struggle to develop and/or maintain these relationships due to impairments in the social domain; this can subsequently lead to sexual offending behaviour due to the individual's inability to appropriately express themselves or inability to read responses from the other person (Murrie et al., 2002) and can be a direct contributor to offending behaviour (Bosch et al., 2020). Individuals diagnosed with ASD have been noted to have a tendency to engage in private acts, such as indecent exposure or masturbation, in a public area (Kalyva, 2010). This has been found to be the most prevalent type of sexual offence within those diagnosed with ASD (Sevlever et al., 2013).

Often, those diagnosed with ASD have other comorbid diagnoses, including mental health difficulties such as **PTSD,** which is disproportionate in comparison to neurotypical individuals (Hossain et al., 2020). PTSD is an anxiety disorder that can develop following traumatic experiences. An individual with PTSD can often relive the traumatic event through nightmares or flashbacks; it can affect the normal life and functioning of the individual resulting in further symptomology such as poor concentration and insomnia.

Individuals with ASD have been found to have reduced hemispheric laterality, meaning that the hemispheres of the brain are functionally different; this has been found to be a precipitating factor in the development of PTSD (Saltzman et al., 2006). Rumball (2019), in clinical samples of those diagnosed with autism, found that the prevalence of PTSD in people with ASD is 2–17% in comparison with 3% of the neurotypical population. This may however be an underestimate of prevalence as trauma symptomology is not always screened for in those with an ASD diagnosis (Kerns et al., 2020), meaning that PTSD can go unnoticed or undiagnosed. Given the characteristics of individuals with ASD, it is highly likely that their experiences of trauma would be exacerbated by their ASD traits (such as sensory processing disorder); examples of such trauma could be bullying or being misunderstood by others (Fisher et al., 2022).

PTSD was previously referred to as 'battle fatigue' and directly linked to experiences in the military. This was only added to the DSM (version 3; APA, 1980) in 1980, as a specific diagnosis. However, there is now the recognition that PTSD is not solely fear based; it is now classified under trauma and stress-related disorders in the DSM 5 (APA, 2013). Foa et al. (2009) noted that **cognitive behavioural therapy (CBT)** and medication were the most successful methods to treat PTSD. However, **eye movement desensitisation and reprocessing** (EMDR; Shapiro, 1989) is a National Institute for Health and Care Excellence (NICE, 2018) primary recommendation for treating PTSD and has been found to be effective in treating trauma (Valiente-Gómez et al., 2017).

EMDR is a psychotherapy aimed to treat trauma. During EMDR therapy, the client works through emotionally disturbing material in brief sequential doses while simultaneously focusing on an external stimulus. Therapist-directed lateral eye movements are the most commonly used external stimulus, but a variety of other stimuli including hand-tapping and audio stimulation can instead be used (Shapiro, 1991). EMDR allows for the traumatic memory to be processed and reinforces a more adaptive style of thinking to manage any residual emotional distress. EMDR therapy uses a three-pronged protocol:

- The dysfunctional past/traumatic events are processed, forging new associative links with adaptive information.

- The current circumstances that elicit distress are targeted; internal and external triggers are desensitised.
- Future templates of potential events are incorporated; this helps the individual to acquire the skills needed for adaptive functioning.

EMDR has been identified as a suitable therapeutic intervention for people diagnosed with ASD and PTSD (Lobregt-van Buuren et al., 2019; Fisher & van Diest, 2022). EMDR follows a scripted protocol; however, due to the flexible nature of EMDR, it can be easily accessible for individuals diagnosed with ASD, in particular due to the potential difficulties that someone with ASD may have in making connections between current symptomology and previous traumatic experiences, when compared to other 'scripted' protocol-based therapies. Fisher et al. (2022) found that adaptations fell into three broad principles: flexibility, clear communication, and awareness of individual differences. Despite this, there is minimal research into utilising EMDR with those with ASD, although the research to date indicates positive effects (Kosatka & Ona, 2014; Lobregt-van Buuren et al., 2019). However, studies noted common themes for EMDR for patients with ASD, including therapy requiring an increased rapport building period, additional or alternative options for bilateral stimulation to eye movements being required (such as hand-tapping), less emphasis on identifying positive and negative cognitions being needed, options such as a 'menu' of emotions to aid emotional recognition needing to be offered, and variation in the session length being required (Fisher et al., 2022). Stark et al. (2020) recommend that the therapeutic modality is discussed with the individual to ensure that the approach would be of most benefit.

Patient history

This current case study involves treatment of a forensic inpatient with ASD and PTSD. Jeffrey's name and some details have been changed to maintain confidentiality. Jeffrey was a resident in a forensic inpatient secure service at the time of treatment.

Referral

Jeffrey had been referred by his clinical team for psychotherapy to help address behavioural difficulties and historical trauma. He presented with acute behavioural outbursts and complex historical trauma; these issues had been identified as problematic over the last ten years. Jeffrey was referred for trauma-focused therapy following a comprehensive period of psychotherapy, utilising CBT and **attachment theory** to enable cognitive restructuring; this lasted for approximately 14 months. Jeffrey was subsequently referred for discussion about the most appropriate direction for his treatment pathway in terms of his PTSD symptomology.

Jeffrey had been assessed throughout his psychotherapy utilising a battery of psychometrics to measure progress and treatment gain. These are described in detail later but were able to provide a baseline measure prior to starting trauma-focused work. Approaches for trauma-focused work were discussed with Jeffrey; based on his engagement with treatment to that point, it was considered essential that he felt some autonomy over his treatment to enable him to engage fully in the process. Before treatment commenced, Jeffrey's case files were reviewed, risk was reviewed utilising structured professional judgement tools, and his **clinical case formulation** was revisited to ensure that therapeutic intervention was tailored appropriately to meet both his risk and need.

Background

Jeffrey was a 32-year-old male, who was detained in hospital under Section 37 of the MHA at the time of treatment. He had two younger sisters. Jeffrey had a good relationship with his sisters; however, this became more fractured as his ASD symptomology became more prevalent in his adolescence.

Jeffrey spent much of his formative years alone, seemingly preferring isolated activities such as reading, playing with Lego, and watching TV. Jeffrey struggled to form friendships and would focus his time on collecting 'Matchbox' cars. When he attended school, Jeffrey became further isolated from his peers due to recognising that he was 'different' to others and his view that they would not understand him. Subsequently, Jeffrey was bullied and abused at school, both physically and sexually. Jeffrey's experiences led to him attempting to take his own life.

Jeffrey's mother also experienced mental ill health; this significantly affected him during his formative years. Jeffrey had reported traumatic memories relating to his mother's attitude and behaviour towards him. It was thought that as a result, Jeffrey had been left with intrinsic paranoid ideation and may have internalised maladaptive coping strategies to deal with both intrapersonal and interpersonal conflict by being verbally and physically aggressive to match the level of the perceived external threat. Jeffrey's father was regularly absent from home due to his work commitments throughout Jeffrey's childhood; this appeared to significantly affect his ability to develop and maintain secure attachments.

Jeffrey was diagnosed with ASD when he was 17 years old. ASD had resulted in Jeffrey having heightened anxiety within social situations, difficulty tolerating loud and/or background noise, and impulsive reactivity resulting in poor behavioural and emotional control. Jeffrey's emotional reactions could be triggered by a number of seemingly low-level situations, including people coughing, laughing, and blowing; Jeffrey became paranoid and would react irresponsibly resulting in him placing himself and/or others at risk through a series of ASD-related 'meltdowns'.

Jeffrey had lived independently but with the support of professionals for approximately ten years prior to admission to hospital. However, he became isolated and reported feeling lonely which affected the way he engaged with support staff; he would focus only on males and attempted to blur boundaries by attempting to initiate contact with staff members outside of the professional working relationship. As a result of the symptomology of his ASD, he had been unable to hold down formal employment and had never had an intimate relationship.

Jeffrey has experienced numerous hospitalisations under the MHA, primarily as a result of verbally and physically violent behavioural presentations. His first psychiatric contact was at the age of 13 years due to these behavioural problems. Jeffrey believed he had been forcefully overmedicated during adolescence and held his first psychiatrist to account for this; this directly linked to his trauma-related experiences, and Jeffrey felt that he had lost many of his formative years as a result of being sedated with medication. Jeffrey believed that this affected his academic attainment and prevented him from developing an intimate relationship.

Offending history

Jeffrey had no previous convictions, however, there had been several incidents which had resulted in him being detained under the MHA. Incidents involved damage to his own and others' property, as well as verbal and physical violence and aggression towards others, including his mother and various members of support staff prior to his hospital admission. Jeffrey moreover presented with socially unacceptable behaviour, such as obsessive behaviour focused on males and episodes of indecent exposure; the latter eventually leading to him receiving a criminal conviction.

Most recent offending behaviour

Jeffrey was convicted of two counts of indecent exposure resulting in him being detained under the MHA under Section 37 and being required to sign on to the **sex offender register** for ten years. Jeffrey is reported to have exposed his genitals and stretched his penis in view of members of the public on a bus.

Previous offending

Despite an absence of formal convictions prior to the index offence, Jeffrey had previously engaged in several incidents of a sexual nature. He had removed his clothing in public places, asked members of the public to have sex with him, had become obsessive with male taxi drivers, and exposed himself in a crowded place.

Clinical case formulation of sexual offending

Prior to treatment, Jeffrey's risk had been assessed and formulated using the risk for sexual violence protocol instrument (RSVP; Hart et al., 2003). A case formulation provides hypotheses about a person's problems, so that the problem can be understood and treatment/support offered.

In Jeffrey's case, the area being considered as the 'problem' or 'presenting issue' was his index offences of indecent exposure, which were considered as being sexually motivated offences. In addition to his indecent exposure offences, Jeffrey had also presented with socially maladaptive behaviours throughout his adolescence and adulthood; likely a result of his ASD-related traits. He had exhibited physical violence towards others, including family members, damaged property such as staff members' cars, threatened physical violence, secreted weapons, intimidated others (in the form of obsessive behaviours), and had engaged in inappropriate sexual behaviours towards others.

Predisposing factors: These are factors which are likely to have played a role in the development of Jeffrey's difficulties. Jeffrey experienced considerable disruption during his childhood, which may in part have been influenced by the presence of rigid rules for living having been imposed by his mother, coupled with an absent father. Jeffrey had reported that his mother was overly strict with him, often comparing him to other young people regarding academic achievement and social ability; this may have significantly affected his socio-emotional functioning. Socio-emotional functioning is defined by the abilities to form and sustain positive relationships; experience, manage, and express emotions; and explore and engage with the environment in a prosocial manner. Problems in this area were evident in Jeffrey's historical presentations and antisocial conduct patterns, whereby he had not expressed his emotions in a prosocial way.

Jeffrey's father was frequently absent during Jeffrey's formative years due to his work commitments; this is likely to have influenced Jeffrey's development and attachment style. Research suggests that males with no father-figure are at increased risk of coming into contact with the criminal justice system (McLanahan et al., 2013). It is likely that the lack of these caregivers in his life had subjected Jeffrey to social and emotional deficits, resulting in the development of maladaptive conduct patterns. In addition to this, Jeffrey's ASD led to problems with reciprocal relationships resulting in a lack of friendships and absence of intimate relationships. His resultant behavioural profile correlates with these difficulties; their influence on his development may have set a precursor for his difficult social behaviours.

The combination of a chaotic familial dynamic, coupled with his ASD, has likely diminished **attunement** between Jeffrey and his caregivers, which could have affected the development of a healthy attachment, ultimately instilling an insecure attachment style. Furthermore, this complex combination of factors is likely to have regularly activated his **Acute Stress Response** or the 'flight or fight' pathways in his brain. Consequently, Jeffrey's baseline levels of arousal were elevated, meaning that he may have perceived minimal stressors to be greater than other people may have experienced them to be, which may explain some of his aggressive reactions when his needs were not immediately met or when he felt he was not in control of a situation.

Jeffrey's historical presentation was characterised by externalising behaviours including verbal and physical aggression, oppositional behaviour, and delinquency. This may have contributed to Jeffrey's level of insight; by using aggressive means, he may have believed that his care staff would immediately acquiesce whereas in reality, they implemented boundaries and regulations which ultimately may have triggered Jeffrey's stress response, thus causing an escalation in the severity and/or intensity of behaviours. Given his admission to hospital with subsequent deprivation of liberty, and in light of his view that his previous psychiatric medication regime was oppressive and negatively affected his life, it is likely that his threat perceptions were further exacerbated which resulted in a difficult-to-break cycle of problem-externalised behaviour.

A further plausible trigger for Jeffrey's conduct is inconsistent parenting/caregiving. Research suggests that lack of consistency in the home can contribute to affect dysregulation in children and young people (Dvir et al., 2014). Lack of consistency can instil insecurity and confusion in children due to the omission of structured, regulated activities, ultimately skewing the level of trust for the primary caregiver(s). Furthermore, the absence of familial boundaries can result in anxiety and fear manifesting in the child due to unstructured rules for living. It may be that due to the chaotic environment that Jeffrey had experienced, coupled with his parents' difficulties with consistent, regimented parenting in educating their child on what is and is not socially acceptable, he experienced increased anxiety as he was unsure whether to expect praise or punishment for his conduct. Ultimately, this may have led to rebellion, using maladaptive coping strategies and negative risk-taking behaviours to communicate hurt, anger, and fear towards those involved in his care.

Our **Internal Working Model** (IWM; Bowlby, 1982) affects how we perceive and interpret different situations and the environments that we are exposed to can help reshape this model. Jeffrey's IWM is likely to have been negative because of his life experiences. Consequently, this may have affected his behavioural responses to threats, which subsequently maintained his maladaptive coping mechanisms in a perseverative loop. This cycle was hypothesised as follows:

- Jeffrey perceiving a threat;
- Hyperarousal due to increase baseline levels of threat;
- Responding with (harmful) behaviours internally justified as equal to threat;
- Needs are met to appease and de-escalate severity/intensity of behaviours;
- Maladaptive coping strategies are positively reinforced;
- Jeffrey receives positive feedback in terms of the assuaging of anxiety and fear, concreting existing attitudes, and thus a feedback loop is constructed.

Jeffrey's vicariously reinforced aggressive behaviours likely exacerbated this cycle due to his cognitive justification that they served a purpose in his life; achieving dominance and control, which ultimately served as self-defence mechanisms and anxiety management techniques against his past traumatic and inconsistent experiences, whereby he was out of control.

Jeffrey expressed confusion about his sexual offending in that he did not perceive it to be a sexually related or sexually motivated action. It was initially hypothesised that Jeffrey's sexual offending was underpinned by his traumatic experiences, with his responses to trauma distress being confounded by his ASD; it was deemed likely that his distress was being responded to by Jeffrey using a sexual behaviour to self-soothe. Although it was considered that this required further exploration during treatment to enhance understanding of Jeffrey's risk-related case formulation, trauma intervention was considered essential for risk management purposes. Consideration of the risk formulation was therefore considered to be an aim of treatment alongside treatment of trauma symptomology.

Intervention

Jeffrey attended two, 60-minute, therapy sessions per week. Four sessions were spent on EMDR resourcing, which built on his period of psychotherapy. Two sessions were spent identifying traumatic events to be worked on during the processing phase of EMDR. The EMDR processing phase lasted for 30 sessions (15 weeks). Following this, 40 sessions were spent on maintenance, consolidation, and transition planning up to when Jeffrey was discharged from hospital into the community. The intervention lasted 38 weeks in total. Jeffrey attended all sessions offered to him.

The focus of the therapy was on Jeffrey's historical trauma related to bullying, being the victim of physical abuse from peers (which had included sexual elements), memories related to his first psychiatrist and family related issues. The primary focus was on the time that Jeffrey attempted to take his own life; this was a significant traumatic memory, which was underpinned by a number of unprocessed traumatic memories.

Several psychometric tests were administered prior to intervention to have a baseline measurement from which to measure any progress. The measures used were the Emotional Problems Scale-Behaviour Report Scale (EPS-BRS; Prout & Strohmer, 1991), the DSM-5 Self-Rated Level 1 Cross-Cutting Symptom Measure (APA, 2013), and the Impact of Events Scale–Revised (IES-R; Horowitz et al., 1979). These will be explored further later.

ASD adaptations

A number of adaptations were made to EMDR to meet Jeffrey's needs; this included slight change to protocol (discussed later) due to Jeffrey's inability to generalise processing from one trauma to another trauma (which may be easier for neurotypical individuals); in Jeffrey's case, each trauma required processing individually as a result of the impact his ASD had on his ability to apply the same learning to other situations.

Jeffrey had good cognitive ability; however, due to his ASD resulting in 'black and white' thinking, explanations of the approach and processes during EMDR needed to be concrete rather than abstract. An example of this literal thinking was that during processing, Jeffrey was instructed to "follow my fingers" during the processing phase and was then asked what he "noticed"; Jeffrey subsequently commented on the movement of my fingers rather than what he noticed about the memory. Jeffrey would often be led away on a tangent related to his specific interests (such as music or literature); therefore, a cognitively demanding task was introduced to prevent him overthinking whilst engaging in the eye movements for processing. Over time, Jeffrey was able to engage without this. Jeffrey's feedback was often very descriptive. He would also evidence reactions such as expressive facial movements and rubbing his face/head during processing and at times would speak in Latin or would sing.

Jeffrey initially struggled to express how disturbing the memory was following processing; he took the query very literally in that he felt the memory was still disturbing and always would be; adaptation was therefore required to assess reduction in memory disturbance. For example reduction was often considered through cognitive description and visualisation as opposed to a rating scale so that Jeffrey could explore "how far away the memory was" in comparison to pre-treatment.

Response to intervention

Jeffrey attended every session offered to him, and through observation of his engagement it was considered that he engaged well with the EMDR protocol. Jeffrey moreover reported a reduction in PTSD-related symptomology in terms of frequency and intensity of symptoms. He reported an improved ability to manage his behaviour on a day-to-day basis, feeling less affected by his historical trauma; this was also observed by his clinical team.

Pre- and post-EMDR psychometric assessment was completed with Jeffrey, which was considered alongside staff and therapist observations of his behaviour. The EPS-BRS (Prout & Strohmer, 1991) is an observational assessment instrument, completed by clinicians. It is designed for use as part of a comprehensive clinical evaluation of individuals aged 14 years and older with mild intellectual disability or borderline intelligence. The 135-item BRS has subscales relating to thought/behaviour disorders (TD), physical aggression (PA), non-compliance (NC), anxiety (AN), distractibility (DS), depression (DP), hyperactivity (HY), withdrawal (WD), low self-esteem (SE), verbal aggression (VA), somatic concerns (SC), and sexual maladjustment (SX). The results for Jeffrey's pre- and post-intervention are presented in Figure 7.1.

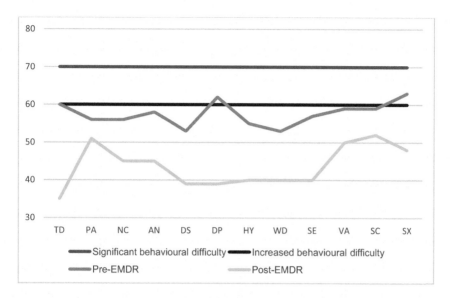

Figure 7.1 Jeffrey's EPS scores (pre- and post-EMDR)

As can be seen in Figure 7.1, there was a clear reduction in all scales from pre- to post-treatment, with no domains falling into the behavioural difficulty range following completion of EMDR therapy. This was reflective of Jeffrey's behavioural presentation in hospital, also evidenced by a significant reduction in incidents.

The DSM-5 Cross-Cutting Symptoms Measure (APA, 2013) was another measure administered pre- and post-EMDR therapy (Figure 7.2). This is a self-report instrument, which required Jeffrey to consider his symptoms in the two weeks immediately prior to the assessment. Subscales of this measure are depression (DP), anger (A), mania (M), anxiety (AN), somatic symptoms (SS), suicidal ideation (SI), psychosis (P), sleep problems (SP), memory (MM), repetitive thoughts and behaviours (RB), dissociation (D), personality functioning (PF), and substance use (SU).

As evidenced from Figure 7.2, there was a decrease in symptomology on most areas aside from anxiety and sleep problems, which increased; however, Jeffrey attributed the increase in these two areas to a recent assessment for a community-based residence which was affecting his mood. Jeffrey was keen to be discharged from hospital but also evidenced anxiety about the decision-making process in terms of finding the most appropriate community placement to best meet his needs, as opposed to accepting the first placement identified. Jeffrey's narrative was consistent with the view of the clinical team, which also noted that his anxiety and subsequent lack of sleep were related to discharge planning.

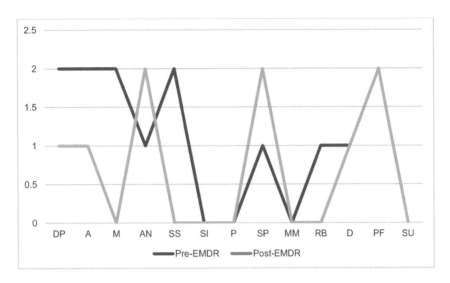

Figure 7.2 Jeffrey's recent DSM-5 Cross-Cutting Symptoms Measure scores (pre- and post-EMDR)

Pre-treatment, Jeffrey scored very highly on the IES-R (Horowitz et al., 1979), which measures trauma symptomatology. His score was considerably high and according to the IES-R may represent a level of PTSD symptoms severe enough to have immunosuppressive effects. Post-treatment, Jeffrey's score was significantly reduced and no longer within the PTSD symptomology range. This was consistent with Jeffrey's behavioural presentation in hospital as well as during his **Section 17 leave** in the community. Jeffrey noted that prior to the intervention his trauma symptoms and an emotion-led behavioural response were triggered more frequently; however, this dissipated during therapy, and Jeffrey was subsequently risk assessed as suitable for unescorted leave in the community and accessed this without issue or concern.

During the period of psychotherapy that he had engaged in prior to EMDR, Jeffrey had been open in discussing the sexual offences, which led to his detention under Section 37 of the MHA. This had provided a good base on which exploration of the circumstances around his offending as well as the function of these behaviours could take place during the period of EMDR therapy. As a result, the clinical case formulation of his offending risk was further developed. Following this exploration in treatment, prosocial coping strategies were also discussed with the aim of Jeffrey being more able to manage risk–related issues in the future. As mentioned, the clinical case formulation of his indecent exposure offences was discussed with Jeffrey; this collaborative working helped further consider his risk and the functions of his offending. Through this, it was hypothesised that Jeffrey's indecent exposure was not underpinned by sexual desire/arousal per se; moreover, it was related to an extreme sensory-based method to manage and soothe anxieties (previously Jeffrey would bite his hands or scratch them). Scratching, rubbing, and biting can be an atypical symptom related to self-stimulation for those with an ASD. Jeffrey also regularly stretched and 'cracked' his bones/joints. The nature of these behaviours could be considered to be akin to the movement and stimulation provided by masturbation or touching/stretching the penis.

Jeffrey described his act of indecent exposure as an extreme soothing act. The link between this and his trauma was that when his emotions were triggered by trauma symptoms, Jeffrey felt the need to self-soothe, and this therefore raised his risk of committing further sexual offending through engaging in behaviours similar to those which resulted in his convictions for indecent exposure. Any sexual elements behind his behaviours were explored and this led to a hypothesis that his offending was not primarily driven by deviant sexual interest, for example a specific interest in exhibitionism/exposure. In counter evidence, Jeffrey cited the importance of dating and romanticism in relation to developing a relationship and embarking on a sexual encounter. Jeffrey was open about never having had a sexual relationship; when this was explored further, Jeffrey was very clear about what consent was and the importance of developing appropriate intimate relationships. Jeffrey was very intent on having a relationship in the future; his lack of experience remained a recurring discussion point; however, this did not lead his clinical team to believe he posed an imminent risk of sexually offending at the time of treatment.

The results of the aforementioned assessments were critical in measuring pre- and post-therapeutic progress and also further informed his formulation. Psychometric testing, self-report, and observational evidence indicated significant progress in relation to PTSD symptomology, which also underpinned his sexual offending. This was considered by his clinical team to be an essential intervention to determine suitability for discharge into the community, to explore how best a transition should take place, and to inform how those supporting him in the community should best work with him.

Following his treatment, which was overall considered to have been successful, Jeffrey was assessed as suitable for discharge from hospital, and a suitable community placement was sourced. Various recommendations were made for those working with Jeffrey, considering his historical difficulties and the likely re-emergence of anxiety and/or PTSD symptomology due to significantly reduced restrictions in the community. For this to be an effective discharge to the community, it was essential that those working with Jeffrey understood the nature of his forensic history alongside his mental health presentation; therefore, a training package, co-produced by Jeffrey, was delivered to the receiving mental health and support team. Those working with Jeffrey in future were also advised to take a trauma-focused approach to working with him so that he could be appropriately supported with any potential re-emergence of PTSD symptomology.

Discussion

EMDR was utilised as a therapeutic intervention to support Jeffrey to process historical trauma and subsequently reduce PTSD symptomology and to in turn aid his risk reduction in relation to sexual offending. As noted by Fisher et al. (2022), there were adaptions required to increase the accessibility of the therapy due to Jeffrey's ASD. In particular, Jeffrey was able to engage better when he had a sense of control and autonomy and when the instructions were adapted in a concrete manner. This was linked to his past experiences of treatment and his often literal and concrete thinking. Of particular note, EMDR with Jeffrey took longer than initially anticipated; this was due to Jeffrey's inability to generalise processing to other traumatic events, likely linked to his ASD-related presentation. For Jeffrey, unlike neurotypical individuals, each trauma event had to be processed separately, in line with the research by Fisher et al. (2022) which emphasised the same. To confidently apply the adaptations, it was essential for the therapist to discuss this in supervision and for the supervisor to have knowledge of ASD alongside EMDR to increase confidence and competence when working with the ASD population (Corden et al., 2021). In this case, there was a significant reduction in PTSD symptomology, in line with research by Lobregt-van Buuren et al. (2019), indicating that when delivered with the necessary adaptations, EMDR can be effective with those with ASD. Furthermore, in relation to Jeffrey, given that his trauma responses were considered to be linked to his risk of sexual offending, these adaptations to enable treatment gain were also central to his risk reduction and management.

In Jeffrey's case, he had a strong desire for a sexually intimate relationship, and whilst this did not appear to drive his sexual offending forward, it was clear that the trauma he experienced throughout adolescence and adulthood underpinned his incidents of indecent exposure and were confounded by his difficulties related to the symptomology of his ASD; primarily his desire for intimacy and difficulties in appropriately communicating this (Murrie et al., 2002). He therefore resorted to extreme measures to both be noticed and to escape the situation he was in on the bus; the public nature of the sexual offending did not appear to be a driving factor as noted in Kalyva's (2010) research; rather it was a response to internal impulses with an aim to shock as opposed to being sexually motivated. Dewinter et al. (2013) reiterated the limited information known about the development processes for individuals with ASD in relation to sexual behaviour and relationships. As Murrie et al. (2002) noted, further exploration is required to separate out sexual offending behaviour and sexually inappropriate behaviour in relation to social reciprocity according to the individual with ASD.

Conclusions

This case explored the utilisation of EMDR with an inpatient diagnosed with ASD and PTSD. Adaptations of the EMDR protocol were explored and utilised to make the therapeutic modality more accessible for Jeffrey. The available evidence, consisting of psychometric testing, self-report, and behavioural observation, highlighted the effectiveness of EMDR in reducing PTSD symptomology and enhanced understanding of Jeffrey's case formulation. In relation to the formulation of the function of the indecent exposure, EMDR enabled an increase in knowledge of the function of the behaviour for Jeffrey, and it was concluded that it was unlikely that Jeffrey's sexual offending was primarily driven by a sexual deviance for indecent exposure. It is important to note that Jeffrey's ASD and trauma presentation, specifically the hypothesis that his indecent exposure linked to his trauma response, which was affected by his ASD presentation, does not provide an 'excuse' for the offending behaviour. Rather, the information revealed in therapy provided useful risk-related information to consider which factors needed support, treatment, and management to keep the public safe.

The enhanced case formulation of Jeffrey helped inform the clinical team so that treatment and support strategies could be put in place to help manage risk in the longer term, which in the time period of the treatment and the proceeding months proved successful, as Jeffrey was discharged into the community in a risk-informed placement and did not engage in sexual risk behaviours during that time despite increased 'freedom' (due to reduced restrictions). It is hoped that this case study provides some inspiration both in relation to adaptations for accessible EMDR therapy for those with ASD and in relation to how for some patients with sexual risk, this may aid risk reduction.

Steven Lovatt, psychotherapist, is acknowledged for his valuable contribution to the treatment and initial formulation of Jeffrey.

References

American Psychiatric Association. (1980). *Diagnostic and statistical manual of mental disorders* (3rd ed.). Author.
American Psychiatric Association. (2000). *Diagnostic and statistical manual of mental disorders* (4th ed., Text Revision). Author.
American Psychiatric Association. (2013). *Diagnostic and statistical manual of mental disorders* (5th ed.). American Psychiatric Publishing.
Bosch, R., Chakhssi, F., & Hummelen, K. (2020). Inpatient aggression in forensic psychiatric patients with autism spectrum disorder: The role of risk and protective factors. *Journal of Intellectual Disabilities and Offending Behaviour, 11*(2), 93–100. https://doi.org/10.1108/JIDOB-05-2019-0008.
Bowlby, J. (1982). Attachment and loss: Retrospect and prospect. *American Journal of Orthopsychiatry, 52*, 664. https://doi.org/10.1111/j.1939-0025.1982.tb01456.x.

Corden, K., Brewer, R., & Cage, E. (2021). A systematic review of healthcare professionals' knowledge, self-efficacy and attitudes towards working with autistic people. *Review Journal of Autism and Developmental Disorders*, 1–14. https://doi.org/10.1007/s40489-021-00263-w.

Dein, K., & Woodbury-Smith, M. (2010). Asperger syndrome and criminal behaviour. *Advances in Psychiatric Treatment*, *16*(1), 37–43. https://doi.org/10.1192/apt.bp.107.005082.

Dewinter, J., Vermeiren, R., Vanwesenbeeck, I., & Nieuwenhuizen, C. (2013). Autism and normative sexual development: A narrative review. *Journal of Clinical Nursing*, *22*(23–24), 3467–3483. https://doi.org/10.1111/jocn.12397.

Dvir, Y., Ford, J. D., Hill, M., & Frazier, J. A. (2014). Childhood maltreatment, emotional dysregulation, and psychiatric comorbidities. *Harvard Review of Psychiatry*, *22*(3), 149. https://doi.org/10.1097/HRP.0000000000000014.

Elvish, J. (2007). *The exploration of autistic spectrum disorder characteristics in individuals within a secure service for people with learning disabilities* (Doctoral dissertation, Thesis for Doctorate in Clinical Psychology, The Tizard Centre, University of Kent).

Fisher, N., & van Diest, C. (2022). Eye Movement Desensitisation and Reprocessing (EMDR). In D. Spain, F. Musich, & S. W. White (Eds.), *Psychological therapies for adults with autism* (pp. 192–205). Oxford University Press. https://doi.org/10.1177/13623613221080254.

Fisher, N., van Diest, C., Leoni, M., & Spain, D. (2022). Using EMDR with autistic individuals: A Delphi survey with EMDR therapists. *Autism Online*, 1–11. https://doi.org/10.1177/13623613221080254.

Foa, E. B., Keane, T. M., Friedman, M. J., & Cohen, J. A. (Eds.). (2009). *Effective treatments for PTSD* (2nd ed.). Guilford.

Glaser, W., & Florio, D. (2004). Beyond specialist programmes: A study of the needs of offenders with intellectual disability requiring psychiatric attention. *Journal of Intellectual Disability Research*, *48*, 591–602. https://doi.org/10.1111/j.1365-2788.2004.00628.x.

Hare, R. D. (1999). Psychopathy as a risk factor for violence. *Psychiatric Quarterly*, *70*(3), 181–197. https://doi.org/10.1023/A:1022094925150.

Hart, S. D., Kropp, P. R., Laws, D. R., Klaver, J., Logan, C., & Watt, K. A. (2003). *The risk for sexual violence protocol (RSVP)*. The Mental Health, Law, and Policy Institute of Simon Fraser University.

Higgs, T., & Carter, A. J. (2015). Autism spectrum disorder and sexual offending: Responsivity in forensic interventions. *Aggression and Violent Behavior*, *22*, 112–119. https://doi.org/10.1016/j.avb.2015.04.003.

Horowitz, M., Wilner, N., & Alvarez, W. (1979). Impact of event scale: A measure of subjective stress. *Psychosomatic Medicine*, *41*(3), 209–218. https://doi.org/10.1097/00006842-197905000-00004.

Hossain, M., Khan, N., Sultana, A., Ma, P., McKyer, E., Ahmed, H., & Purohit, N. (2020). Prevalence of comorbid psychiatric disorders among people with autism spectrum disorder: An umbrella review of systematic reviews and meta-analyses. *Psychiatry Research*, *287*. https://doi.org/10.1016/j.psychres.2020.112922.

Kalyva, E. (2010). Teachers' perspectives of the sexuality of children with autism spectrum disorders. *Research in Autism Spectrum Disorders*, *4*(3), 433–437. https://doi.org/10.1016/j.rasd.2009.10.014.

Kerns, C., Berkowitz, S., Moskowitz, L., Drahota, A., Lerner, M., & Usual Care for Autism Study (UCAS) Consortium Newschaffer, C. (2020). Screening and treatment of trauma-related symptoms in youth with autism spectrum disorder among community providers in the United States. *Autism, 24*(2), 515–525. https://doi. org/10.1177/1362361319847908.

Kosatka, D., & Ona, C. (2014). Eye movement desensitization and reprocessing in a patient with Asperger's disorder: Case report. *Journal of EMDR Practice and Research, 8*(1), 13. https://doi.org/10.1891/1933–3196.8.1.13.

Lobregt-van Buuren, E., Sizoo, B., Mevissen, L., & de Jongh, A. (2019). Eye Movement Desensitization and Reprocessing (EMDR) therapy as a feasible and potential effective treatment for adults with autism spectrum disorder (ASD) and a history of adverse events. *Journal of Autism and Developmental Disorders, 49*(1), 151–164. https://doi. org/10.1007/s10803-018-3687-6.

Loomes, R., Hull, L., & Mandy, W. P. L. (2017). What is the male-to-female ratio in autism spectrum disorder? A systematic review and meta-analysis. *Journal of the American Academy of Child & Adolescent Psychiatry, 56*(6), 466–474. https://doi.org/10.1016/j. jaac.2017.03.013.

McLanahan, S., Tach, L., & Schneider, D. (2013). The causal effects of father absence. *Annual Review of Sociology, 39,* 399–427. https://doi.org/10.1146/annurev-soc-071312–145704.

Mental Health Act. (1983). C20. Government of the United Kingdom.

Mental Health Act. (2007). C12. Government of the United Kingdom. www.opsi.gov.uk/ acts/acts2007/ukpga_20070012_en_1.

Murphy, D. (2007). Hare psychopathy checklist revised profiles of male patients with Asperger's syndrome detained in high security psychiatric care. *The Journal of Forensic Psychiatry & Psychology, 18*(1), 120–126. https://doi.org/10.1080/14789940601014777.

Murrie, D. C., Warren, J. I., Kristiansson, M., & Dietz, P. E. (2002). Asperger's syndrome in forensic settings. *International Journal of Forensic Mental Health, 1*(1), 59–70. https://doi.org/ 10.1080/14999013.2002.10471161.

National Institute for Health and Care Excellence (NICE). (2018). *Post Traumatic Stress Disorder* [NICE Guideline No. 116]. https://222.nice.orj.uk/guidance/ng116

National Institute of Mental Health. (2018). *Autism Spectrum Disorder.* Author: USA. www. nimh.nih.gov/sites/default/files/documents/health/publications/autism-spectrum-disorder/22-MH-8084-Autism-Spectrum-Disorder.pdf.

Prout, H. T., & Strohmer, D. C. (1991). *EPS: Emotional problems scales professional manual for behavior rating scales and the self-report inventory.* Psychological Assessment Resources, Incorporated.

Rumball, F. (2019). A systematic review of the assessment and treatment of posttraumatic stress disorder in individuals with autism spectrum disorders. *Review Journal of Autism and Developmental Disorders, 6*(3), 294–324. https://doi.org/1-.1007/s40489-018-0133-9.

Saltzman, K. M., Weems, C. F., Reiss, A. L., & Carrión, V. G. (2006). Mixed lateral preference in posttraumatic stress disorder. *The Journal of Nervous and Mental Disease, 194*(2), 142–144. https://doi.org/10.1097/01.nmd.0000198201.59824.37.

Sevlever, M., Roth, M. E., & Gillis, J. M. (2013). Sexual abuse and offending in autism spectrum disorders. *Sexuality and Disability, 31*(2), 189–200. https://doi.org/10.1007/ s11195-013-9286-8.

Shapiro, F. (1989). Eye movement desensitization: A new treatment for post-traumatic stress disorder. *Journal of Behavior Therapy and Experimental Psychiatry, 20*(3), 211–217. https:// doi.org/10.1016/0005-7916(89)90025-6.

Shapiro, S. (1991). *Foundations without foundationalism: A case for second-order logic* (Vol. 17). Clarendon Press.

Shelton, L. (2019). Neurodevelopmental disorder: Learning disability in secure forensic psychiatric services. In R. Tully & J. Bamford (Eds.), *Case studies in forensic psychology: Clinical assessment and treatment*. Routledge.

Stark, E., Ali, D., Ayre, A., Schneider, N., Parveen, S., Marais, K., Holmes, N., & Pender, R. (2020). Psychological therapy for autistic adults: A curious approach. Cited in Fisher, N., van Diest, C., Leoni, M., & Spain, D. (2022). Using EMDR with autistic individuals: A Delphi survey with EMDR therapists. *Autism*. https://doi.org/10.1177/13623613221080254

Valiente-Gómez, A., Moreno-Alcázar, A., Treen, D., Cedrón, C., Colom, F., Perez, V., & Amann, B. L. (2017). EMDR beyond PTSD: A systematic literature review. *Frontiers in Psychology, 8*(1668). https://doi.org/10.3389/fpsyg.2017.01668.

8 A case study examining the use of functional analysis to understand behavioural and emotional instability in an adult male with an acquired brain injury

Sarah Ashworth

Introduction

At times, within **neuropsychology**, the typical psychological practices of talking with a client, collaboratively exploring potential triggers, reinforcers, and patterns of behaviour are not possible. This may be for a constellation of reasons, including lack of engagement, low levels of insight, communication difficulties, and risk factors. This difficulty is not solely experienced within neuropsychology, as this problem is also often faced within **intellectual disability** and within other clinical populations. However, such barriers may be inherently linked to an individual's brain functioning and as such must be considered.

When working with people in the clinical setting, factors that may be impacting upon behaviour that are typically considered include thoughts, emotions, and interpersonal dynamics. However, less traditional factors such as physiological states (e.g. hunger, pain, fatigue) and external factors (e.g. noise, temperature, weather) may also need to be considered to fully understand behaviour. To consider hypotheses generated in a systematic and evidence-based manner, overarching principles are needed to guide and structure evaluations, such as functional analysis (FA). This chapter explores FA in more detail and in the context of acquired brain injury.

Functional analysis

Although typically applied within the context of intellectual disability and a range of clinical settings, FA can be particularly useful within fields where client engagement is limited. Functional analysis can be defined as "the identification of important, controllable, causal functional relationships applicable to specified behaviors for an individual" (Haynes, 2000). It is a behavioural approach in which the laws of **operant conditioning** and **classical conditioning** are applied to explore potential relationships between certain stimuli and responses (Yoman, 2008). FA is commonly used in psychotherapy to better understand behaviour and in some cases to subsequently facilitate behavioural

DOI: 10.4324/9781003213116-8

change. In cognitive behaviour therapy (CBT), the reasons behind the behaviours are called *functions* (O'Donohue & Fisher, 2009), because it is hypothesised that such behaviours serve a function, or purpose, for the individual.

Examples of clinical application of FA in addition to CBT include behavioural activation (Kanter et al., 2005) and third-wave therapies such as dialectical behaviour therapy (DBT; Linehan, 1993) and acceptance and commitment therapy (ACT; Sturmey, 2008). Generally, maladaptive or **challenging behaviours** (such as self-harm, aggression, or compulsive behaviour) are targeted, and the antecedents, behaviours, and consequences are fully explored (Bakker, 2008). The factors that potentially maintain such behaviours (through reinforcement strategies) are considered.

Jamison et al. (2016) highlight four common functions of challenging behaviour which include increasing access to social attention (e.g. getting attention from a caregiver; Cooper Heron & Heward, 2007), increasing access to certain items or activities (e.g. to obtain a tangible reward such as money or food), to facilitate escape and/or avoidance of unpleasant stimuli or tasks (e.g. to avoid a difficult appointment; Miltenberger, 2008), and/or for sensory stimulation (e.g. to gain physiological release; O'Neill et al., 1997). At times, a single behaviour can serve multiple functions. For example self-harm can be driven by a need for sensory stimulation (e.g. to experience the physiological reduction in blood pressure in response to the sight of blood) and simultaneously, this behaviour may also serve to increase access to social attention (e.g. attention of healthcare providers in treating the wound).

Once the function has been identified, and the patterns through which the behaviours are reinforced and/or maintained, a plan can be developed which attempts to meet the outstanding need in an adaptive manner without the client resorting to the challenging or maladaptive behaviour. To identify potential functions, analysts must consider a range of factors which may be relevant to the individual. These may be internal or external to the individual in question and can include a range of emotional (e.g. anxiety, anger), physiological (e.g. hunger, pain), social (e.g. grief, loneliness), or environmental (e.g. noise) factors.

There are several advantages to using FA. Generally, the method of data collection within FA involves informant observation of the client within their regular environment, utilising objective measures (e.g. reporting frequencies of certain behaviours). This approach allows for a more reliable account of the antecedent behaviour itself and the consequences than more traditional talking therapies where the client is encouraged to reflect upon their perceptions of possible triggers and consequences, which may be impacted upon by limited insight, cognitive bias, impression management, and/or self-deception.

However, FA could also be considered to be a relatively reductionist approach to psychological analysis and intervention, which is associated with some limitations. There are no standard methods for determining potential behaviour functions, which can lead to interpreter bias affecting outcomes. As such, evaluating effectiveness is difficult, limiting opportunities for establishing a solid evidence base using randomised controlled studies and meta-analyses.

Furthermore, the literature is limited generally, with much being focused upon children with developmental difficulties (Beqiraj et al., 2022). This means that for potential populations for whom FA may be beneficial in principle, there is not a robust evidence base available to support application. One such clinical area is that of **acquired brain injury** (ABI).

Acquired brain injury

Increasing numbers of adults in the UK suffer from an ABI. Of those affected, many require immediate medical care and longer-term rehabilitative and social care. Behavioural change, disturbance, and challenging or violent behaviours are common consequences of an ABI (Gould et al., 2021), particularly associated with moderate to severe ABI (Holth et al., 2021). **Traumatic brain injury** (TBI) specifically has been found to be a risk factor for earlier onset, more violent, offending (Williams et al., 2018). Furthermore, TBI is associated with poor treatment engagement, in-custody infractions, and increased rates of reconviction (Williams et al., 2018). Individuals with brain injury engage in challenging behaviours at low frequencies (i.e. threatening suicide, making unwanted sexual advances, or walking out in traffic); however, such behaviours may have very serious consequences. Therefore, those involved need to be able to quickly and accurately understand the factors related to these behaviours to reduce risk ((Dixon et al., 2020).

Alderman and Wood (2013) hypothesise that factors resulting from ABI such as executive and attentional dysfunction, poor insight, problems of awareness and social judgement, labile mood, altered emotional expression, and poor impulse control are all influential factors in increasing behavioural disturbance. Despite having a range of physical, psychological, social, and behavioural needs, people with ABI are often overlooked in policy, guidance, and the development of psychological interventions. There are no evidence-based guidelines for managing challenging behaviours as a result of an ABI. The lack of clinical resources to guide practice has been highlighted by researchers (Gould et al., 2021).

Guidance which has accompanied the Care Act (Department of Health, 2014) in the UK mentions ABI in relation to **mental capacity**. The guidance notes that people with ABI may have difficulties in communicating their "views, wishes and feelings" (Department of Health, 2014, p. 95). Therefore, many who suffer from an ABI experience a range of communication difficulties and may struggle to engage in the types of psychological intervention and treatment that are more typically offered. Due to these difficulties, suggestions regarding the implementation, or adaptation, of existing psychological interventions have been made. These include **Positive Behaviour Support** guidelines (e.g. PBS+ PLUS; Gould et al., 2021), behavioural approaches (e.g. neuro-behavioural rehabilitation; Alderman & Wood, 2013), and FA.

Initial evaluation of the utility of FA in identifying effective interventions for severe problem behaviour in very young children with TBI indicated that analysis of behavioural function may play an important role in developing effective interventions for this group (Moore et al., 2010). However, the application of FA within the field of neuropsychology and ABI is still relatively limited. Dixon et al. (2020) state that "functional assessment and analysis following brain injury should be approached the same way a clinician would attempt to understand function of any other psychological disorder" (p. 271), and they go on to explain how clinicians should attempt to identify external events in the environment with large effects upon the challenging behaviours. This case study will examine the application of FA principles with a case involving an individual with an ABI who was displaying challenging behaviour.

Patient history

This clinical case study summarises neuropsychological assessment, FA, and formulation completed with a male in his forties who was detained under Section 3 of the Mental Health Act (1983, 2007) within a locked neuropsychiatric inpatient rehabilitation setting. Throughout the case study, the client will be referred to as David, and some details have been changed to maintain anonymity. As David was unable to provide informed consent for this case study due to his lack of capacity, a best interests meeting was conducted with his team and documented, in line with British Psychological Society (BPS) guidance (BPS, 2021) and Health Care Professionals Council standards (HCPC, 2015). As a result, in line with furthering others' practice in the area of FA and neurorehabilitation, this case study was produced.

Client background: There was very limited information regarding David's background history before he became an inpatient. He had not been in contact with services previously and his ability to provide a reliable account of his history was limited. Some information had been gained from his parents.

David attended mainstream education and there were no significant concerns regarding behavioural issues; however, it was noted that he was not very academically focused. He left school with no qualifications at the age of 16 years old. Following leaving school, David obtained employment and he lived independently in a council flat close to his parents who provided significant support. David's father looked after his money as David developed an alcohol addiction. There had been reports that David was documented to have a history of seizures related to his alcohol intake, which was managed with anti-epileptic medication; however, his compliance with this tended to fluctuate. David tended to live an isolated lifestyle. There was no documented history of offending behaviour or instances of particularly aggressive, disruptive, or violent behaviour prior to his ABI.

Referral: David was assaulted by several men with baseball bats whilst in his home resulting in head injury. As he was alone in his home at the time, he was not found for several days following the assault and he experienced significant withdrawal from alcohol during this time, further exacerbating his cognitive impairment. His parents reported that he had not been taking his anti-epileptic medication consistently for over a year prior to his admission to neuropsychiatric services.

David was taken to accident and emergency department, and his **Glasgow Coma Scale** (Teasdale & Jennett, 1974) indicated moderate brain injury. His injuries included soft tissue injures and bruising to his head and several areas of his body, lacerations to his face and body, and broken bones. His initial injuries were medically managed within a high dependency unit (HDU). After a period of six months, David was assessed as being medically fit for discharge from hospital. However, due to safeguarding concerns regarding his vulnerability, it was agreed that he could not return to his former residence and temporary accommodation was found with a plan to rehouse him. However, the discharge was unsuccessful due to his erratic and challenging behaviour, and he was returned to HDU two days later. His family members reported that his behaviour had deteriorated dramatically; he had become disruptive, aggressive, and also at times lethargic. Furthermore, David was refusing to eat and was suspicious of his family and other people.

As an inpatient in the HDU, David presented with moderate/severe cognitive impairment (as per the assessments discussed later) and challenging behaviour including verbal and physical aggression towards people and objects, wandering, and attempts to abscond. None of these behaviours had been reported prior to the assault. There were times when members of security staff were required to attend the ward to stop David from leaving it and also to redirect him back to his bed space when being verbally aggressive towards nurses. He had been disorientated in time and place and had **retrograde amnesia**. At these times, he was documented as being confused and requested to be allowed off the ward for him to attend work (he was not in employment). At other times, he presented as amenable.

David's mood was observed to fluctuate throughout the day, and his emotional lability manifested in rapidly changing facial expressions, body language, tone, and posture (e.g. smiling and laughing one minute, shouting and swearing the next with no obvious trigger observed by staff members). He was occasionally able to have a conversation with staff members. However, at other times, he would become verbally aggressive and sexually disinhibited if approached by staff for interaction (e.g. making inappropriate sexual comments or threats). David had also been physically aggressive towards staff, such as by elbowing them in the face. He had also hit a family member during a visit.

Initially, David would spend most of his time pacing the corridor or lying on his bed in the dark. Over time, David became more independent with his personal hygiene and moderately attended to this himself. His mobility fluctuated and he was considered at high risk of falls due to losing his balance. It was noted that he had not experienced any sensory loss. As discussed earlier, David had a history of seizures due to alcohol intake, with poor medication compliance. He experienced **generalised tonic–clonic seizures** one-month post-brain injury, which were treated with medication. It was six months post-assault when David was referred to and accepted for admission by a locked rehabilitation unit for clients with ABI and neuropsychiatric disorders, alongside comorbid mental health conditions. This was the setting of the current case study.

The role of a psychologist in a neuropsychiatric locked rehabilitation unit is varied and can involve training, consultancy, supervision, assessment, and treatment. Upon admission, David was referred to me as the ward psychologist for assessment by his clinical team to produce an overview of his current cognitive functioning, a comprehensive assessment of risk, psychological formulation, and recommendations regarding his rehabilitation potential.

Assessments

Cognitive functioning: Whilst David was unable to engage with formal assessment of current intellectual functioning (such as the Wechsler Adult Intelligence Scale, 2008) due to his attentional and behavioural challenges, he was able to tolerate and engage with a less demanding assessment providing a general picture of his current level of functioning. The Addenbrookes Cognitive Examination third version (ACE-III; Mathuranath et al., 2000) is a useful brief assessment which is applied with people to gain a general picture of changes in cognitive skills. An overall score can be calculated as well as individual scores for orientation, memory, attention, fluency, language, and visuospatial skills. As the test can be applied regularly (it can be repeated every four months), it can be used for monitoring progress or decline.

David engaged with routine assessment of his cognitive functioning infrequently, and results indicated that he had difficulty across all areas of cognitive functioning assessed, specifically memory, but with a relative strength in the area of visuospatial skills. It was notable that his memory did not improve with the recognition options that were presented in the test, suggesting that there would be little benefit of utilising reminders and prompts in day-to-day life. Repeated assessment indicated that there appeared to have been a slight improvement regarding his overall cognitive functioning, specifically regarding orientation and attention but not by much. This is a common process in the period following brain injury as natural healing occurs, particularly, when someone is within a stable placement as the individual familiarises themselves with the environment. There was also a move towards a more consistent profile, meaning that over time, there was less variance between subdomains. Findings of the cognitive functioning assessment were incorporated into the psychological formulation and helped to guide care and treatment planning.

Test of premorbid functioning: The Test of Premorbid Functioning (TOPF; Wechsler, 2011) estimates an individual's premorbid (i.e. pre-injury) cognitive and memory functioning. This tool was completed with David to consider his likely level of cognitive functioning prior to brain injury and as such give an indication of rehabilitation potential and cognitive reserve. The results suggested that his overall IQ was likely to have been in the 'low average' range prior to brain injury. Comparing this to his post-ABI level of functioning suggested significant deterioration.

Risk: The Short-Term Assessment of Risk and Treatability (START; Webster et al., 2004) is a risk assessment tool that contains 20 items for clinicians to consider when assessing risk across seven domains. START risk estimates take into account the current environment of the person although this tool has been demonstrated to have mixed inter-rater reliability findings in a UK study (Timmins et al., 2018). The START was completed regularly by the clinical team, and generally the areas of increased risk were identified as being risk of violence, self-neglect, victimisation from others, and case-specific areas of inappropriate sexual behaviour (including sexualised comments, verbal threats, and sexual touching of others). Findings of the risk assessment were incorporated into the psychological formulation and guided care and treatment planning.

Functional analysis of David

As David was presenting with behaviours that could have harmed himself or others, FA was utilised to examine the causes and consequences of risk behaviour. In line with FA principals, information regarding instances of challenging behaviour was collected including how often (frequency), when (temporal locus), and how long for (temporal extent) as guided by best practice (Johnston & Pennypacker, 1993). A worksheet which promoted 'ABC' analysis (Hanley et al., 2003) was used to collect information about what came before the behaviour (A; antecedents), the behaviour itself (B), and the consequences of the behaviour (C). ABC worksheets were completed following every incident of challenging behaviour observed by nursing staff to consider the range of risk behaviours that David presented with. These were recorded and analysed by members of the psychology team and support staff to ensure reliability.

After David had been an inpatient for 20 months, a review was held which was when this case study begins. The review indicated that within preceding six months (months 14–20 of his admission), there had been an increase in the number of risk incidents recorded (120 incidents) as compared to the six months prior to that when there had been approximately 60 incidents (months 9–13). It was noted that despite the increased frequency, generally, these behaviours were of a similar nature and level of severity. The majority of these incidents involved verbal and physical aggression; however, there had been some instances of inappropriate sexual behaviour or comments in the previous two months, which David had not been presenting with previously as an inpatient. These were generally related to sexualised insults, gestures, and threats but also involved sexualised touching of staff members' breasts and buttocks (e.g. slapping a nurse's bottom).

A retrospective analysis incident profile was developed at that point, covering 20 months, to examine whether there were any months of the year in which David was more likely to display challenging behaviours (see Figure 8.1). It was considered that this profile could help the clinical team understand David's behaviour more effectively in respect of understanding patterns, so that informed recommendations and support could be offered. Figure 8.1 details this analysis.

Additionally, a profile demonstrating the frequency of behavioural incidents by the time of day when they occurred was also completed. This was to examine whether there were any times of day when David was more likely to display challenging behaviours. This included the data collected from a 12-month period. Figure 8.2 depicts the findings.

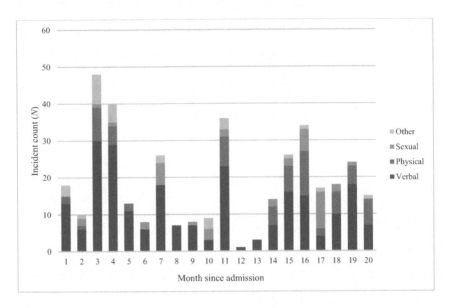

Figure 8.1 Incident profile

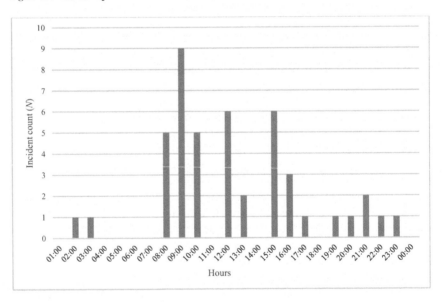

Figure 8.2 Temporal incident profile

Of note, as part of the behavioural analysis and observations, nursing staff fed back that they had noticed that David's challenging behaviour had tended to occur when it had been raining. Given this interesting observation, a basic profile of David's incident profile and average UK rainfall since his admission

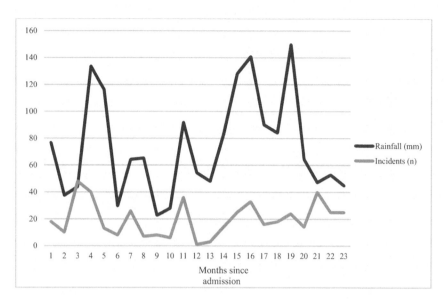

Figure 8.3 Incident count and average rainfall comparison

was completed. This analysis did reveal what appeared to represent a pattern of higher numbers of recorded risk incidents during, or just after, months with higher millimetres of rain; see Figure 8.3.

Incidents were documented to:

- consist of behaviours including violence and aggression (verbal and physical towards other people and objects);
- have taken place in the communal areas of the ward;
- occurred following some sort of interaction with David (such as offering medication, offering drinks, getting meals etc.);
- often be coupled with observations of confusion/disorientation; and
- be followed by periods of withdrawal and low engagement on the ward.

From a review of the data, the following observations were made:

- There were notable peaks in frequency during months 3–4, 7, 11, and 16.
- There were notable increases in frequency during certain hours of the day, specifically 08:00–10:00, 12:00–13:00, and 15:00–14:00.
- There appeared to be a close correlation between UK rainfall and incident frequency, which was hypothesised to possibly be a pre-cursory relationship related to a drop in atmospheric pressure which occurs prior to rain (Maini & Schuster, 2019).

A brief FA of David's challenging behaviour was completed, and the following themes were noted as being potential functions of his behaviour:

- Expression of negative emotions (e.g. sadness, fear, confusion, abandonment, rejection) potentially related to limited contact with family members; increased incidents are noted to have occurred during limited contact with David's parents (e.g. months 3–4 and 15–16).
- Attempts to reduce cognitive overload; increases are noted during interactions, which David may have found cognitively taxing.
- Threat response/defence mechanism; an increase in incidents was noted during interactions that may have been perceived as threatening due to David's history of trauma.
- An attempt to obtain food; an increase in incidents around mealtimes was noted. Further to this, it was hypothesised that reduced blood sugar levels may have played a role in exacerbating the behaviour.
- An attempt to reduce experience of pain/headaches by seeking attention from others; atmospheric pressure generally drops before rainfall which may cause headaches (Maini & Schuster, 2019).

Recommendations

Through discussion with the multidisciplinary team, the findings of the FA and discussion were used to inform specific recommendations for David's care, treatment, and management. David's PBS plan (Gore et al., 2013) was updated to incorporate these recommendations.

Initially, there were to be regular nursing assessments of David's mood and mental state, structured within nursing daily risk assessments, the findings of which were to be communicated to the team advising them of increased risk and effectiveness of management strategies. Staff were advised to maintain a minimal interaction approach during periods of agitation and increased risk highlighted from the analysis (e.g. mealtimes and medication times, limited contact with parents, poor weather/low pressure). Therefore, staff were to ensure that interaction with David was upon a needs-led basis, as it may be that interaction with David was perceived as threatening and initiating a threat response, albeit attempting to ensure that self-isolation is not necessarily encouraged as this could also have had potential negative consequences. Further to this, to minimise potential threat response triggers, staff were advised to maintain some physical distance between David and peers wherever possible.

A proactive approach from nursing staff was recommended, ensuring David had access to food and fluids in line with his current care plans regarding fluid and diet intake, to proactively offer/provide pain relief if considered necessary due to the potential link between challenging behaviour and pain/headaches, and to proactively offer video/telephone contact with family if they were unable to visit in person. The team was advised to monitor weather patterns and atmospheric pressure and consider alongside other information to inform risk assessment. This information was to be provided at nursing handovers and staff members were to be made aware of the patten of increased incidents at times around heavier rainfall. Another recommendation was that if David did present with challenging behaviour (such as verbal aggression, shouting, swearing, or making threats), staff were to reduce confronting this challenging behaviour to a minimum, where safely possible, and use a minimal intervention approach.

Further to the aforementioned recommendations, staff were encouraged to continue to complete accurate and comprehensive ABC monitoring to provide up-to-date information following any instance of David's challenging behaviour. This was so that data could be collected to evaluate the effectiveness of the implementation of the recommendations and to review and update the management plans as necessary.

The findings of this analysis were incorporated into David's care plan relating to management of violence and aggression. They were also included in his updated PBS plan. The team continued to monitor and analyse David's behaviour in relation to potential patterns, relationships, and functions which guided care and treatment planning.

Outcomes

The phenomenon of rainfall and the other factors hypothesised through FA were explored with behavioural data (a key component of FA) and formed the focus of team discussions aimed to increase flexible and exploratory thinking regarding potential functions of challenging behaviour. This led to increased confidence in anticipating and subsequently preventing, or managing, instances of challenging behaviour in line with PBS principles. In team discussions, nursing staff reported that they felt that whilst they did not necessarily understand all the functions of David's challenging behaviour, they felt equipped with the skills to observe, examine, and interpret potential functions of behaviour to minimise risk to David and others around him.

The process of FA allowed for specific recommendations to be made regarding David's behaviour. This facilitated a greater understanding of David's behaviour and an increased ability of staff to anticipate, proactively address, and as such avoid instances of challenging behaviour. Once these recommendations were implemented, a reduction in instances of David engaging in challenging behaviour was noted. Within the following month only three recorded instances of challenging behaviour were noted, as compared to 25 incidents recorded each month in the two months prior. Ultimately, this increased behavioural stability led to a referral, and successful transition, to a residential service for David where he had more freedom and was supported in his resettlement into community living.

Whilst David's transfer to a less restrictive service was a progressive and positive move, it prevented the current team from being able to follow-up and examine the frequency and severity of David's challenging behaviour whilst the recommendations were being implemented over a longer period to provide a more robust evaluation of efficacy; this can often be the case in forensic and neuropsychiatric settings where a patient moves to another service and the original team is no longer involved in their care. However, the short-term positive impact upon David's challenging behaviour in terms of reduced frequency, the reported increase in understanding, confidence, and resilience in the staff team in relation to David's challenging behaviour, and the application of a science-practitioner approach and subsequent reflection and learning were all initially very promising. Importantly, the FA and recommendations also provided the service that David transitioned to a basis on which to work and continue to analyse David's behaviour and progress to continue to aid his care and recovery whilst minimising risk to David and others around him.

Discussion

This chapter has presented a case study detailing application of FA principles for an individual with an ABI who displayed challenging behaviours. FA in this case allowed for a systematic examination of instances of challenging behaviour; a range of hypotheses regarding potential triggers, functions, and related factors were identified and explored. This process can allow for innovative thinking regarding complex and challenging cases in neuropsychology.

Dixon et al. (2020) suggest that too much emphasis on speculative internal mechanisms that may underlie challenging behaviour for individuals with ABI may not have as much clinical utility as if the environment is the focus. As such, clinicians are urged to consider the external environment as much as possible when identifying function for individuals with ABI.

In this case, staff members had noticed that it often rained around the time when David was presenting as particularly emotionally labile and was displaying increased instances of challenging behaviour. It is a long-held belief that the weather affects human behaviour (Harley, 2018). Often in conversation with professionals, comments are made relating the behaviour of individuals within their care, exploring the potential relationship with weather changes (e.g. "the ward was so unsettled last night, I think a storm is coming"). Regarding cognition, the meteorological variables that have the greatest effect on mood and memory are hours of sunshine, temperature, and humidity; however, a commonly highlighted meteorological phenomenon as impacting upon human behaviour is that of rain (Harley, 2018). There is some evidence that falling barometric pressure increases misbehaviour in student populations (Staut, 2001), and there is rapidly falling pressure before and during rainfall. There is a traditional belief that falling pressure affects the blood flow to the brain, but this belief is not supported by evidence (Harley, 2018). Research has indicated that changes in atmospheric pressure may be contributing factors when considering headaches, although the direction of the association appears inconsistent (Maini & Schuster, 2019). It is hypothesised that relevant mechanisms include **neuronal excitation, vasoconstriction, barotrauma**, and **hypoxia**. However, there are no randomised controlled trials examining effective acute or preventive treatments and further research is needed in this area.

Changes in barometric pressure seem unlikely to be a key influencing factor in many individuals' challenging behaviour, and thus this individual factor may not be generalisable to the ABI population as a whole. However, this case study aims to encourage the consideration of applying psychological approaches that are commonly used with other clinical populations, such as FA, to the field of ABI and challenging behaviours. Dixon et al. (2020) highlight that whilst factors such as historical events, injury location, and interactions between neurological, physical, and psychological deficits may play a role in the manifestation of a challenging behaviour, such factors may not be modifiable. Following identification of fixed factors (such as weather in this case), questions should be asked about potential contingencies maintaining the challenging behaviours. Potential examples of maintaining factors within this case study may have included the attention received by David from staff following instances of challenging behaviour making him feel cared for, or conversely, it may have been the space and reduced interaction David received following instances of challenging behaviour which made him feel safe and less threatened. Dixon et al. (2020) discuss that efforts should be made to minimise hypothesising, speculating, and inferring causes of behaviour and instead clinicians should utilise objective methods of exploration to confirm or refute potential function. If David had remained at the locked rehabilitation service, there may have been clinical utility in exploring these further.

Conclusion

It is hoped that this case study has served to highlight the utility of thinking creatively and innovatively within clinical practice. A key lesson from this case study was to listen to what seemed like anecdotal observations by staff members, such as their observations about the weather, as well as attending to more typically observed issues when dealing with challenging or violent behaviour such as apparent mood state and interactions with others. Through taking on board an additional but less typical factor such as the rainfall, patterns were able to be monitored and observed to aid his clinical team in more fully understanding behaviour. In David's case, the clinical team responsible for his care and management considered that this information contributed to keeping him and others safe, highlighting the value of FA in the field of ABI and challenging or harmful behaviour.

References

Alderman, N., & Wood, R. L. (2013). Neurobehavioural approaches to the rehabilitation of challenging behaviour. *NeuroRehabilitation, 32*(4), 761–770.

Bakker, G. (2008). *Practical CBT: Using functional analysis and standardised homework in everyday therapy.* Australian Academic Press.

Beqiraj, L., Denne, L. D., Hastings, R. P., & Paris, A. (2022). Positive behavioural support for children and young people with developmental disabilities in special education settings: A systematic review. *Journal of Applied Research in Intellectual Disabilities, 35*(3), 719–735.

British Psychological Society (BPS). (2021). Code of ethics and conduct. Author.

Cooper, J., Heron, T., & Heward, W. (2007). *Applied behaviour analysis.* Pearson Education.

Department of Health. (2014). *Care and support statutory guidance: Issued under the Care Act 2014.* Author.

Dixon, M. R., Hinman, J. M., & Bihler, H. L. (2020). Overview of brain injury. In *Functional analysis in clinical treatment. Practical resources for the mental health professional* (pp. 271–292). Academic Press.

Gore, N., McGill, P., Toogood, S., Allen, D., Hughes, J. C., Baker, P., Hastings, R., Noone, S., & Denne, L. (2013). Definition and scope for positive behaviour support. *International Journal of Positive Behavioural Support, 3*(2), 14–23.

Gould, K. R., Ponsford, J. L., Hicks, A. J., Hopwood, M., Renison, B., & Feeney, T. J. (2021). Positive behaviour support for challenging behaviour after acquired brain injury: An introduction to PBS+ PLUS and three case studies. *Neuropsychological Rehabilitation, 31*(1), 57–91.

Hanley, G. P., Iwata, B. A., & McCord, B. E. (2003). Functional analysis of problem behavior: A review. *Journal of Applied Behavior Analysis, 36,* 147–185.

Harley, T. (2018). *Weather and behaviour. Taken from 'The Psychology of Weather', from 'The Psychology of Everything' series.* Routledge.

Haynes, S. N. (2000). Chapter 19; Behavioural assessment of adults. In G. Goldstein & M. Hersen (Eds.), *Handbook of psychological assessment* (3rd ed.). Elsevier Science Ltd.

Health and Care Professions Council (HCPC). (2015). Standards of proficiency – practitioner psychologist. Author.

Holth, K., Gould, K. R., Hicks, A. J., Analytis, P., Feeney, T. J., & Ponsford, J. L. (2021). "I've never been positive . . . I am now": Participant perspectives of a Positive Behaviour Support Intervention (PBS+ PLUS) for community-living individuals with ABI and their close others. *Neuropsychological Rehabilitation,* 1–18.

Jamison, W. J., Hard, A., Allen, T. C., Clark, J., & Hagy, S. (2016). ABA in 2016. [PowerPoint slides]. Obtained from www.masteraba.com/functions-of-behavior.

Johnston, J. M., & Pennypacker, H. S. (1993). *Readings for strategies and tactics of behavioral research* (2nd ed.). Erlbaum.

Kanter, J. W., Cautilli, J. D., Busch, A. M., & Baruch, D. E. (2005). Toward a comprehensive functional analysis of depressive behavior: Five environmental factors and a possible sixth and seventh. *The Behavior Analyst Today, 6*(1), 65–81.

Linehan, M. (1993). *Skills training manual for treating borderline personality disorder.* Guildford Press.

Maini, K., & Schuster, N. M. (2019). Headache and barometric pressure: A narrative review. *Current Pain and Headache Reports, 23*(11), 87.

Mathuranath, P. S., Nestor, P. J., Berrios, G. E., Rakowicz, W., & Hodges, J. R. (2000). A brief cognitive test battery to differentiate Alzheimer's disease and frontotemporal dementia. *Neurology, 55*(11), 1613–1620.

Mental Health Act. (1983). C20. Government of the United Kingdom.

Mental Health Act. (2007). C12. Government of the United Kingdom. www.opsi.gov.uk/acts/acts2007/ukpga_20070012_en_1.

Miltenberger, R. (2008). *Behaviour modification.* Wadsworth Publishing.

Moore, T. R., Gilles, E., McComas, J. J., & Symons, F. J. (2010). Functional analysis and treatment of self-injurious behaviour in a young child with traumatic brain injury. *Brain Injury, 24*(12), 1511–1518.

O'Donohue, W. T., & Fisher, J. E. (2009). *General principles and empirically supported techniques of cognitive behavior therapy.* John Wiley & Sons.

O'Neill, R., Horner, R., Albin, R., Sprague, J., Storey, K., & Newton, J. (1997). *Functional assessment and programme development for problem behaviour: A practical handbook.* Brooks/Cole Publishing Company.

Staut, A. J. (2001). *The effects of barometric pressure on elementary school students' behavior.* The Graduate School University of Wisconsin-Stout.

Sturmey, P. (2008). *Behavioral case formulation and intervention: A functional analytic approach.* John Wiley & Sons.

Teasdale, G., & Jennett, B. (1974). Assessment of coma and impaired consciousness. A practical scale. *Lancet, 2,* 81–84.

Timmins, K. L. E., Evans, L., & Tully, R. J. (2018). Inter-rater reliability of the Short-Term Assessment of Risk and Treatability (START). *The Journal of Forensic Psychiatry & Psychology, 29*(6), 968–988.

Webster, C. D., Martin, M., Brink, J., Nicholls, T. L., & Middleton, C. (2004). *Short-Term Assessment of Risk and Treatability (START).* St. Josephs Healthcare, Hamilton and British Columbia Mental Health and Addiction Services.

Wechsler, D. (2008). *Wechsler adult intelligence scale* (4th ed.). Pearson Publishing.

Wechsler, D. (2011). *The test of premorbid function (TOPF).* The Psychological Corporation.

Williams, W. H., Chitsabesan, P., Fazel, S., McMillan, T., Hughes, N., Parsonage, M., & Tonks, J. (2018). Traumatic brain injury: A potential cause of violent crime? *The Lancet Psychiatry, 5*(10), 836–844.

Yoman, J. (2008). A primer on functional analysis. *Cognitive and Behavioral Practice, 15*(3), 325–340.

9 Clinical and forensic assessment of firesetting

Faye Horsley

Introduction

Psychological literature addressing the misuse of fire most commonly refers to either 'arson' or 'firesetting'. The former is a legal term (Daykin & Hamilton, 2012), whereas the latter constitutes "all deliberate acts of setting fire that are not recreational in nature" (Gannon & Barrowcliffe, 2012, p. 2). Horsley (2021, 2022) notes that these terms are often used interchangeably in the forensic, psychological, and criminological literature, which can be problematic. In this chapter, the term firesetting is applied, except where reference is specifically being made to the criminal offence of arson.

The literature base on firesetting is narrower than that relating to other offence types, although, encouragingly, empirical research has grown over the past decade (for examples see Gannon et al., 2013; Ó Ciardha et al., 2015; Tyler et al., 2015; Gannon & Barrowcliffe, 2012; Barrowcliffe & Gannon, 2015, 2016; Butler & Gannon, 2020; Horsley, 2021, 2022). In 2012, the multi-trajectory theory of adult firesetting (M-TTAF; Gannon, Ó'Ciardha, Doley & Alleyne) was published, which has progressed theoretical understanding of the behaviour. Even more recently, Horsley proposed the continuum of fire use theory (CoFU, Horsley, 2021, 2022), which calls for a re-conceptualisation of firesetting (more accurately, 'fire use', as referred to by Horsley) from a categorical to dimensional construct.

The growth in the firesetting knowledge base has informed the development of a treatment programme specifically designed for firesetters in prison (the firesetter intervention programme for prisoners [FIPP]; Gannon, 2012, as cited in Gannon et al., 2015). This improves on the previous 'one size fits all' approach to treating firesetters (Horsley, 2022). That being said, Horsley (2022) discusses the evolutionary significance of fire and the challenges this poses when considering rehabilitative approaches with adults. Whilst progress has been made in the treatment arena, the same cannot be said with respect to firesetter assessment, epitomised by the fact that there are currently no validated risk assessment tools specifically designed for adults who set fires (Watt & Ong, 2015). This poses a challenge for practitioners because research evidence suggests that firesetters present somewhat of a different psychological picture to

DOI: 10.4324/9781003213116-9

that of their violent and non-violent offending counterparts (for example see Edwards & Grace, 2014).

The complexities surrounding the forensic psychological assessment of firesetters formed the basis of the idiosyncratic approach taken in the assessment of 'Carl' (not his real name), outlined in this chapter. The case study of Carl has been chosen to exemplify the nuances and challenges of assessment in cases of firesetting.

Client background

Referral

Carl was aged 35 at the time of assessment. He was referred for an independent psychological risk assessment via his legal representative for the purpose of his first parole review. Carl was serving an indeterminate sentence for public protection (IPP) for the offence of arson with intent to endanger life, with a minimum custodial prison term of just under six years. Carl's file information was reviewed, which included his parole dossier containing past and recent reports, and he was interviewed for approximately five hours. Carl was residing in a closed prison, having recently been transferred back to **closed prison** from **open prison** conditions for security reasons (detailed later). Prior to being interviewed, written information about the psychological assessment was provided to Carl, and this was discussed. He provided his signed consent to take part.

Childhood and family

Until the age of ten, Carl lived with his biological parents and his younger brother. He described family life as "chaotic" because his father was a drinker and had a bad temper. Carl's father was physically abusive towards his mother, which Carl regularly witnessed. His parents separated when he was around ten years old. Although his father's behaviour had been difficult, Carl described his life following the separation of his parents as "worse" because it made him feel that he no longer had a family. The two siblings moved, with their mother, into a small flat and contact with their father abruptly ceased. Their mother soon became involved with another man, whom Carl described as a "druggie". From this point onwards, his mother started using drugs, and became neglectful of her sons. When Carl was aged 12, he and his brother were taken into care, where Carl was physically and sexually abused. He reported during interview that he perceived going in to care as rejection by his mother. At the age of 16, he left the care system and stayed with friends.

Previous experience of fire

This area was explored in detail during clinical interviews. Carl described childhood memories of the whole family sitting around the coal fire in their home, which he said was the only time his father was "in a good mood", and everybody felt "happy". He enjoyed watching the flames change colour and remembered feeling comforted, safe, and relaxed. In essence, these times were a temporary respite from the chaos and conflict of everyday family life. Whilst most of Carl's fire-memories were positive, Carl has one memory which he described as "really bad". By the time Carl was ten, his parents' relationship had deteriorated, and, on one occasion, his mother threw some of his father's belongings into the lit fireplace. Importantly, Carl noted that it was after this incident that his parents separated.

From a young age, Carl said that he and his brother would steal matches from shops, go to local fields, and light "campfires". They would throw objects into the fire to "see how they burned", starting with crisp packets but progressing to aerosol cans, which he enjoyed because of the "flashes, and bangs". Carl said that when he was aged 12, they "accidentally" set a barn on fire. A local resident called the Fire and Rescue Service (FRS), and the brothers watched them arrive from a distance. Carl said he felt "shocked, scared, and excited". Carl's first arson conviction was at the age of 15, which took place in a care home (described later).

Education and employment

Carl was expelled from primary school for throwing a chair at a teacher. From the age of 12–16, his education was coordinated via the care system. He found school difficult, and he did not pass any exams. At the age of 16, he enrolled at college to study a qualification in catering, but he left after a week, stating that it was "boring". Carl has no record of paid employment in the community. Carl's prison employment record had been inconsistent, and he had been dismissed from a number of positions. Most recently, he was employed in the prison kitchen but he self-harmed by deliberately scalding his skin, leading to a dismissal. He was unemployed in the prison at the time of assessment.

Intimate relationships

Carl met Laura, whom he described as his first "serious" girlfriend, in the care system when they were both 14. Carl described this as a "happy" relationship, which ended after about a year because they "grew apart". His self-report is, however, discrepant with the file information because according to probation reports Carl was described as "clingy, jealous, and possessive" of Laura, and the relationship ended because she found a new partner. Carl's behaviour towards Laura following the breakdown of their relationship was described as "harassment" in one report and involved an instance of firesetting (see later). He was subsequently moved to a different care placement as a result.

Carl denied having had any further intimate relationships until he met Amy, the victim of his most recent offence. However, his conviction history includes a harassment offence, against a woman named Mary, when he was 24, for which a restraining order was issued. Carl described Mary as a friend during interview for this assessment, and he denied having any recollection of the offence. The limited file information available indicated that they may have had a short-term relationship, which Carl struggled to accept was over, resulting in him repeatedly following her to work and shouting threats at her.

At the age of 27, Carl met Amy, the victim of the most recent offence, whom he described as "the love of my life". Within a year the couple were living together. According to Carl's account, Amy was a heavy drinker, and so his own alcohol consumption increased. They survived on unemployment benefits and spent most of their time intoxicated. Reports by probation made reference to a number of police call-outs to the couple's home as a result of verbal altercations, although he denied this during interview. After a year, Amy informed Carl that she had met someone else and no longer wanted to be in a relationship with him.

Carl admitted to having had a brief relationship with his male cell mate in a previous establishment earlier on this sentence. When asked about his sexual orientation, Carl said this is something he is "still battling with", adding that he is "probably bi-sexual or gay". He said it is difficult to admit to himself that he has "feelings for men".

Substance misuse

Carl first tried alcohol at the age of eight when his father took him and his younger brother to a local public house. Carl started to drink cider on a daily basis in his mid-teens. He recognised that alcohol was a "coping" mechanism to manage the impact of his chaotic family background as well as the abuse he suffered in care. Carl continued to drink into adulthood but started to prefer spirits. As referred to previously, he and his partner Amy together drank on a daily basis, and he admits to having been "addicted" to alcohol at this point in his life. There was no evidence that Carl ever misused drugs.

Mental health

According to a psychiatric assessment, which was completed at the time of sentencing, there was no evidence of mental illness or psychopathic disorder, but the author made reference to a history of mild depressive episodes relating to relationship difficulties and alcohol use. Importantly, the report also highlighted "significant personality difficulties" in Carl's case, namely developing dependent relationships, possessiveness, jealousy, an unclear sense of his own identity, and emotional instability. At the time of the current psychological assessment, Carl was taking an anti-depressant medication. Carl described feelings of "flatness" but said that these fluctuate rapidly, and he can experience "happiness followed by anger" very regularly. This was corroborated by reports within the parole dossier, albeit his presentation has been more stable in recent years compared to earlier in his sentence. Prison records indicated that Carl had a history of self-harming behaviour, most recently about three months prior to this psychological assessment. He has most commonly self-harmed in prison by pouring boiling water onto his arms, which he explained was because he enjoys the "burning sensation".

In the current psychological assessment, using the *Diagnostic and statistical manual for mental disorders*, fifth edition (DSM-V; APA, 2013), a cluster of personality characteristics associated with borderline personality disorder (BPD) was noted as being relevant in Carl's case. The central features of BPD according to the DSM-V is "a pervasive pattern of instability of interpersonal relationships, self-image, and affects, marked impulsivity that begins in early adulthood and is present in a variety of contexts" (p. 663).

Most recent offence

Carl was sentenced to an indeterminate sentence for public protection (IPP) for the offence of arson with intent to endanger life. His minimum custodial term of just under six years had recently expired at the time of referral. This meant that his case was being considered by the parole board for their assessment of suitability for transfer to an open prison or release into the community. The details of the offence were as follows: Carl had been in a relationship with the victim, Amy, for about a year. Amy ended the relationship, informing Carl that she had found another partner. Carl left their flat and moved in with a friend where he spent the next few weeks drinking very heavily. He tried to call Amy, but she did not answer her phone, and he sent her threatening text messages, which resulted in a harassment order being issued.

At about midnight on the night of the offence, Carl decided to go to Amy's home. He knocked on the door but there was no reply, although lights came on in the property while he was outside. At that point he left, went to a local 24-hour garage, and bought a cigarette lighter, an aerosol deodorant, and newspapers. He returned to the flat, lit the newspapers, and pushed them through the letter box. He also pushed the aerosol can through, which exploded. He left the immediate vicinity but remained close by, watching the property. Amy was in the property at the time and escaped out of her bedroom window and was unharmed. However, the fire caused a great deal of damage to the home. She called the FRS, and Carl watched as they arrived at the scene. He was arrested in the early hours of that morning.

During interview for the current psychological assessment Carl denied intending to harm Amy. He said he lit the fire to bring some "closure" to their relationship and to "cleanse all of the bad memories". He expanded to say that he saw the fire as a way of "drawing a line" under everything that had happened between them. He conceded that he took some enjoyment out of watching the fire take hold before the FRS arrived at the scene. In particular, he noted the size and colour of the flames, which he could see through the window and added that they made him feel "peaceful, and happy".

Previous offending

When Carl was 15 years old, he was sentenced to a nine-month referral order for the offence of arson. According to official documentation, he set fire to a duvet cover in the bedroom of a resident of the same care home he was living in at the time. The bedroom belonged to Laura, with whom he had been in a relationship. The act was, reportedly, in response to Laura ending their relationship and occurred after a series of threats made towards her over the preceding weeks. Laura was not present in the building at the time.

There are two other arson offences on Carl's record. When he was aged 18, he was convicted of arson after setting fire to a neighbour's shed following a verbal altercation, and three years later he received another arson conviction for setting fire to a refuse bin outside of a public house, after being asked to leave by a member of staff (reportedly owing to his intoxicated state). In addition to the aforementioned arsons, Carl has a criminal damage conviction, dating back to his early twenties, which relates to him reportedly smashing a friend's window following an argument. As referred to earlier, he has a conviction for harassment against a woman named Mary.

Progress in prison

Carl had four prison adjudications on record; three relate to failing alcohol tests earlier in his sentence, and one related to damaging prison property, which occurred during an altercation with a prison officer three years ago. Overall, his day-to-day conduct in prison had been reasonably good; he was described as compliant and polite. The main concerns in the closed prison estate were around his self-injurious behaviour.

In the year prior to the current assessment Carl was transferred to an open prison but there were concerns about his behaviour almost immediately. Intelligence accumulated pertaining to alcohol use, and one month after he had transferred to the prison, he failed an alcohol test. When his Prison Offender Manager (POM) attempted to discuss this, Carl became verbally abusive and issued threats about burning down the POM's house. This led to a transfer back to closed conditions, where he was residing at the time of the psychological assessment.

Carl completed two treatment programmes during his sentence: one targeting substance misuse and the other managing emotions. Feedback from treatment facilitators was generally positive; Carl's attitude was commended, and he was thought to have gained from the interventions. However, not long after completing the managing emotions programme Carl self-harmed, suggesting that emotional regulation was an ongoing issue.

Assessment of risk

Two formal risk assessment tools were employed for the purpose of Carl's psychological assessment. The HCR-20v3 (Douglas et al., 2013) was used to assess general risk of violence. The HCR-20 is a flexible clinical checklist of 20 risk factors, identified through empirical research as significant correlates of violence recidivism. The HCR-20v3 defines violence as "the actual, attempted or threatened infliction of bodily harm of another person" (p. 2). This definition may include threats of harm where they are clear and unambiguous or behaviours likely to induce fear such as stalking. The HCR-20v3 tool is a method to structure clinical judgement about a client's relevant risk factors with a view to guiding risk management. In administering the HCR-20v3, clinicians are required to evaluate and document the presence of each of the 20 risk factors and its relevance to violence.

The HCR-20v3 was considered to be suitable as a risk assessment method in Carl's case because he has a history of violence, and so it was necessary to consider the risk he might pose in the future. It is worth noting that arson is included within the HCR-20v3 definition of violence. There were, however, a number of important considerations in relation to Carl. First, although the HCR-20v3 is suitable for use with those convicted of arson, research indicates there are some key differences between arsonists and other violent offenders (for examples see Gannon et al., 2013; Edwards & Grace, 2014; Wilpert et al., 2017). Therefore, it has been suggested that standard violence risk assessment tools may not be wholly informative when used with arsonists (Edwards & Grace, 2014). As such, Horsley (2022) recommends that reviewing additional factors (i.e. factors over and above those included in a general risk tool like the HCR-20) is best practice when working with those who set fires. Second, for Carl, it was prudent to consider whether an intimate partner violence (IPV)-specific risk assessment tool should also be employed, given that the target of the index offence was an ex-partner, along with the harassment conviction on record. However, information pertaining to Carl's relationships was sparse, and it was therefore determined that the use of an IPV tool would be speculative and unreliable. The HCR-20v3, as a measure of general violence, supplemented with firesetting considerations, was considered the optimal choice.

HCR-20v3 assessment

Historical items

The HCR-20v3 is separated into three sections. The first of these contains ten historical factors, with the option for additional items to be considered where necessary. Historical items are coded across the person's whole lifetime up until the day of assessment, both in terms of their presence and their relevance

Table 9.1 Summary of historical items

Past problems with	Presence	Relevance
H1: Serious violence	Present	High
H2: Non-violent antisocial behaviour	Present	High
H3: Relationship instability	Present	High
H4: Employment	Present	High
H5: Substance misuse	Present	High
H6: Major mental illness	Partially present	Moderate
H7: Personality disorder	Possibly present	Moderate
H8: Traumatic experiences	Present	High
H9: Violent attitudes	Partially present	Moderate
H10: Treatment or supervision response	Present	High

Table 9.2 Summary of clinical items

Recent problems with	Presence	Relevance
C1: Insight	Partially present	Moderate
C2: Violent ideation or intent	Partially present	Moderate
C3: Symptoms of major mental illness	Partially present	Moderate
C4: Instability	Present	High
C5: Treatment or supervision response	Partially present	Moderate

to risk management. The coding of items in relation to Carl is included in Table 9.1.

Clinical items

The second section of the HCR-20v3 presents clinical items, which pertain to the client's presentation in the past six months. Five clinical items are included, but the clinician has the option to make additional considerations if applicable. Table 9.2 presents a summary of the ratings for Carl.

Risk management items

The final section of the HCR-20v3 contains five items relating to potential future problems. There is some conceptual overlap with the historical and clinical sections but, importantly, risk management items relate specifically to the future; usually the next 12 months. In rating these items, clinicians should consider the most likely situation/s for the client in the next 12 months. In Carl's case, owing to the purpose of the assessment, risk management items were rated from three possible perspectives, namely if he were residing in a closed prison, an open prison, or in the community because all of these were potential

Table 9.3 Risk management items

Future problems with	Closed prison conditions		Open prison conditions		Community	
	Presence	Relevance	Presence	Relevance	Presence	Relevance
R1: Professional services and plans	Absent	Low	Partially present	Moderate	Absent	Low
R2: Living situation	Absent	Low	Present	High	Partially present	Moderate
R3: Personal support	Absent	Low	Partially present	Moderate	Partially present	Moderate
R4: Treatment or supervision response	Partially present	Moderate	Partially present	High	Partially present	High
R5: Stress	Partially present	Moderate	Partially present	High	Partially present	High

outcomes of the parole review. In some instances, considering these different outcomes resulted in separate ratings for an item. For other items, the rating was the same, irrespective of the outcome of the parole process. Table 9.3 summarises the ratings for Carl.

Fire-specific risk considerations

As referred to earlier, Horsley (2022) suggests that reviewing additional factors (i.e. over and above those included in a general risk tool like the HCR-20v3) is best practice when working with those who set fires in accordance with the latest psychological literature. The considerations made in the assessment of Carl are outlined in the following sections.

Arson offending history

Research has indicated a number of static/historical factors, which could warrant assessment for those convicted of arson (Edwards & Grace, 2014). Each of these was reviewed in Carl's case as follows: (i) *multiple arsons (i.e. charges for arson) at the time of the court appearance for the index offence* – according to Edwards and Grace, the more charges for arson at the time of the most recent court appearance, the greater the risk of arson recidivism. This item was not present in Carl's case because he was charged with only one arson, rather than multiple offences at the time of his court appearance for the most recent offence; (ii) *age at first arson offence* – those aged 18 years or younger were more likely to commit another arson according to the research by Edwards and Grace. Carl was 15 when first convicted for arson, and so this factor was considered to be present in his case; (iii) *prior vandalism offences* – Edwards and Grace found that having this type of offence on record was predictive of arson recidivism. This item was considered present in Carl's case owing to a conviction for criminal damage which related to the breaking of a window at the home a friend. In summary, two of the three static factors referred to earlier were present in Carl's case, which highlighted an inflated risk of committing a future arson offence. However, it is important to note that the strongest predictor of future offending (multiple arsons) as determined through the study by Edwards and Grace was not present in Carl's case.

Psychological characteristics

Gannon et al. (2013) propose that firesetters are specialists, that is they present a different psychological picture to other types of offenders and therefore should be assessed and treated differently. In their research, they found that a number of psychological characteristics can distinguish between firesetters and other offenders. Therefore, consideration of these distinguishing features can augment a general violence risk assessment, such as the HCR-20v3. Each of these factors was explored in the assessment of Carl's risk as described in the following sections.

Fire-related factors

According to Gannon et al. (2013), when compared with non-firesetters, there was more evidence of an *interest in fire, attitudes supportive of firesetting*, and *identification with fire* in a sample of firesetters. There was at least partial evidence of *fire-interest* in Carl's past. When recounting his early experience of the family coal fire, Carl made reference to the sensory aspects, such as the colours of the flames. Also, he recalled emotive aspects of the experience of sitting by the fire and finding it calming. Furthermore, he recalled some reckless firesetting, for instance throwing aerosols into fires and setting a barn on fire, albeit he claims the latter was an accident. In addition, Carl remained at the scene of his most recent offence, which he said he enjoyed. In response to all of these past experiences, Carl described physiological arousal. At the time of assessment there was some indication of an ongoing interest in fire in Carl's case. This can be difficult to assess in prison because prisoners do not routinely have access to sources of fire both for safety and security reasons. Therefore, Horsley (2022) discusses the importance of looking carefully for **risk paralleling behaviours (RPBs)** in firesetters.

In Carl's case, repeated self-harm through the use of boiling water was considered as, potentially, risk paralleling and, thus, evidence of ongoing fire interest. When asked about this he said that he liked to "feel the heat" on his skin, and that it made him feel "calm". In the absence of easy access to literal forms of fire in prison (i.e. a naked flame; smoking materials and therefore lighters/matches are banned in prisons in England and Wales), it is possible that Carl has used sources of heat as an alternative to evoke the feelings he has previously associated with firesetting. Notwithstanding his self-harm, when Carl was asked directly about his current views of fire, he conveyed ambivalence. For example in response to questions about the Grenfell Tower disaster in London, which was a widely reported and devastating fire that he would have seen on the news, he focused on his perception of mistakes made by the FRS rather than the fire itself, showing no indication of inappropriate emotional arousal. It was considered possible that, in Carl's case, he might be interested in the fire/heat that he controls himself but less so when it occurs elsewhere and involves other people. However, at the time of assessment, there had been no systematic monitoring by prison staff of Carl's behaviour and attitudes specifically in relation to fire and, thus, whether or not he still had an interest in fire was not entirely clear.

There was definite evidence of attitudes supportive of firesetting in Carl's history. Carl's account of the most recent offence, namely that he believed firesetting was the best way to bring "closure" on the ending of the relationship with Amy, is suggestive of firesetting-supportive attitudes, and specifically beliefs about the utility, and power of fire. Whilst he denied that the offence was a form of revenge, this was not discounted as a possibility in the psychological assessment. If revenge did feature as a motivator, then this could represent a view, on Carl's part, that fire can be used to punish and as a way of communicating feelings. From an attitudinal perspective, Carl's ongoing self-harm was conceptualised as risk paralleling in that it broadly represents the same views about the utility of fire (or heat in this case) as a means through which to communicate and manage feelings/self-soothe. Moreover, the events leading up to Carl's transfer back to closed conditions from the open prison prior to the psychological assessment were considered here. Carl behaved in a threatening manner towards a member of staff and specifically made a threat to burn their house down. Again, this suggests that he continued to view fire (albeit in the form of a threat) as a powerful tool to send a clear message and to harm others.

Identification with fire is also highlighted as relevant in the firesetting research by Gannon et al. (2013), as well as in fire use more broadly (Horsley, 2021). There was some evidence of this factor in Carl's case. During interview he reported feeling a "connection" with fire when he was a child because of the association with what he described as mostly calm and happy family memories. With respect to the present day, Carl denied any ongoing identification with fire; however, given the aforementioned methods of self-harming and the verbal threat in open conditions, the possibility could not be discounted.

Emotional regulation and self-concept

In their research, Gannon et al. (2013) found that when compared with non-firesetters, firesetters demonstrated more difficulty in regulating emotions such as anger. This was considered relevant in Carl's case as demonstrated by his ongoing self-harm and losing his temper with staff. Likewise, a weak **self-concept** was more prevalent in the firesetter group in Gannon et al.'s research.

This, too, is relevant in Carl's case, for example with respect to his uncertainty over his sexual identity.

Pyromania

Pyromania is a mental disorder characterised by a set of criteria. Given Carl's presentation, firesetting history, and his self-reported feelings and reactions around firesetting, pyromania was considered a possible diagnosis in his case. However, it was determined that irrespective of whether or not he met the 'diagnostic threshold' for this mental disorder the risk assessment conclusions and treatment recommendations would remain the same and, thus, no formal assessment was undertaken.

Theoretical considerations

Gannon et al. (2012) present a theoretical framework for understanding fire-setters entitled the multi-trajectory theory of adult firesetting (M-TTAF). In addition to the comprehensive etiological theory of firesetting, they propose five associated prototypical firesetting trajectories, which represent different 'types' of firesetters based on their characteristics. Consideration of which trajectory best represents an individual's behaviour can be helpful because it can guide the identification of treatment needs. Carl's presentation was best aligned with the fifth trajectory – called the multifaceted trajectory – in that there was evidence of an interest in fire but also general risk factors such as emotional regulation difficulties. That being said, Carl was not a 'typical' case for the mul-tifaceted trajectory given that his non-firesetting offending is minimal and most of his offence-supportive thinking was closely intertwined with fire.

Clinical case formulation

Formulation was conducted in respect of further understanding Carl's risk, and importantly also to communicate this psychological understanding to the parole board which was required to decide about his continued detention.

There is no universally agreed-upon definition of formulation within the psy-chological literature. According to Douglas et al. (2013) it is "intended to facili-tate clinicians' conceptualisation of the roots of a person's problems with an eye toward intervention". In essence, formulation could be thought of as the process of summarising a client's 'life story' to understand their problems and offending behaviour. A common approach in psychology is known as 'four-p' (predispos-ing, precipitating, perpetuating, and protective) or 'five-p', which includes iden-tification of the presenting problem (see Tully, 2019, for a summary). Through adopting the 'p framework' in forensic psychological assessments, clinicians iden-tify the factors, which are thought to have contributed to the client's offend-ing behaviour and responsivity issues. The five-p framework was adopted for Carl's assessment. However, as highlighted by Tully (2019), simply listing relevant factors could limit understanding into the client's presentation. Therefore, a fuller narrative was developed in Carl's formulation so that it was chronological, and coherent. The formulation is presented in the following sections.

Predisposing factors

Instability was a key feature of Carl's childhood and adolescence. He was exposed to violence in the home, and he found the breakdown of his parents' relationship difficult. He perceived being placed in care as rejection by his mother. He was, moreover, the victim of physical and sexual abuse whilst in care, which is likely to have led to mistrust on his part, affected his attachment style, and to have reinforced an already developing view that the world is a dangerous place in which he cannot trust others. At times, Carl's parents struggled to regulate their emotions and misused substances. Therefore, they demonstrated poor emotional management, and in the absence of any prosocial role model to counter this for Carl both in the family home and in the care setting, he did not learn how to manage his own emotions. Moreover, the unstable home environment was likely perceived by Carl as invalidating, insecure, and threatening, which may have contributed to an unstable sense of self and, ultimately, to the emergence of personality characteristics associated with BPD. A lack of understanding into his emotions and lack of adult support meant that Carl was unable to effectively process the negative events in his life. Further, Carl's interpersonal skills were underdeveloped, resulting in a difficulty in expressing himself and a lack of conflict management skills.

It seemed likely that perception of rejection from his mother led to the development of a fear of abandonment. This, coupled with the aforementioned mistreatment and emotional issues, resulted in poor self-esteem, low mood, and anxiety. Furthermore, Carl described himself as a "loner" and so is likely to have had a sense of social ineffectiveness as a child. In other words, he considered himself to be of no importance and felt he was ignored by others; this is highlighted in the psychological literature as an antecedent to arson by Jackson et al. (1987).

Crucially, the calmest moments of Carl's early life were in the presence of fire, as his family gathered around the coal fire. However, on one occasion, he observed the destructive nature of fire as his mother burnt his father's belongings, which was the catalyst to the breakdown of their relationship. Carl may therefore have acquired conflicting messages about fire. On the one hand, it could be used to soothe and calm, but on the other it can damage and destroy. Importantly, he may also have learnt that fire represents endings.

Carl experimented with fire in childhood. He was physiologically aroused by it, which is highlighted as a feature of firesetting (Gannon et al., 2012) and fire use more generally (Horsley, 2021) in the empirical literature. For Carl, this arousal was further reinforcing and strengthened his association with fire. It is possible that **pyromania** is a relevant diagnosis in his case, which is characterised by interest in fire and physiological arousal connected to it. Some of Carl's earliest uses of fire, for example setting a barn on fire and the arson when he was 15, further reinforced its power and destructive nature. It is therefore possible that fire and aggression became merged; this is described as a fire-aggression fusion script by Gannon et al. (2012). It is likely that fire use soon became one of Carl's 'go-to' coping strategies, meaning that he turned to it whenever he faced a problem. Ultimately, fire was arousing and interesting to him, in addition to providing a useful route for the expression of aggression, communication, and emotional management. For these reasons, his presentation is well-aligned with the multifaceted firesetter trajectory (Gannon et al., 2012). As a result of his early experiences, it could be said that Carl had, therefore, formed a maladaptive relationship with fire (see Horsley, 2022 for discussion).

Precipitating factors

Prior to the index offence, Carl's relationship with his partner broke down. He had made attempts to contact her, but these were unsuccessful. He already had a history of harassing ex-partners, probably driven by a fear of abandonment, which developed after he was placed into care and, thus, he resorted to the same behaviour again. Amy's repeated rejection of him in the weeks leading up to the offence likely led to feelings of anger and fear, alongside low mood and anxiety. Carl was unable to manage these emotions, nor could he effectively communicate how he was feeling. To cope, his alcohol use increased, leaving him even less emotionally regulated. At this point he called upon firesetting as a previously learnt coping mechanism and committed the offence. There were likely several factors influencing his decision. Carl already viewed fire as a way of soothing and calming himself, but he also associated it with endings, and this is consistent with his account of the motivation for the offence as being a way of "drawing a line" under what had happened with his relationship. Although he denied it, another motivating factor in the offence may have been a desire to seek revenge on Amy, underpinned by the aforementioned fire-aggression fusion script.

Perpetuating factors

Perpetuating factors are those which maintain the problem behaviour. Early fire-related learning may explain why Carl has multiple arson convictions; the first one dating back to when he was 15. Chronic emotion regulation difficulties, underdeveloped interpersonal problem-solving/communication skills, alcohol misuse, a lack of structure in his life, and the absence of meaningful goals were also identified as important perpetuating factors, in addition to a fear of abandonment. Furthermore, Carl's BPD characteristics could explain the longevity of his difficulties and maladaptive behaviour. All of these factors relate to Carl's perception of, and behaviour, in respect of intimate and non-intimate relationships. The instability, combined with his problems managing stress seems to have perpetuated risk. These factors therefore were considered important to change or manage in relation to future risk of firesetting.

Protective factors

In recent decades, there has been a gradual shift in forensic psychology from a focus solely on risk to one which also considers positive characteristics, otherwise termed protective factors (see Towl & Crighton, 1996; Ward, 2017). The Structured Assessment of Protective Factors (SAPROF; De Vogal et al., 2012) is a structured professional judgement tool designed to aid clinicians in assessing characteristics of a person and their environment, which may reduce or mitigate the risk of reoffending. The SAPROF comprises 17 items, organised into three categories: (i) *internal items* – relating to individual characteristics; (ii) *motivational items* – relating to the person's willingness to behave in a positive and law-abiding way; and (iii) *external items* – referring to environmental characteristics.

Unfortunately, few protective factors were considered present in Carl's case; these were limited to: (a) *intelligence* – there was no evidence of issues with Carl's intellectual or cognitive functioning; (b) *professional care* – at the time of assessment, Carl had access to and contact with appropriate professional services; (c) *living circumstances* – the closed prison environment where Carl was residing was suitable, albeit it could, at times, be a source of stress; and (d) *external controls* – the prison setting was generally considered to be containing with respect to Carl's risk.

Risk scenarios

The HCR-20v3 tool, which provided the main basis of Carl's assessment, provides a framework for future scenarios of violence to be developed. Scenarios are not an attempt to predict the person's future, rather, they enable the clinician to highlight how future violence could manifest if it were to occur. In Carl's case, two scenarios were outlined.

Scenario 1 – firesetting

Firesetting was considered the most likely form of future violence. More specifically, Carl was considered to be at risk of setting fire to a property, in response to a perceived wrongdoing on the part of a person or persons. The most recent offence was committed against an intimate partner, and so future partners could be at risk if conflict were to arise and/or if the relationship broke down. However, Carl also targeted non-intimate partners in previous arson offences, and he has threatened firesetting against prison staff. Therefore, members of the public, staff, associates, and friends were also identified as potential victims. Any instance of firesetting in Carl's future could be driven by a number of motives including a need to express his emotions, anger, a desire for revenge/retribution, and a wish to communicate a message, as outlined in the clinical case formulation. The overall likelihood of a repeat firesetting offence in the future was, at the time of assessment, considered to be moderate, and the risk of serious harm was high, on the basis of the nature of the index offence. The imminence of risk was assessed as moderate to high in the event that Carl was released, which was based, in part, on the recency of the threat of firesetting while Carl was in open conditions as well as the presence of important risk factors that needed attention, for example some problems with insight and instability.

Scenario 2 – harassment of an intimate partner

Harassment in the form of verbal comments/threats, abusive text messages, and/or physically following an intimate partner/ex-intimate partner was also considered to be a possible trajectory for future violence in Carl's case. If this were to occur, this was deemed to be most likely in the aftermath of a relationship breakdown. The motivation would be a desire to be 'heard' by the victim and/or a reluctance to accept that the relationship had come to an end. An inability to regulate his emotions, which may include anger was also highlighted as possible motivator. The overall likelihood of this behaviour was considered to be moderate, with a moderate risk of serious harm. The imminence was assessed as low, given that Carl was not in a relationship at the time of assessment. Of particular relevance in Carl's case was that this scenario of harassment could potentially be a precursor to scenario 1 (firesetting), as was the case with the index offence. It was considered possible that firesetting could represent an escalation from verbal threats; this would need to be considered by those tasked with monitoring Carl in the community.

Risk and manageability

The HCR-20 was used to assess Carl's overall risk of violence, with additional consideration given to fire-specific factors. The SAPROF was employed to assess protective factors. A formulation was developed, along with scenarios, to highlight the most likely roots to violence in Carl's case. On the basis of this assessment, it was concluded that overall, Carl posed a moderate risk of violence in the community, with a high risk of serious harm. Firesetting was considered to be the most likely form of violence. The imminence of risk was assessed as moderate to high outside of the closed prison environment. On the basis of the assessment, Carl was not considered suitable for a transfer to open conditions or release at the time of the assessment.

A number of outstanding need areas were highlighted from this assessment. With respect to general psychological functioning, ongoing emotional regulation difficulties were identified, as well as interpersonal problem-solving deficits. Two factors were of particular concern in Carl's case, namely self-harm through scalding his skin and the recent threat to burn down his POM's home. Both of these were conceptualised as risk paralleling, and, thus, potentially indicative of ongoing fire interest and fire-related attitudes. Two recommendations were made – one pertaining to the monitoring of Carl's firesetting risk and one in relation to risk reduction.

Monitoring and treatment

As cited earlier, Horsley (2022) highlights the difficulty with accurately assessing certain fire-specific risk factors in a secure setting, in part because those in prison do not routinely have access to fire in the form of a naked flame. With this in mind, a period of concerted monitoring of fire-related attitudes and behaviour was recommended, given the ongoing concerns about risk paralleling behaviour and fire interest/fire-supportive attitudes. For example it was suggested that staff should observe and record Carl's reactions to any fire-related news stories, any signs of arousal to fire or heat-related stimuli, and his response to alarms being activated on the wing.

The firesetting intervention programme for prisoners (FIPP; see Gannon, 2013; as cited in Gannon et al., 2015) is a manualised treatment programme specifically designed to meet the needs of those with a firesetting history. The FIPP targets four areas, which have been found through research to be associated with firesetting, namely fire-related factors, offence-supportive cognition, emotional regulation, and social competence (Gannon et al., 2015). A referral to the FIPP was recommended for Carl. This was considered suitable to address the fire-specific concerns in his case, as well as general functioning needs such as emotional management and interpersonal problem-solving. Although he had completed some psychological treatment related to emotions and substance misuse, it was the opinion of the assessor that this had not fully addressed the core factors underpinning the firesetting risk identified within the case formulation. Although the FIPP was considered the best option for Carl, Horsley's extensive discussion on the evolutionary significance of fire (2022), namely the extent to which we may all be 'hardwired' to find it appealing, should be considered in terms of setting realistic goals for treatment.

Conclusion and discussion

The forensic psychological literature on firesetting is lagging behind that of other offence types, such as sexually violent and violent offending behaviour. Although the literature base has seen exponential growth over the past decade, there is still no validated risk assessment tool specifically designed for adults who set fires (Watt & Ong, 2015). As discussed by Horsley (2020, 2022), this poses a challenge for practitioner forensic psychologists and allied professionals because it means that there is no consensus on exactly what factors need to be considered when assessing firesetters. Another obstacle to effective firesetting assessment is the lack of opportunity for natural observation of prisoners interacting with fire. This is quite unique to this type of offence because, in other cases, the behaviour someone displays in prison can be used to assess how they might behave once released. For example if a prisoner is serving a sentence for a violent offence against a male acquaintance, then how they interact with peers on the prison wing could be relevant. In the case of fire, however, prisoners have little access to it or even to sources of heat. Firesetting cases can be complicated even further if the individual appears to have formed a 'relationship' with fire (see Horsley, 2022 for discussion on the human–fire relationship), particularly if this is maladaptive. As has been highlighted in this chapter, it is important to consider the relevance of such a relationship in an individual's life and, indeed, how this has developed across their lifespan.

The many challenges of assessing firesetters were illuminated in the case of Carl because of his complex history and presentation and the presence of fire-specific factors. This chapter has demonstrated how the HCR-20 and the SAPROF tools can be supplemented through reference to the best available research evidence. Fire-specific static risk factors, as highlighted in the work of Edwards and Grace (2014), were applied to Carl to determine whether the nature of his previous firesetting could inform his future risk. Furthermore, dynamic factors were considered through drawing on the work of Gannon et al. (2013). Theoretical perspectives were also useful in making sense of Carl's offending and presentation, namely through application of the M-TTAF (Gannon et al., 2013). However, there was not an exact 'fit' between Carl's case and the trajectory thought to be most closely aligned with his presentation – the multifaceted trajectory. This highlights that there remain many 'unknowns' with respect to firesetters and that this affects clinical practice with, and risk management of, this group of people.

Along with the many challenges associated with assessing firesetters, the case of Carl has demonstrated the complexity of identifying an appropriate treatment pathway, particularly where an interest in fire is relevant. The development of the FIPP (see Gannon, 2013; as cited in Gannon et al., 2015) marks a sea change in firesetting treatment, moving from a crude 'one size fits all' approach to one which is much better tailored towards a person's needs. Carl was considered to be an ideal candidate for the FIPP because of the combination of general and fire-specific dynamic risk factors. However, Horsley's discussion on the evolutionary significance of fire (2022) is a reminder that humans may, to some extent, be 'hardwired' to find fire attractive. In cases where an adult has already formed a maladaptive relationship with it, this highlights significant challenges pertaining to rehabilitative interventions for firesetters.

In conclusion, Carl's case highlights the complex process of assessing someone with a history of setting fires. The HCR-20 and SAPROF were useful in identifying general risk and protective factors; however, it was necessary to augment the assessment through drawing upon the latest psychological firesetting literature. Even through using this approach, however, there are still many 'unknowns', for example the extent to which fire's appeal is 'hardwired' and how to monitor risk-paralleling behaviour in custodial settings where access to fire is very limited. These questions are yet to be answered, highlighting just some of the areas where further research is required and demonstrating the need for a careful and considered risk assessment approach that is needed with firesetters.

References

American Psychiatric Association. (2013). *Diagnostic and statistical manual of mental disorders* (5th ed.). American Psychiatric Publishing.

Barrowcliffe, E. R., & Gannon, T. A. (2015). The characteristics of un-apprehended firesetters living in the UK community. *Psychology, Crime & Law, 21*(9), 836–853. https://doi.org/10.1080/1068316X.2015.1054385.

Barrowcliffe, E. R., & Gannon, T. A. (2016). Comparing the psychological characteristics of un-apprehended firesetters and non-firesetters living in the UK. *Psychology, Crime & Law, 22*(4), 382–404. https://doi.org/10.1080/1068316X.2015.1111365.

Butler, H., & Gannon, T. A. (2020). Do deliberate firesetters hold fire-related scripts and expertise? A quantitative investigation using fire service personnel as comparisons. *Psychology, Crime & Law*, 1–21.

Daykin, A., & Hamilton, L. (2012). Arson. In B. Winder & P. Banyard (Eds.), *A psychologist's casebook of crime: From Arson to Voyeurism*. Palgrave Macmillan.

De Vogal, V., de Ruiter, C., Bouman, Y., & de Vries Robbé, M. (2012). *SAPROF: Guidelines for the assessment of protective factors for violence risk, Version 2*. Van der Hoeven Kliniek.

Douglas, K. S., Hart, S. D., Webster, C. D., & Belfrage, H. (2013). *HCR-20: Assessing risk for violence version 3*. Mental Health, Law and Policy Institute.

Edwards, M. J., & Grace, R. C. (2014). The development of an actuarial model for arson recidivism. *Psychiatry, Psychology and Law, 21*(2), 218–230. https://doi.org/10.1080/13218719.2013.803277.

Gannon, T. A., Alleyne, E., Butler, H., Danby, H., Kapoor, A., Lovell, T, Mozova, E., Spruin, E., Tostevin, T., Tylr, N., & Ciardha, C. Ó. (2015). Specialist group therapy for psychological factors associated with firesetting: Evidence of a treatment effect from a non-randomized trial with male prisoners. *Behaviour Research and Therapy, 73*, 42–51.

Gannon, T. A., & Barrowcliffe, E. (2012). Firesetting in the general population: The development and validation of the fire setting and fire proclivity scales. *Legal and Criminological Psychology, 17*(1), 105–122. https://doi.org/10.1348/135532510X523203.

Gannon, T. A., Ciardha, C. Ó., Barnoux, M. F., Tyler, N., Mozova, K., & Alleyne, E. K. (2013). Male imprisoned firesetters have different characteristics than other imprisoned offenders and require specialist treatment. *Psychiatry: Interpersonal and Biological Processes, 76*(4), 349–364. https://doi.org/10.1521/psyc.2013.76.4.349.

Gannon, T. A., Ciardha, C. Ó., Doley, R. M., & Alleyne, E. (2012). The multi-trajectory theory of adult firesetting (M-TTAF). *Aggression and Violent Behavior, 17*(2), 107–121. https://doi.org/10.1016/j.avb.2011.08.001.

Horsley, F. K. (2020). *Arson reconceptualised: The continuum of fire use* (Unpublished doctoral dissertation, Durham University).

Horsley, F. K. (2021). Arson and firesetting: A new conceptualization. In D. A. Crighton & G. J. Towl (Eds.), *Forensic psychology* (3rd ed.). Wiley.

Horsley, F. K. (2022). *New perspectives on Arson and firesetting: The human-fire relationship.* Routledge.

Jackson, H. F., Hope, S., & Glass, C. (1987). Why are arsonists not violent offenders? *International Journal of Offender Therapy and Comparative Criminology, 31*(2), 143–151. doi:10.1 177%2F0306624X8703100207

Ó Ciardha, C., Barnoux, M. F., Alleyne, E. K., Tyler, N., Mozova, K., & Gannon, T. A. (2015). Multiple factors in the assessment of firesetters' fire interest and attitudes. *Legal and Criminological Psychology, 20*(1), 37–47. https://doi.org/10.1111/lcrp.12065.

Towl, G. J., & Crighton, D. A. (1996). *The handbook of psychology for forensic practitioners.* Routledge.

Tully, R. J. (2019). Sexual deviancy: Assessment for court. In R. J. Tully & J. Bamford (Eds.), *Case studies in forensic psychology* (pp. 25–47). Routledge.

Tyler, N., Gannon, T. A., Dickens, G. L., & Lockerbie, L. (2015). Characteristics that predict firesetting in male and female mentally disordered offenders. *Psychology, Crime & Law, 21*(8), 776–797.

Ward, T. (2017). Prediction and agency: The role of protective factors in correctional rehabilitation and desistance. *Aggression and Violent Behavior, 32*, 19–28. doi: 10.1016/j. avb.2016.11.012

Watt, B. D., & Ong, S. (2015). Current directions of risk assessment in deliberate firesetters. In R. M. Doley, G. L. Dickens, & T. A. Gannon (Eds.), *The psychology of arson: A practical guide to understanding and managing deliberate firesetters* (pp. 167–184). Routledge.

Wilpert, J., van Horn, J., & Eisenberg, M. (2017). Arsonists and violent offenders compared: Two peas in a pod? *International Journal of Offender Therapy and Comparative Criminology, 61*(12), 1354–1368.

10 Conclusion

Ruth J. Tully and Jennifer Bamford

Why more case studies?

In 2019, we published our first book of case studies in forensic psychology, and we were humbled by the offers of contributing chapters from professionals in the field. What it demonstrated is that so many of us are working in contexts and sub-specialisms of forensic and clinical psychology within which we need to adapt to the needs of our client and/or the service we are working in. These adaptations (and their success or otherwise) offer helpful learning experiences for each other, hence the high value of clinical case studies in describing and evaluating the work we do. Within this second book of case studies, we have aimed to offer some more of these examples. This has been done in the hope that this may inspire practitioners and researchers to further examine the various topic areas included in this book.

Whilst case studies are often seen as lacking in empirical rigour compared with other methods, such as systematic reviews, it is recognised that in areas of psychology where research is limited, case studies can offer useful building blocks (Eisenhardt, 1989). It is however important to recognise what is arguably the most obvious limitation of case studies – the lack of generalisability. However, within this book, we hope to be clear that whilst the case studies are unique, what was a consistent theme was that there were complex considerations that required 'doing something differently' based on the clinical presentation of the person being assessed or treated. We do not aim to use these case studies to posit new ways of approaching a whole population of clients but rather as examples of creative ways of accounting for the unique aspects of a case in line with the general principle that shared effective clinical practice aids the development of clinical and forensic psychology as a whole.

In this book, Dr Arsuffi explored the importance of considering and measuring a range of types of recovery for a patient in a secure hospital setting in the process of assessing treatment outcome and readiness for move-on; this chapter emphasised the need to consider treatment in the medium to long term for some people accessing forensic services. Dr Patel promoted the importance of multidisciplinary working and the value of helping the wider team to understand the clinical needs of a patient with a diagnosis of paranoid schizophrenia. Another

DOI: 10.4324/9781003213116-10

chapter considered the effectiveness of bespoke therapy during a period of investigation for an individual who had committed online sexual offending but who remained in the community; as technologically assisted sexual offending develops along with technology, considering what the unique needs of people who offend in this way are as compared to those who commit contact sexual offences will need further research. Dr Horsley helped us understand how to consider the unique elements of firesetting risk in the absence of a specific risk assessment tool. It will be of interest to consider if in several years' time, a tool has been developed and validated for use with this unique population. Dr Ashworth described the use of functional analysis with a patient with ABI and how this helped to identify patterns to help understand the patient's challenging behaviour more effectively, showing the value of such analysis. Ms Shelton offered useful insight into the practical applications of adaptations for EMDR therapy to treat trauma symptoms for a patient with ASD. Dr Holt and Mr Warkcup considered the importance of a whole systems approach to trauma-informed care for a young person. Each chapter of this book highlights the need to continue to adapt our approaches to responsivity with every person we work with and not to assume that what works for one individual with a specific presentation, diagnosis, or offending history will work for all of those with the same features.

Assessing and treating during the COVID-19 pandemic

This book was completed during the global COVID-19 pandemic at a time when a range of unprecedented difficulties were present for psychologists and clients. Whilst for much of the world, the pandemic brought with it a sense of imprisonment through national and regional lockdown, many of our detained clients suffered even more social deprivation and isolation. For example, prisoners reported that they were confined to their cells for 23 hours per day for weeks or months at a time in an effort to prevent the spread of the virus. This brought with it understandable concerns regarding the well-being of those detained, such as a decline in mental health and higher suicide risk (Stephenson et al., 2021), alongside the very real concern about an airborne virus within institutions with known overcrowding, poor ventilation, and limited access to healthcare (World Health Organization: Regional Office for Europe, 2020). At the time of writing, we are still seeing the psychological consequences of COVID-19 and the necessary response to this by services, and we would expect that we will continue to see this over the coming months and years as we recover from this difficult time. These consequences will have an impact on the lives of forensic service users and people who are detained, as well as the staff members working with them and could affect the psychological treatment and risk reduction of service users over time.

During the pandemic, many forensic services and prisons had to significantly reduce or cease all planned therapeutic activities, leaving some clinically vulnerable patients potentially at risk to themselves and others, and leaving many prisoners behind in progressing through their sentence planning or risk reduction objectives. Once restrictions were eased, waiting lists for therapeutic intervention had understandably grown longer in many services. Prisoners who were dependent on intervention to demonstrate risk reduction have faced delays to parole hearings, and frustration has grown regarding continued deprivation of liberty due to reasons that were outside of their and others' control. Those who were motivated to change their behaviour and to not create further victims had been delayed or prevented from accessing risk reduction treatment. We have seen that some people in prison have shown regression in their behaviours, possibly due to the long periods alone or locked in their cell and not being able to have visits from their families, resulting in even further delays to their progress in custody. Those who secured release from prison or were discharged from hospital during the pandemic came out to a world shut down to them, with even fewer employment, social, and support opportunities available to them, and with new restrictions to their everyday life that they quickly needed to navigate. Many authorities were unable to drug test (with this usually involving access to bodily fluids from a client), potentially curtailing effective risk management for some, and reduced or remote supervision from community-based services (such as video or phone calls with probation instead of in-person appointments) was present for many people.

Whilst this situation was understandably frustrating and worrying to those residing in secure settings, those working in these settings have, in our experience, also felt the pressure of trying to repair (as much as they could) the damage the pandemic caused. Staff on the front line in these services were doing their best to meet clinical needs in a safe way, whilst also managing their own anxiety and often also their personal losses associated with the pandemic. There were ever-changing rules and restrictions in services to react to the rise and fall in COVID-19 positive cases; court/parole hearings and meetings were cancelled at the last minute and many people were off sick. Working in forensic and clinical services through the pandemic has been a considerable challenge for many and there are emerging clinical studies that are revealing some of the consequences for frontline staff working during the COVID-19 pandemic. These studies, primarily conducted within hospital staff samples, have concluded high anticipatory anxiety (Digby et al., 2021) and found concerns about providing high-quality patient care (Holton et al., 2021). Studies have further highlighted the need for psychological services to help manage the mental health of frontline staff (Zaka et al., 2020).

However, staying at home was not safe for everyone, with victims of domestic violence facing increased vulnerability during the period of lockdown (Usher et al., 2020) and with rates of domestic abuse increasing across a number of countries (Kourti et al., 2021). Also, we saw some interesting changes in crime itself during this period, with crime rates for many offence categories sharply declining in the first full month of lockdown (Langton et al., 2021) but with the rate of cybercrime increasing (Interpol, 2020; Buil-Gil et al., 2021) likely in response to the majority of the population staying at home and becoming reliant on the internet to work, socialise, and shop.

Despite the undeniable negative consequences of the COVID-19 pandemic, this period offered the opportunity for adaptation and creativity and in some ways, brought out the best in those willing and able to adjust to the 'new normal' in supporting the people they work with. We saw the quick implementation of remote assessment using videolink technologies as a response to not being able to sit with someone in person. Whilst we are sure that an entire chapter or even a book could be devoted to the advantages and disadvantages of remote assessment, what it did allow us to do was to try to carry on. The British Psychological Society quickly responded to the rise in remote assessments with helpful guidance for practitioners (e.g. BPS, 2020) and teams shared helpful resources, contacts, and guidance on how to set up and manage remote assessment. It may be that psychologists and other mental health professionals became collectively more technologically capable and being able to be 'present' remotely offered a new opportunity that was no longer limited by location. Psychologists could see clients hundreds of miles away or attend conferences or training in locations previously unattainable by distance. Travel time no longer needed to be factored into the completion of treatment or assessments, allowing more time for clinical activity. Clinically, we encountered clients who said they preferred meeting remotely, with some saying that it felt less psychologically threatening and reduced their anxiety not to be in the same room. Some community clients with severe anxiety or travel limitations were able to engage when they may not otherwise have felt able to. The implementation of remote or hybrid parole and court hearings reduced the cost of travel and in many cases with this being funded by public money, this in theory could provide opportunity to invest in more clinical services.

That being said, what we then needed to navigate was a range of difficulties with videolink assessments likely not considered before. This included the risk of increased dishonesty (Buchanan et al., 2005), distraction in our clients (Germain et al., 2009), poor quality in connections impairing assessment of vocal tone (Jones et al., 2001), and technical issues impairing motivation/engagement (Luxton et al., 2012). Additionally, use of videolink was seen by many as a last resort, not a preference, and clients may have felt pressured into a remote assessment if there was no other option (Hyler et al., 2005). Assessing those with acute clinical issues also represented a challenge; for those with paranoid presentations for example there may have been a concern about the privacy of the assessor (Rogers, 2001). In our experience, there are also limitations to the psychological assessment of people via video, such as a lack of ability to fully observe body language, some reduced opportunity for 'small talk', and the person being interviewed not being able to see assessor body language which could have helped put them at ease. Some psychological testing is not possible or appropriate to do remotely due to how some tests are developed and validated or due to them requiring some physical elements, as is often seen for instance in psychometric tests of memory functioning.

It was a steep learning curve for many adjusting to these new considerations and in our experience at times made aspects of assessing and treating someone's psychological presentation much more difficult. It is in our view crucial to consider, to attempt to respond to, and to acknowledge the limitations of remote assessment and treatment in the forensic and clinical context. It is not known if treatment is as effective via remote means when compared to in-person treatment, and it may not be known if something significant has been missed due to remote interview methods as part of psychological assessment. For some patients, a psychologist is one of the few people they feel comfortable talking to and some elements of rapport building and maintenance, and the development of feelings of trust could be lost due to remote means of interview/therapy. Research and insight into the impact of adjusted methods of service delivery during the COVID-19 pandemic is needed to further inform the work we do.

The way that the pandemic was responded to by psychological and mental health professionals is another example of the collective ability of our colleagues to adapt in ways required to meet the needs of others. We observed people doing their best in very challenging circumstances. It should be acknowledged that despite the personal struggles, stress, and losses each professional may have been experiencing due to the pandemic and associated restrictions, they were working hard to provide psychological services to others. Professionals were sometimes treating service users remotely or in person whilst not being able to see their family, whilst family members were sick, whilst their patients were worried or who became sick, and many professionals themselves contracted COVID-19. Several of the case studies in this book were conducted at the time of the pandemic, and it is our shared view that there is a lot to be proud of regarding how clinical teams and the services that work with forensic patients and those with histories of offending worked together to meet the needs of the individuals they care for.

References

British Psychological Society. (2020). *Guidelines: Psychological assessment undertaken remotely.* Author.

Buchanan, T., Johnson, J. A., & Goldberg, L. R. (2005). Implementing a five-factor personality inventory for use on the internet. *European Journal of Psychological Assessment, 21,* 115–127.

Buil-Gil, D., Miro-Llinares, F., Moneva, A., Kemp, S., & Diaz-Castano, N. (2021). Cybercrime and shifts in opportunities during COVID-19: A preliminary analysis in the UK. *European Societies, 23*(1), 47–59.

Digby, R., Winton-Brown, T., Finlayson, F., Dobson, H., & Bucknall, T. (2021). Hospital staff well-being during the first wave of COVID-19: Staff perspectives. *International Journal of Mental Health Nursing, 30,* 440–450.

Eisenhardt, K. M. (1989). Building theories from case study research. *Academy of Management Review, 14*(4), 532–550.

Germain, V., Marchand, A., Bouchard, S., Drouin, M. S., & Guay, S. (2009). Effectiveness of cognitive behavioural therapy administered by videoconference for posttraumatic stress disorder. *Cognitive Behaviour Therapy, 38,* 42–53.

Holton, S., Wynter, K., Trueman, M., Bruce, S., Sweeney, S., Crowe, S., Dabscheck, A., Eleftheriou, P., Booth, S., Hitch, D., Said, C., Haines, K., & Rasmussen, B. (2021).

Immediate impact of the COVID-19 pandemic on the work and personal lives of Australian hospital clinical staff. *Australian Health Review, 45*(6), 656–666.

Hyler, S. E., Gangure, D. P., & Batchelder, S. T. (2005). Can telepsychiatry replace in-person psychiatric assessments? A review and meta-analysis of comparison studies. *CNS Spectrums, 10,* 403–413.

Interpol. (2020). *Cybercrime: COVID-19 impact.* www.interpol.int/content/download/15526/file/COVID-19%20Cybercrime%20Analysis%20Report-%20August%202020.pdf. Accessed 20 June 2022.

Jones, B. N., Johnston, D., Reboussin, B., & McCall, W. V. (2001). Reliability of telepsychiatry assessments: Subjective versus observational ratings. *Journal of Geriatric Psychiatry and Neurology, 14,* 66–71.

Kourti, A., Stavridou, A., Panagouli, E., Psaltopoulou, T., Spiliopoulou, C., Tsolia, M., Sergentanis, T., & Tsitsika, A. (2021). Domestic violence during the COVID-19 pandemic: A systematic review. *Trauma, Violence & Abuse.* Online article. https://doi.org/10.1177/15248380211038690.

Langton, S., Dixon, A., & Farrell, G. (2021). Six months in: Pandemic crime trends in England and Wales. *Crime Science, 10,* 6.

Luxton, D. D., Kayl, R. A., & Mishkind, M. C. (2012). Health data security: The need for HIPAA-compliant standardization. *Telemedicine and e-Health, 18,* 284–288.

Rogers, R. (2001). *Handbook of diagnostic and structured interviewing.* The Guilford Press.

Stephenson, T., Leaman, J., O'Moore, E, Tran, A., & Plugge, A. (2021). Time out of cell and time in purposeful activity and adverse mental health outcomes amongst people in prison: A literature review. *International Journal of Prisoner Health, 17*(1), 54–68.

Usher, K., Bhullar, N., Durking, J., Gyamfi, N., & Jackson, D. (2020). Family violence and COVID-19: Increased vulnerability and reduced options for support. *International Journal of Mental Health Nursing, 29,* 549–552.

World Health Organization: Regional Office for Europe. (2020). *Preparedness, prevention and control of COVID-19 in prisons and other places of detention: Interim guidance.* www.euro.who.int/__data/assets/pdf_file/0019/434026/Preparedness-prevention-and-control-of-COVID-19-in-prisons.pdf?ua=1.

Zaka, A., Shamloo, S. E., Fiorente, P., & Tafuri, A. (2020). COVID-19 pandemic as a watershed moment: A call for systematic psychological health care for frontline medical staff. *Journal of Health Psychology, 25*(7), 883–887.

Global glossary

Active monitoring is regular monitoring of a person who has symptoms of a condition but who is not currently having clinical intervention. It is also referred to as 'watchful waiting'.

Acute stress response centres on the physiological reaction to threats to our safety, either by fight, flight, or freeze.

Acquired brain injury is any type of damage to the brain that happens after birth. Causes can include disease, assault or injury to the head, substance misuse, or lack of oxygen.

Adverse childhood experiences (ACEs) are highly stressful and potentially traumatic events or situations that occur during childhood and/or adolescence. They can be a single event, or prolonged threats to, and breaches of, the child's safety, security, trust, or bodily integrity. Examples include abuse of any kind (e.g. physical, sexual, emotional), living with someone who abused drugs or alcohol, exposure to domestic violence, and living with someone with serious mental illness.

Anti-psychotic medication is a type of psychiatric medication which is used to treat psychosis.

Assertive outreach teams are part of community mental health services but are separate from the traditional community mental health teams (CMHTs). They are specialist teams set up to work with people with mental illness or personality disorder, who have previously been admitted to hospital and who might have other problems such as violence, self-harm, homelessness, or substance abuse. They offer intensive and long-term support, which can help to overcome the trust issues presented by forensic mental health patients and develop robust working alliances with them.

Attachment theory is a psychological, evolutionary, and ethological theory that provides a descriptive and explanatory framework for understanding interpersonal relationships between human beings.

Attunement is based on the idea that a primary caregiver has to be available and emotionally receptive to their child, which provides a solid base for that child to explore their world.

Barotrauma is a condition which affects the middle ear resulting from sudden changes in air pressure.

Body scan is a mindfulness practice which involves 'checking in' with one's body by mentally scanning oneself from head to toe, bringing awareness to every part of the body in turn.

Borderline personality disorder. It used to be thought that those with borderline personality disorder (BPD) were on the 'border' of neurosis and psychosis, hence the name of the disorder; however, it is now known that this is not an accurate description. The term 'borderline' within the diagnosis is often misunderstood due to its origin or due to its dictionary meaning. BPD is a disorder of mood and interpersonal interactions and can also be called **emotionally unstable personality disorder**. In everyday language it is perhaps better described this way. Symptoms can include overwhelming distress, anxiety, worthlessness or anger, difficulty managing feelings without self-harming/drug use, having difficulty sustaining stable relationships, sometimes losing contact with reality, and in some cases those with this disorder can threaten to harm others as well as themselves.

Categories of indecent images: In England and Wales, the courts rely on the categorisation of indecent images when considering the seriousness of the image. Category A images are those that involve images of penetrative sexual activity, sexual activity with an animal, or sadism. Category B images are those that involve non-penetrative sexual activity. Category C images are those that involve indecent images not falling within categories A or B.

Challenging behaviour (or **behaviours which challenge**) refer to any behaviour with the potential to cause physical or psychological harm to another person, self, or property.

Child and Adolescent Mental Health Services (CAMHS) is a name used for mental healthcare services provided in the UK for children, generally up until 18 years old, who are having difficulties with their mental health and emotional well-being.

Child protection plan is a written record for parents, carers, and professionals, which sets out key information such as including the outline of concerns, who the social worker is, what work needs to be done to reduce the concerns, what needs the child has and how they can be met, what needs the parent has and how they can be supported, and a time frame for when the work should happen.

Child Sexual Exploitation Material (CSEM) refers to images or videos which show a person who is a child engaged in or is depicted as being engaged in explicit sexual activity. This is a term often used interchangeably in the literature and clinical practice with 'indecent images of children' (IIOC).

Classical conditioning   (also called **respondent conditioning)** is a learning process that occurs when two stimuli are paired. The response which is at first caused by the second stimulus is after time caused by the first stimulus.

Clinical case formulation   is an individualised integration of multiple hypotheses about a person's problems and goals, the causal variables that most strongly influence them, and additional variables that can affect the focus, strategies, and results of treatment.

Closed prison   is a custodial environment which is designed to make escape extremely difficult. Closed prisons house offenders considered to pose the greatest risk to the public. In England and Wales, prisons that are built to house 'Category A', 'Category B', and 'Category C' prisoners are 'closed prisons', and those built for 'Category D' prisoners are referred to as 'open prisons'.

Cognitive behavioural therapy (CBT)   is a talking therapy that can help individuals manage problems by changing the way they think and behave and learning about the relationship between thoughts, emotions, and behaviours. It is most commonly used to treat anxiety and depression.

Cognitive distortions   are unhelpful thinking styles that can bias logical ways of thinking. In an offending context, cognitive distortions can sometimes be used to justify, minimise, and/or maintain offending behaviour. They can be described as irrational beliefs that contribute to uncomfortable emotions and exaggerated pattern of thoughts that are not based on factual information and are sometimes also referred to as '**thinking errors**'.

Command hallucinations   are auditory hallucinations that instruct a person to act in specific ways; these commands can range in seriousness from innocuous to life threatening.

Depersonalisation   is a state in which a person's thoughts and feelings seem unreal or not to belong to them.

Depression   is a mood disorder that causes a persistent feeling of sadness and loss of interest. Also referred to as major depressive disorder or clinical depression, it affects how people feel, think, and behave. Depression can lead to a variety of emotional and physical problems and people with depression may have trouble doing normal day-to-day activities and sometimes may feel as if life isn't worth living. Depression may require long-term treatment including medication, psychotherapy, or both.

Developmental theory.   There are various theories within developmental psychology which focus on human development across the lifespan. They encompass physical, cognitive, social, intellectual, perceptual, personality, and emotional growth and are key to understanding how people learn, mature, and adapt.

Dialectical behaviour therapy (DBT) is based on CBT but has been adapted to meet the particular needs of people who experience emotions very intensely. It is mainly used to treat problems associated with borderline personality disorder (BPD), such as repeated self-harming, emotional instability, risk-taking behaviour. The skills training element of treatment focuses on four key areas: acceptance, distress tolerance, interpersonal effectiveness, and emotional regulation.

Emotionally Unstable Personality Disorder (EUPD): See 'borderline personality disorder' (BPD).

EMDR is an acronym for 'Eye Movement Desensitisation and Reprocessing' and is often recommended for treating PTSD. EMDR is a powerful psychological treatment method that was developed by an American psychologist Dr Francine Shapiro in the 1980s. A wealth of research is available demonstrating its benefits in treating psychological trauma arising from a range of diverse traumatic experiences.

Factor analysis is a technique that is used to reduce a large number of variables into fewer numbers of factors that is more understandable.

Generalised tonic-clonic seizures are generalised seizures involving unconsciousness and violent muscle contractions.

Glasgow Coma Scale (GCS) is a clinical scale used to measure an individual's level of consciousness following a head injury.

Good lives model is a strengths-based rehabilitation theory that assists clients to develop and implement meaningful life plans that could be protective against future offending.

Historical Clinical Risk-20 (HCR-20): A 20-item structured clinical guide for the assessment of violence risk.

Hypoxia is a condition in which the body or a region of the body (such as the brain) is without adequate oxygen supply at the tissue level.

Insecure attachment style is a relational pattern that stems from negative experiences during childhood when a child's needs are not met. It can result in difficulties developing and sustaining meaningful relationships with others.

Intellectual disability is a learning disability characterised by significant impairment of intellectual functioning, significant impairment of adaptive functioning. Deficits usually begin early in the developmental period.

Interim care order is a temporary arrangement that ensures a child is safe during care proceedings. When an interim care order is applied for, the local authority will be required to detail their plan for the child, including placement and contact. This may be for placement in foster care, with other friends/family members, and in some cases the child can remain at home with exclusion requirements in place that prevent certain individuals from entering the home or seeing the child.

Internet Sex Offender Treatment Programme (i-SOTP)   is a group-based programme that was historically designed to treat those convicted of internet-facilitated sexual offending.

Lapse   can be considered to be a temporary failure of concentration, memory, or judgement. The key word in the definition of a lapse is temporary. It differs from a relapse, which by definition is a verb meaning to suffer deterioration after a period of improvement. In simpler terms, a relapse is a full-blown resumption of an addiction that was at one time stopped or the person attempted to stop it.

Looked after child: In England and Wales, the term 'looked after children' is defined in law under the Children Act 1989. A child is 'looked after' by a local authority if he or she is in the care of or is provided with accommodation for more than 24 hours by the authority.

Mental capacity   refers to a person's ability to make decisions for themselves at the required time.

Mental Health Act 2007   is the legislation governing the compulsory treatment of people who have a 'mental disorder' within the definition of the Act. The Mental Health Act 2007 amends the previous legislation, namely the Mental Health Act 1983. The Act is largely concerned with the circumstances in which a person with a 'mental disorder' can be detained for treatment for that disorder without their consent. It sets out the processes that must be followed and the safeguards for patients. The main purpose of the legislation is to ensure that people with serious 'mental disorders' which threaten their health or safety, or the safety of the public, can be treated even without the person's consent, where it is deemed necessary to prevent them from harming themselves or others.

Mental Health Act Section 2   is part of the civil sections under the Mental Health Act. It provides for someone to be detained in hospital under a legal framework for an assessment and treatment of their mental disorder.

Mental Health Act Section 47/49   involves a transfer of a person from prison to hospital with restrictions.

Mindfulness   is a meditative practice in which an individual is tasked with focusing entirely on what they are sensing and feeling in the moment, without interpretation or judgement. It can often involve breathing techniques, guided imagery, and other practices to relax the mind and help reduce stress.

Multi-agency risk assessment conference (MARAC)   is a regular meeting where agencies discuss high-risk domestic abuse cases and develop a safety plan for the victim and their children. Agencies taking part can include police, independent domestic violence advisors (IDVAs), children's social services, health visitors, and GPs, amongst others.

Multidisciplinary team (MDT) is a care professional team that involves a group of professionals from one or more clinical disciplines who together make decisions regarding recommended treatment of individual patients.

Neuronal excitability refers to the readiness of a neural circuit or nerve cell to respond to a stimulus, usually in the form of an action potential, which is a transient change of electrical charge (polarisation) of the neuronal membrane.

Neuropsychology is the study of the relationship between brain functions and behaviours, emotions, and cognitions.

NICE guidelines are evidence-based recommendations for health and social care in England. They set out the care and services suitable for most people with a specific condition or need and people in particular circumstances or settings. The guidelines help health and social care professionals to prevent ill health, promote and protect good health, improve the quality of care and services, and adapt and provide health and social care services.

Open prison is a custodial environment which has less physical and often relational security than a closed prison. These establishments house prisoners who can be reasonably trusted not to attempt to escape and who are considered to pose a lower risk to the public than those in closed prison. They are also designed to enable prisoners to begin to reintegrate with the community.

Operant conditioning (also called instrumental conditioning) is a learning process where the strength of a behaviour is shaped by reinforcement or punishment.

Paranoid schizophrenia is a severe long-term mental health condition. It causes a range of different psychological symptoms whereby the person may not always be able to distinguish their own thoughts and ideas from reality.

Parasympathetic nervous system (PNS) is one of two major divisions of the larger autonomic nervous system. It is responsible for maintaining the resting heart rate and stimulating digestion, among other things, which helps the body to calm down. It is frequently referred to as the 'rest and digest' system.

Persecutory delusions occur when someone believes others are out to harm them which are not based on reality and/or despite evidence to the contrary.

Person-centred counselling is a humanistic approach to therapy which is based on three elements offered by a therapist; unconditional positive regard (accepting and valuing the client), congruence (being honest and transparent in how they experience the client and their world), and empathic understanding (seeing the client's viewpoint as if they were them).

Play therapists   are trained professionals who work with children (and their families) to support them to deal with difficult situations and experiences through the use of play.

Post-traumatic stress disorder (PTSD)   is an anxiety disorder caused by very stressful, frightening, or distressing events. Causes can vary and PTSD symptoms can develop immediately or even years after the event occurs. Symptoms include nightmares, flashbacks, feelings of isolation, irritability, and guilt. The person may have poor concentration and suffer from insomnia. Symptoms are often persistent, severe, and impact on the person's day-to-day life.

Processing speed   is the ability to mentally process simple or routine visual information without making errors.

Psychosis   is when people lose some contact with reality. This might involve seeing or hearing things that other people cannot see or hear (hallucinations) and believing things that are not actually true (delusions).

Pyromania   is an uncommon mental disorder which is characterised by a set of diagnostic criteria, namely: (i) a history of firesetting (i.e. on more than one occasion); (ii) tension and emotional arousal before firesetting; (iii) fascination with/interest in, and/or attraction to fire; (iv) pleasure, gratification, or relief when setting fires; (v) there is no other obvious reason for the firesetting, such as financial gain.

Psychological formulation   is a provisional explanation or hypothesis based on psychological theory and summation and integration of the knowledge about the person. It provides a framework for describing a problem, how it developed, and is being maintained. There are various models of psychological formulation.

Retrograde amnesia   refers to a loss of memory for events, or information that was learned, in the past.

Risk of Sexual Violence Protocol (RSVP)   is a set of structured professional judgement guidelines for comprehensive assessment and management of risk for sexual violence.

Risk paralleling behaviour (RPB)   is often also called 'offence paralleling behaviour'. It is behaviour which serves the same function as an offence or known risk behaviour for the person. The behaviour may be similar or different to the original behaviour; the function is important to consider.

Scaffolding can refer to a range of techniques and forms of support that assist an individual to learn new skills. Scaffolding can include experiences that foster a sense of safety and may involve temporary forms of support that promote skill development and goal attainment.

Section 17 leave is the term used where detained patients have leave from the hospital which must be approved by their responsible clinician.

Sense of salience is the term used for anything that is prominent, conspicuous, or otherwise noticeable compared with its surroundings.

Self-concept is a psychological term referring to how a person views themselves, with respect to their identity. Someone with a weak self-concept is unclear about who they are and who they want to be in the future.

Sex offender register is a police record of certain sexual offenders who are required to notify the police of personal information about them and to notify the police of any changes. There is no public access to the register, but in some circumstances some members of the public can formally request the record to be checked as to whether a specific person has a record for child sexual offences.

Sexual Harm Prevention Order (SHPO), previously known as a sexual offence prevention order (SOPO), is a court order that can be requested by the police or court when there is a concern that an individual may be at risk of committing a sexual offence. The order contains various conditions an individual will need to comply with over a specified period of time.

Sexual violence can be defined as any sexual act, attempt to obtain a sexual act, unwanted sexual comments, contact, or advances by any person regardless of their relationship to the victim.

Stabilisation involves learning skills to cope with distressing trauma symptoms such as flashbacks, nightmares, and intrusive memories. Also, it involves thinking about managing emotions and regaining a sense of safety within an individual's own mind and body.

Static/actuarial tools are risk assessment tools that consider static or historical risk factors that have been repeatedly associated with reconviction, for example prior sexual offences. Actuarial sex offender risk assessments take a nomothetic approach, offering probabilistic estimate of sexual offending within a given time frame based on base rates.

Structured professional judgement (SPJ) tools are risk assessment tools where the judgement of clinicians is aided by guidelines designed to support clinical judgement, and the overall decision on risk level is left at the discretion of the professional judgement of the assessor. This can be described as an ideographic approach.

Survival response system is the physiological response activated by the limbic system in response to perceived or real danger. It is often referred to as the 'fight, flight, freeze' response.

Suspended sentence is when a defendant receives a prison sentence from the court but is permitted to serve this sentence time on probation in the community, usually with various conditions. Often, if the conditions are breached, the person can be required to serve their suspended sentence in prison instead.

Sympathetic nervous system (SNS) is one of two major divisions of the larger autonomic nervous system. It is essential for preparing the body for action, including emergencies, and is frequently referred to as the 'fight-or-flight' responses.

Tactile hallucinations involve an abnormal or false sensation of touch or perception of movement on the skin or inside the body.

Therapeutic alliance relates to how the client and a therapist connect, behave, and engage with each other.

Thinking errors. See 'cognitive distortions'.

Thought insertion is a delusion in which the individual believes that thoughts have been forced into their mind and ascribes these thoughts to outside sources.

Thought withdrawal is a delusion that occurs when a person believes that a person or entity has removed thoughts from their mind.

Three-minute breathing space is a three-step **mindfulness** practice that usually involves: (1) actively attending broadly to one's experience, noting it, but without the need to change what is being observed; (2) narrowing the field of attention to a single, pointed focus on the breath in the body; (3) widening attention again to include the body as a whole and any sensations that are present.

Transactional analysis is a style of talking therapy where a therapist will explore an individual's personality and how this has been shaped by their lived experiences. It is based on the theory that each person has three ego-states: parent, adult, and child. A therapist will work with a client to consider how these ego-states play out in their relationships/communication with others and to provide opportunities for the client to change unhelpful patterns of relating.

Trauma-informed care (TIC) is an approach to providing services that assumes that all individuals (service users and staff) are more likely than not to have a history of trauma. TIC recognises the presence of trauma symptoms, acknowledges the role trauma may play in an individual's life, and endeavours to best support an individual's needs whilst avoiding re-traumatisation.

Traumatic brain injury refers to a head injury which causes damage to the brain by an external force.

Vasoconstriction is the narrowing of blood vessels resulting from contraction of the muscular vessel walls.

Index

Page numbers in *italics* refer to figures. Page numbers in **bold** refer to tables.